An Introduction to Political Theory

An Introduction to Political Theory

Toward the Next Century

Robert Booth Fowler

University of Wisconsin–Madison

Jeffrey R. Orenstein

Kent State University

HarperCollins*CollegePublishers*

Executive Editor: Lauren Silverman
Project Editor: Shuli Traub
Design Supervisor/Cover Design: John Callahan
Cover Illustration: Miro, Joan. *The Song of the Vowels*. Palma, April 24, 1966. Oil on canvas, 12′1/8″ × 45′1/4″. Collection, The Museum of Modern Art, New York. Mrs. Simon Guggenheim Fund, special contribution in honor of Dorothy C. Miller. Photograph © 1992 The Museum of Modern Art, New York.
Production Manager/Assistant: Willie Lane/Sunaina Sehwani
Compositor: Circle Graphics Typographers
Printer and Binder: R. R. Donnelley & Sons Company
Cover Printer: The Lehigh Press, Inc.

An Introduction to Political Theory: Toward the Next Century

Library of Congress Cataloging-in-Publication Data

Fowler, Robert Booth, 1940–
    An introduction to political theory : toward the next century /
Robert Booth Fowler, Jeffrey R. Orenstein.
        p.   cm.
    Includes bibliographical references and index.
    ISBN 0–06–042168–1
    1. Political science.   I. Orenstein, Jeffrey R.   II. Title.
JA71.F63   1993
320—dc20   92–30211
                                                    CIP

93 94 95 9 8 7 6 5 4 3 2

To those in our families with us and departed who have provided so much so that we could become what we are today we dedicate our memories, our friendship, and this book.

Contents

Preface

This book reflects our conviction that political theory is not something that belongs in a museum but is a living enterprise that helps us to examine and make decisions about the ends and means of politics and government. It represents our current thinking about political theory and is not a new edition of any of our other works. It has been started from scratch because we have tried for the first time to integrate the past and the present of political theory in looking toward the twenty-first century of the current calendar, the twenty-sixth after Socrates and Plato.

We hope that you share our enthusiasm with this approach to political thought. We have tried in these pages to share the joy and pride we take in political theory and what it can accomplish for our lives as citizens. We have also tried to share some of the insights and perspectives that we may have gleaned from political theory. Our aim is to communicate with you the sense of optimism and opportunity we see in the future. The twenty-first century of our calendar and the twenty-sixth century of political theory are dawning, and we want you to share our appreciation of what can be accomplished by those who think seriously about the prospects of public interaction.

We hope that you enjoy using this text. In each chapter, we have included both a Glossary of Key Terms and Suggestions for Further Reading as study aids for you. We have tried to write clearly and define terms in context so that you can understand what political theorists do instead of struggling with their sometimes arcane language. Most of all, we hope that you will use what you have learned in these pages as a springboard to your own political thinking and commitment. We do not think political theory requires any one approach or dogma. In fact, we two agree on many issues and approaches and disagree on others. But we do hope that you will come to agree with us that the historical and analytical insights of political theory are a good starting place to develop your own ideas. We urge you to try them and modify them in any way that seems appropriate for you, no matter where life takes you.

We wish to thank Lauren Silverman of HarperCollins Publishers for her invaluable assistance in this project and our colleagues who have helped us with their welcome criticisms and insights (particularly anthropologist John Harkness). We also gratefully acknowledge the following reviewers: Robert E. Calvert, DePauw University; Bertil L. Hanson, Oklahoma State University; Ceferina G. Hess, Lander College; and Andrew Raposa, Westfield State College. Finally, we thank our many students over the years who have challenged us and made us think about vital political norms and questions.

Robert Booth Fowler

Jeffrey R. Orenstein

Chapter
1

On Political Theory

*P*olitics and government in some form have been part of the human cultural legacy since the beginnings of human association. Inevitably, these political bonds among people raise questions about what kind of politics is best and what we ought to do about the issues and institutions of our collective interactions. The history of these questions and their answers (as we have been writing them down for approximately twenty-six centuries) forms the cultural legacy known as political theory that is the subject of this book.

Political theory is the search for wisdom and understanding about the ends and means of political life. It is an activity concerned with the search for the best possible political and social lives of today's citizens. It has always occupied a central role in people's lives precisely because it concerns such vital and unavoidable topics as the issues and institutions that form the fabric of our collective existence.

Political theory affects and beckons us today as it has from the dawn of recorded history. For example, in our century the rise and collapse of the Soviet Union and its communist ideology are momentous political events that do not merely fascinate us. They require us to make moral and political sense of them in order to deal with their consequences. So too were the decline and fall of Athens and the rise of the Roman empire to ancient Greeks and Romans. And just as these ancient events drew some of society's best minds to political theory to attempt to make sense, our century's events have held the same lure to some of our best minds. Surely, the next century will have similar momentous political events and just as much political theory in response. Political theory does not stop or decline with time any more than do politics and history.

As we discuss in the pages that follow, the rise and fall of great empires and the revolutionary changes in political relationships and public institutions have played a central role on the human stage for the last two and a half millennia of written political theory. Since these activities show no signs of abating, we can predict with confidence that political theory will continue to be a craft practiced by those who wish to understand and mold the political events of each age. Thus, we emphasize throughout these pages that because politics—the central focus of political theory—is everywhere, political theory is not the exclusive property of any particular age or people.

While good political theory has rigorous standards and methods,[1] these are not so arcane or complex as to block the intelligent person from understanding and learning to use them. Political theory is a discipline that most of us can learn to do with some facility. While this is not a book on the methodology of doing political theory, we examine the topic to the extent that is needed in order to understand how good political thinkers use ideas and values to search for a better political life.

The fact is that political theory is a necessary discipline to us and will be to our heirs as well. While our age's preoccupation with studying facts is useful and important, it cannot do what our world requires: providing moral consdieration about the ends and means of politics and government. These are only addressed effectively by political theory that focuses on normative (moral) decisions and situations and searches for guidance to understand and deal with them. Such decisions are among the toughest ones that people face because there are the fewest available intellectual supports and methodological roadmaps to guide us. But we cannot avoid making these moral decisions (and neither can our heirs) because not deciding what are the proper ends and means of politics and government can yield potentially horrendous consequences. Without an ability to handle political values and issues thoughtfully and creatively, we surely face wholesale amorality (or, even worse, the nihilism of saying that anything goes, regardless of the human cost) in our public institutions and policies. Political theory allows us to recognize such dangers and guides us toward making the right choices, no matter how tough they might be or how few signposts there are along the way.

The preceding themes constitute our approach to the subject of this book. Political theory is the academic discipline that undertakes the search for wisdom and understanding about what ought to be in political and social life. Political theory, or political philosophy as it is sometimes called, is an activity concerned with what is morally right rather than with the discovery or testing of empirical facts about the world. Thus political theory asks how people should govern themselves; whether we should have a government; when, if ever, we should be obligated to the political community; whether we should have economic equality; and similar questions. Always we ask "should" and "ought," about what is morally legitimate. As political theorists we try to shed light on how to think about such ethical matters and on ways to look for adequate answers to them.

Just as we need to distinguish political theory from studying "the facts," we also must distinguish it from the study of public policies. If facts will help us to think through normative perspectives, so will the ethical positions we develop affect the policies we may choose in trying to accomplish our moral goals. This explains why—in later chapters of this book—we address policies connected with political theories in some detail. Policy and theory need not and inevitably will not be always radically separate. Yet there are often differences between policy and theory. Political theory addresses broad questions of morality—justice, obligation, community—while policy usually directs our attention to specific problems in social welfare, farm incomes, military expenditures, and the like and the connections between these issues and our goals and values.

We see political theory as a conversation or a series of arguments. It involves searching, but it also involves discussing insights and perspectives, talking and arguing about them with other people and other views, past and present. In this sense it is often a highly interactive activity. We can learn from others' thinking and their analyses, and they can learn from ours. It is no wonder that in our enterprise we take many views seriously. The reason is not that we agree with everybody and everything; theories and positions often clash in ways that cannot be resolved. But we are intellectually enriched when we take alternative theories into account and explore, learn from, or argue with them.

While we have given you some idea of what we mean by political theory, we also need to define how we use the concept of politics. The meaning of politics is hardly self-evident and perspectives definitely vary. For us the political involves the public realm in life. We describe politics as the processes by which public decisions are made. We separate the public and the private, understanding the private as the personal world of self, family, and friends. We acknowledge that the line between public and private is not especially distinct or firm, and it varies from time to time and culture to culture. We appreciate that private life can become quite intertwined with the public, political world. School policies, child abuse laws, welfare policies inevitably link the public and private spheres. Equally, attitudes and actions in the private sphere inevitably affect political and collective life. Yet the two realms are not the same, and the distinction is one that many of us cherish.

Some people insist that everything that is personal is also political, that all our "private" relations are really in part relations about governing and power. Such a sentiment is correct in that private relationships and actions do have consequences for the larger society. The old idea of the possibility of a purely private realm or a purely private act is properly dead. But there are degrees of publicness or the political. And, if everything is political, or equally political, then the word *political* has no meaning. For the question then becomes, political as distinct from what?

In sum, we define political theory or philosophy in this book as the ongoing search and discussion, or debate, about what ought to exist in the public realm in life, recognizing that such ideas will have considerable impact on all dimensions of human existence.

THE IMPORTANCE OF POLITICAL THEORY

Political philosophy plays a major role in shaping all of our lives. All governments and all societies have political theories and justifications for the way
they are and are not. Sometimes these are sophisticated, sometimes not, but
they are always there. Some societies operate with just one theory, but more
often there are diverse and conflicting ideas and values. These values influence rulers as well as citizens; they influence all of us. They affect policy
choices and decisions every day. Thus, we dwell in a universe where political
values and normative theories about what is morally right are inescapable
components of existence. Like it or not, political theory is a fact of life and
there is no reason to suspect that it will not be in the fast-approaching twenty-
first century. We have much to gain from studying it.

How much political theory matters in any given setting or in regard to any
particular policy, of course, will vary. Individual personalities and experiences as well as the structures and forces of history, economics, politics, and
religion all play a role in what happens. It is impossible to formulate a general
rule about how much individual psychology or broader social factors matter in
relation to the power of individual or cultural values. Yet none of these
elements, including the role of political theory, can be ignored in appreciating
contemporary politics or in imagining those of the twenty-first century.

We know that we all have values and we all think at times in terms of our
values when we think about politics. We have ideas about what is right and we
apply them to the imperfect world of politics around us. This is simply the way
people are, have been, and will be in the future; it is part of what it means to
be human. While some of us care more about them, all of us have values,
including those who contend that they lack such norms. And all of us have
opinions about what and how values should be translated into politics and
society. Each of us, therefore, is at least potentially something of a political
theorist. We only differ in how much we have developed our insights and
arguments.

In short, political theory, at least in embryonic forms, is not only all
around us but part of all of us as well. This reality makes political theory
important quite apart from its role in the broader canvas of history and
society. Political theory is something that is part of our individual story as well
as the larger story around us. Thus, to understand ourselves as well as to
engage the world around us, we should move toward greater awareness of and
skill in political theory. It summons us both to personal development as moral
people and to greater encounter with our larger social order.

THE HISTORY OF POLITICAL THEORY

We cannot say when or where political theory began. No one knows. We can
be sure that it started when the first person asked if his or her society or
political order was morally right, or perhaps if some action or policy that

happened was right. To question the moral rightness of something in political life is to start down the road of political theory or philosophy. It may seem a simple act, but it can be earthshaking in its consequences, both personal and societal. Perhaps the first questioners, or doubters, faced danger. Since then, many who raised political questions have faced danger and even death. For merely to ask if something is ethical is to imply that it might not be. It is to raise the specter of doubt about the given and the accepted. It is also to suggest the value of the human mind and its capacity to raise doubts over or against society and its time-honored traditions and beliefs.

Among ancient peoples, perhaps there were many moments when political theory was born and reborn in just this fashion. The process often may have been quiet and private. In the absence of written records, we do not know. We do, however, understand when it emerged in written form in the history of the Western world. This epochal event took place twenty-five centuries ago, in the fifth century B.C., in the Greek city-state of Athens. There Socrates and (in the following century) his student, Plato, created political philosophy as an activity that Plato recorded for all time as Socrates, Plato, and their students conducted their brilliant conversations on truth and the good political order.

Plato recounts that Socrates began the discourse of political theory by inquiring of Athenian citizens just what justice meant—in our terms, what it ought to be. Of course there were several opinions, but Socrates rejected every one as inadequate and spurred his students to craft better ideas. The conversation he began continues today and into the future.

Why Socrates and Plato deserve honor is not merely their pioneering practice of political philosophy. Political theory is more than opinions about what ought to be in political and social life. We all have opinions on these issues, but political theory is about carefully considered and argued opinions that bring us insight or truth. Socrates also merits praise because he made insightful arguments on such matters as justice and obligation, presentations that have proven to be of permanent worth (which we discuss in later chapters). The same is true of Plato. Thus political philosophy in the West not only "began" with Socrates and Plato. They were also among the greatest voices in its history.[2]

Much has happened since. Other central political theorists have emerged in the West, from Aristotle to Marx, with many in between. They have propounded new ideals and made new arguments and have discussed old ones with fresh perspectives. They have joined the company of memorable and stimulating political theorists from other cultures, such as Confucius in ancient China or Gandhi in modern India.[3] Among the rest of us, too, forms of political theory continue unabated, as we offer our feelings, opinions, and arguments on justice or obligation, on liberty and equality. Our thoughts may not always be highly organized or as aware of alternative arguments as they might be, but they are first steps toward doing good political theory.

Yet in recent decades, skeptics have questioned whether it is possible to do worthwhile political theory anymore. They grant that people can have opinions, but they wonder if arguments with any depth are possible in our age. Skeptics suspect that there are no longer any secure foundations from which we can found a major moral theory relevant to politics. Our era seems to be one bereft of confidence in Truth while committed to celebration of individual or group interests and goals. There seems little fertile soil for political theory that might transcend one person or one age.

Yet the process of doing political theory clearly goes on today, even flourishes. Its remarkable history helps the process, but political philosophy depends ultimately on the way people behave. Humans always seem to ask what is right or wrong—in politics and elsewhere—a fact we expect to be as characteristic of the twenty-first century as it has been of our own. Political theory likely has a long history ahead.

REFLECTIONS ON POLITICAL THEORY

As we have seen, political theory is the search for and argument about wisdom and truth as these may apply to political and social existence. It is about what ought to be. It is a realm where everything is contested, an activity where opposing understandings and opposing arguments are as routine as they are important. It is not for closed minds, though it attracts more than a few; nor is it for the timid, though anyone can learn to do theory with confidence over time.

Three kinds of political theory are most practiced today. They are normative, analytical, and historical theory. Sometimes they are at war with each other, but often they interweave, each in its own fashion contributing to an overall search for wisdom regarding politics. To understand political theory in our time, and to give a sense of what this book does, we now look briefly at each in turn.

Normative political philosophy concentrates directly on the search for and argument over what ought to be in public life, our collective existence. Those who practice normative political theory are typically interested in the classic, fundamental questions of political theory regarding governance, distribution, and respect within any political community; questions of justice, rulership, and community. We know that "ought" and "should" are the usual forms of normative theory and that, while relevant, facts cannot decide the morally right. What "is" in this world cannot be ignored, but it cannot alone decide what is right or just or good. Normative theory is proudly and inescapably about ideals, and these are often not the same as what may exist or may have existed.

Since argument is so essential to normative theory, we can expect that it usually takes shape in discussion, one thinker arguing with another about the best values, insights, or systems. Argument does not determine whether something is true or not, but it can and does serve to illuminate or justify a position or an insight. Moreover, any position is more worth taking seriously if it can stand the fire of skeptics or outright antagonists. This does not mean that to do normative theory one has to be a contentious or unpleasant personality. Civility and argument can coexist well, but there can be no doubt that normative theory is about discussion and argument.

The greatest political theorists self-consciously argued and were superb at the activity. This was true of Plato in fourth-century-B.C. Athens and of Thomas Hobbes two thousand years later in England; it describes James Madison, principal author of our Constitution and Bill of Rights in eighteenth-century America and Karl Marx in nineteenth-century Paris and London. Each explored and advocated ideas about what was right in the political and social order around him. Each argued his case, creating in the process memorable works of normative theory, from Plato's *Republic* to Hobbes's *Leviathan*, from Madison's *Federalist Papers* to Marx's *Capital*.

Always they presented reasons for their perspective that were as compelling and substantial as possible. Often they engaged opponents and challenged skeptics, sometimes directly, sometimes not. They were not always kind with opposing views, but they accorded them the respect implied in arguing with them instead of just pretending that everyone agreed on the issues in conflict. In the works of these great thinkers, we have a record of political theory at its best. No one expects any of us to match them, yet these thinkers constitute an impressive model for how to do normative political theory.[4]

A second kind of political theory is analytical in nature. (This term is used generically here. In using it, we do not embrace or even evaluate the specific words and concepts of the subfield of philosophy called Analytical Philosophy. This has been amply discussed in the literature of that discipline and can be explored through its sources.) Analytical political theory is about the investigation of the key ideals, concepts, and ideas of political theory. As the name implies, political theorists who practice it explore what makes up theories and arguments. They dissect the parts of theories, their relationship to each other, and their connection with other arguments and discourses. Analysis of political theory, for example, requires us to do what we have done here: discuss and probe the varieties of political theory. Analysis of the concept of justice will require us to probe its contested meanings, the arguments that swirl around them, and the relationship between justice and other values and concepts.

Political theorists with an analytical approach do not necessarily develop a normative stance nor make a normative argument. Their goal is to discuss, clarify, delineate, and reformulate. Much less often do they go further and argue what is morally sound in politics or elsewhere. Thus they often have a different approach than more explicitly normative political theorists. Yet to do normative theory, we must be analytical. We have to know what we are—and are not—talking about when we argue regarding justice or democracy. Such analytic theory can help us be clear about concepts and make distinctions and proceed from there. We have to try to avoid muddled thinking as we reflect on what political life ought to be or when we try to argue with others about crucial political topics, if we want to understand and to be understood.

While the analytic approach to political theory cannot tell us what ought to be, its contributions go a long way toward providing the best possible groundwork for making good normative judgments—and arguments.

While most analytical political theory focuses upon basic concepts such as democracy or obligation, some of it looks in another direction and addresses some of the most basic assumptions in political philosophy. For example, it may ask whether we can discern truth at all, or whether when we take apart all political claims there is much left besides an individual and his or her personal disposition toward the world. Or, it may ask such vexing questions as whether there is anything in the world that is not in some sense political. Such broad queries may sometimes seem only an annoying sidetrack. Yet they have value because they can potentially straighten out our perspectives about what good political theory can and should assume.

A third type of political theory is historical in focus. It recounts the history of past political thinking. Sometimes it concentrates on the past "great" ideas, classic visions of justice or liberty. Sometimes it stresses the "great" political philosophers and their arguments about what ought to be in politics. Sometimes it takes the form of intellectual history: an account of the political views and arguments of the intellectuals in one culture or another.

Theorists with this focus look to the past, of course, but their work contains as much potential value for contemporary political theory as other approaches. Historical theorists open to us the vision of what others have thought as they struggle with questions of political philosophy. These theorists give us perspective and they can save us many steps in our own journey of discovery. Socrates' discussion of political obligation in his *Apology* is a permanent contribution to the debate over political obligation; so are Aristotle's reflections on law in his *Politics*. Equally, John Stuart Mill's defense of freedom is of great value. Whenever theorists consider freedom, they turn to Mill's nineteenth-century classic, *On Liberty*. Contemporary American feminist thought also has a rich history from which it may benefit: for example, feminist thinking in the Progressive Era, 1900–1917. In each case, the past provides us with perspective and a greater chance for wisdom, regardless of whether past arguments convince us.

In practice, of course, most political theorists employ all three styles of political philosophy. Most are normative; they seek wisdom about politics and they undertake to make arguments about what is right in political life. Most are analytic, insistent on the value of clarification of terms and norms, whether in discussing basic concepts or in arguments and discussions about what ought to be in politics. Most are also at least somewhat historical. If they do not directly study the history of political philosophy, in one way or another they draw on the history researched by others. Emphasis differs from thinker to thinker, from person to person. Taken together, all paths of political theory play a part in the common task, the search for insight or truth about what ought to be in common, public experience together.

DOING POLITICAL THEORY

Political theory is an activity, something one does. It is not at all passive, whether we concentrate on normative argument, analytic distinction, historical investigation, or all three. Moreover, it is very much a social activity. We may think or write alone. But whatever we develop regarding political philosophy, we must enter into discussions with others, living and dead, who have faced or are facing the same problems and puzzles. Political theory eventually becomes a conversation and thus a social enterprise for its practitioners.

Exactly how the thinking and the conversation take place, exactly how political theory is done, is not obvious. Nor is there a single, correct route one must travel. Yet there are signposts that can direct us and will be useful for you. Fortunately, while doing political theory may seem daunting, the basic activity is straightforward enough for any intelligent and motivated person to learn how to do it. In fact, once we recall that everyone already has political ideas and opinions, all our suggestions take on a new light. They are really guides toward a better political theory, toward helping you to think and argue more effectively about political values and the good political society.

First, it is essential that we be clear about our position, our problems, and our values. Clarity is crucial from the start and all the way through. We must also honor the rest of the rules of rational thinking. Emotion matters in thinking and in politics, of course, but to make a good argument or to do political theory requires clear, logical, coherent, and organized reason. We must also argue. We have to give reasons as to why anyone should see things the way we do. There is never anything self-evident about our perspective, no matter what it is and no matter how obvious it seems to us. And we must take on those who see things in other ways because other views are likely to strengthen our own as we both learn from and learn to reply to our critics.

Along the way, we must keep remembering that normative arguments are not the same thing as empirical ones, that how the U.S. Congress actually works is not the same thing (necessarily) as how the Congress should work. We must appreciate the cultural and historical setting in which we plan to explore and apply political theory as well. If we are claiming that something is always true or right, we must understand that this is what we are doing and what may be its implications. Or, if we are talking about what is right for our country alone, we need to recognize this and be aware of the particular dilemmas that this may create for us. Always we have to have a sense of context and of mission.

ABSOLUTE FOUNDATIONS OF POLITICAL THEORY

We also have to establish our basic framework in which we propose to argue, our overall perspective from which much will come. We have to know and be clear about our foundation, or lack of foundation. We may want to argue our starting points extensively; we may not. But they enormously affect how we see things.

Though some political theorists are reluctant to respect any basis of thought but their own, there is a huge variety of foundations in political theory. Everyone has such a foundation, or a view on why he or she avoids all foundations. People start somewhere with their arguments and values in politics just as in all areas of moral life. Even the most sophisticated political theories start from some crucial assumptions and/or beliefs. Therefore, in the chapters that follow we conduct arguments about topics such as justice partly by looking at them through the lens of differing foundations. This is why we must have an awareness from the start of alternative foundations in order to do aware political theory.

Utilitarianism is one starting point familiar to all of us. Its premise is that our foundation for normative arguments should be the goal of advancing pleasure or happiness. If the object is the individual, happiness for an individual, we call it individual utilitarianism. If the object is society, the greatest amount of social happiness possible or the greatest good for the greatest number, we term it social utilitarianism.

The advocates of utilitarianism like the fact that, in its reflections on the good society, it takes people into account pretty much as they are. It respects their judgments about what they desire and what kind of society they seek. No wonder its supporters often rally to democracy as the best way to discover what people see as the greatest good for themselves or for society as a whole. Utilitarians also are pleased that their perspective has no higher or grander foundation than people's happiness and their judgments about common happiness. They want to be practical and they see utilitarianism as practical, proceeding in close connection with empirical realities, not shadowy ideals from some undefined place. For utilitarians, dreaming is not a substitute for real desires and a practical common good.

There are problems with this approach, of course, as with all others. The standard in social utilitarianism of the greatest good for the greatest number does not inherently protect unpopular individuals or groups. Social utilitarians could, in the classic example, justify slavery if a majority strongly felt the gain outweighed the suffering of the slaves. Moreover, exactly what is meant by terms such as *the greatest good* or *pleasure* and *pain* and how we should determine their meaning are controversial questions. Answering them poses no small problem to the supposedly practical utilitarians.[5]

Nature as the proper foundation for values is another common approach in our culture. It will certainly remain popular in the next century as environmental concerns grow. We are most used to it in the form of natural rights claims. This is how it appears in our Declaration of Independence and other political statements of our history that invoke nature as the absolute and fitting ground for values: "We hold these truths to be self-evident, that all men . . . are endowed . . . with certain unalienable rights." This is the claim that in nature are certain moral guarantees or rights for each individual, such as the right to life or the right to liberty. This approach is a familiar part of our national political tradition, one congenial to many Americans since natural rights puts individuals before all else, including government or society.

But there are many other ways in which theorists invoke nature as a foundation. Aristotle in ancient Greece held that nature was the proper foundation for the good society and saw nature operating as a series of goal-oriented laws whose moral truth he affirmed.[6] Many others have followed him in having recourse to this approach, holding that politics and society should discover and then follow the natural laws they contend are part of our universe.

We expect that in the twenty-first century nature will greatly expand its appeal as a foundation for political theory. As emphasis on environmentalism and on the survival of planet Earth grows, more and more thinkers will invoke nature as the basis for a good community and a better politics. In this case, though, we can expect that those who appeal to nature will talk less of natural laws and more of nature as a holistic system, each part interdependent on the others. What will not change will be the confident assumption that nature is a proper moral basis for all of human existence, including politics.

Turning to nature as a foundation means today what it has always meant in one way: it is invoking an absolute standard of truth. Of course, what nature teaches depends enormously on who interprets it. This is no minor difficulty, even though the mere presence of conflicting claims does not establish that all such claims are false. One or more might be the correct reading of nature, but for the skeptic it is not clear how we would know. And confident assertions about nature—whether from Aristotle long ago or modern ecologists today—are not a substitute for convincing us what exactly nature's truths are. Indeed, the history of science suggests that perceptions of nature's truths have a decided way of changing over time. Thus we may well suspect that today's truths about nature may soon become tomorrow's errors about nature.

Even if we know the truths of nature, however, another question arises: why should "nature" be our standard for politics and morality? This is the classic question, and one far too rarely propounded by those celebrating nature as their foundation. How does the "is" of natural laws or the ecosphere turn into the "ought" of political and social life?[7]

Religion has played an enormous role as a foundation for ethical and political arguments over the millennia of human existence. No foundation has been more often cited over human history. Christianity is still integral to Western thinking today. But there are many political theorists in the contemporary era who proceed from other traditions as well—Islam, of course, and Judaism, Buddhism, among others—in the world as well as in the United States.

Perhaps the most famous political thinker and activist in recent American history is Martin Luther King, Jr., and there is no doubt that his foundation was religious. As with others for whom religion is their foundation for political argument, King went from his religion to concrete applications in political and moral life. But his Christianity was not—and no Christianity can be—a series of particular solutions to specific problems; it was the framework from which he attempted to formulate specific arguments, answers, and actions. Thus there is plenty of room to argue about King's politics and ethics, but to understand the basis for his arguments, we have to appreciate his Christian background.[8] For him, religion was the foundation for his political theory, no more, no less.

Such is the usual situation with those who argue from a religious foundation. It provides the basis for their thought but not necessarily a pat answer to every dilemma. Again, there is usually room for argument and there must be. Where there is no room for argument, there is no room for doing political theory. Then we are dealing not with thinkers, but with narrow ideologues who are either simpleminded or fanatics. Neither of these types is much use in the search for and argument about truth in politics.

Uneasiness about religious foundations, as with all the others, is real. How do we know that any particular religious foundation is true? This is no silly question, given the plethora of religions in the world. Indeed, how do we know any religious foundation is true? Then, how do we know what follows from a religion in terms of politics and ethics? Christians cannot agree on this matter; nor can followers of Islam; nor Jews; nor any other religious group. And how do religious believers avoid the curse of some religious-political arguments, the temptation to slip into rigid assertions that has led to political and religious persecutions?

All of these are good queries, but for the believer they are not entirely relevant. If one believes in a religion that provides a foundation for life, its truth commands people to build from it toward a better political society. There may be and must be disputes about what that would look like. What there could hardly be is denial that political theory must acknowledge such a foundation.

NONABSOLUTE FOUNDATIONS
OF POLITICAL THEORY

Nature or religion or other foundations that have in common the belief in an absolute truth or truths—or those foundations that are comprehensive systems, such as utilitarianism—are not the only options. Many theorists today prefer foundations that are less convinced of the existence of truth or are at least less sweeping than utilitarianism. They offer foundations or, as many would wish to say, approaches that—while more than just affirmation of personal feeling or opinion—are not tied to impossible or overbroad claims to truth.

There are various such approaches from which political theory and political argument begin. One, for instance, is the famous argument of T. D. Weldon, that in this age the claims about absolutist conceptions of truth are empty, that these truths often sound good but cannot be substantiated in fact. Weldon argues that theorists should just admit this reality and forget pretensions to secure, true foundations. Weldon wants us to substitute what we may call the art critic model. Art critics do not claim to have the truth with a capital

T about what is good art and what is not. Yet they have standards among themselves that—however easygoing—allow considerable agreement as to what is great art and what is not. There are disputes, but art critics are not generally reduced to sheer individual opinions in assessing art.

Why, Weldon asks, cannot political theory do the same? Ideas about what is a good government or a just society do not have to be judged True or False. Political theory can, instead, have its own, less absolute, internal rules that will serve to distinguish the good from the bad in political theory. Perhaps this is already the practice in much of the political theory profession today. Few Truths are announced or defended, but there is no doubt that there are collective rules (albeit broad rules) about what counts as good theory and what does not.[9]

Contextualism at the present time is another example of a popular nonabsolutist approach. It has many adherents, some describing themselves as contextualists, others as "good reasons" thinkers, others as pragmatists.[10] All contextualists share the idea that in fashioning a foundation for political theory, we should deal with the society we are in, its history, and its traditions of values and arguments. Their assumption is that all these are inevitably part of what we do and think and that we cannot and should not try to escape our life context in struggling with the moral dilemmas of politics.

Contextualists do not believe they can provide certain or absolute answers. Nor do they believe there is any point in searching fruitlessly for them in our era. But they believe they can provide insight as we try to discern good political values for the world we know. Some talk in terms of theorizing within the value traditions of our respective time and place, or at least in terms of dialogue with them; others speak of working within the practices of people's lives; still others urge the necessity of operating within the ongoing conversations about political theory. Always the stress is on relating to our specific context and on talking with others.

For contextualists, theory is a connected, interactive process. It draws on all possible insights from the past and present of our individual and collective experience. The assumption is that what is good will change as people's experiences in specific contexts change. They see this fact as a positive good. For them, political theory is not a search for absolute truths, but a flexible search, in interaction with others, for what makes sense in a given place and time.[11]

CONCLUSION

There are two great temptations in doing political theory. One is to grasp for a simple foundation that will somehow answer all the central questions. This is the hope that one approach will tell us in no uncertain terms, and with no shades of gray, just what justice ought to be or when liberty should count more than equality. The other temptation is to give up and declare that one opinion is just as good as another and we should simply offer our personal opinions and walk away. Neither view gets us far. Foundations of one sort or another are always present in doing theory, but they are best seen as a starting point, rather than a finish line. And they always need to be carefully explained and defended.

On the other hand, we can do much better than dismiss everything as a matter of subjective opinion. We can talk with each other and with the past. We can argue with each other and with the past. As we do so, we can move beyond simple opinions into considered arguments and reflections about what ought to be in politics. And "we" is the correct word because political theory is something we can all do successfully to some degree and it is something we all must address if we are to have a future.

GLOSSARY OF KEY TERMS

analytical political theory Investigation of key ideals, concepts, and ideas of political theory.

art critic model An approach to political theory that suggests some nonabsolute standards of experts as criteria for values.

assumptions Concepts and ideas that cannot be proven but which are held to be true because a body of evidence and logic points to their validity. Are found at the basis of virtually all human thought.

city-state The classical Greek polis that encompassed the whole of public life in a given region. A precursor of the modern state.

contextualism An approach to political theory that deals with the effect of the context of society on political theory.

historical political theory Study of past political thinking and its context. Stresses discourse of political theory as it has developed.

logic Canons and principles of reason and validity in thought. Used in political theory extensively.

normative, empirical Different ways of categorizing knowledge. Normative emphasizes values and empirical emphasizes facts.

normative political theory Search for and argument about values in public life.

political theory Search for wisdom and understanding about what ought to be in politics and society. Rigorous thought about the ends and means of politics and government. (Also called political philosophy or political thought.)

politics Process by which public decisions are made and public relationships take place. (Affects private life.)

public policy Goals, decisions, and allocations by government. Usually in the form of laws, regulations, agency actions, and budget allocations.

utilitarianism A political theory stressing the greatest good for the greatest number.

SUGGESTIONS FOR FURTHER READING

Anderson, Charles. *Pragmatic Liberalism.* Chicago: University of Chicago Press, 1990.

Aristotle. *The Politics.*

Bentham, Jeremy. *The Utilitarians: An Introduction to the Principles of Morals and Legislation*. Garden City, N.Y.: Doubleday, 1961.

Bible or Koran and other works of scripture have been of great significance in providing foundations for many theorists.

Gunnell, John. *Between Philosophy and Politics*. Amherst: University of Massachusetts Press, 1986.

Herzog, Don. *Without Foundations: Justification in Political Theory*. Ithaca, N.Y.: Cornell University Press, 1985.

King, Martin Luther, Jr. *A Testament to Hope: The Essential Writings of Martin Luther King, Jr.* Edited by James Melvin Washington. San Francisco: Harper & Row, 1986.

Lyons, David. *Forms and Limits of Utilitarianism*. Oxford: Oxford University Press, 1965.

Nash, Roderick. *The Rights of Nature*. Madison: University of Wisconsin Press, 1989.

Oppenheim, Felix. *Moral Principles in Political Philosophy*. New York: Random House, 1968.

Plato. *The Republic*.

Rorty, Richard. *Contingency, Irony, and Solidarity*. New York: Cambridge University Press, 1989.

Sabine, George. *A History of Political Theory*. 3d ed. New York: Holt, Rinehart, and Winston, 1961.

Weldon, T. D. *A Vocabulary of Politics*. Baltimore: Penguin, 1960.

Wolin, Sheldon. *Politics and Vision; Continuity and Innovation in Western Political Thought*. Boston: Little, Brown, 1960.

NOTES

1. All academic disciplines have a set of standards and methods that have been developed by trial and error. Those found in political theory are no more arcane or any less objective than in any other form of carefully developed study about a specific, complex subject like politics and government.
2. See Plato, *The Republic*. It demonstrates how Plato and Socrates (Plato's chief subject) developed political philosophy and developed a political philosophy of great substance.
3. Some classic guides to the history of political thought might include Sheldon Wolin, *Politics and Vision* (Boston: Little, Brown, 1960); and George Sabine, *A History of Political Theory*, 3d ed. (New York: Holt, Rinehart, and Winston, 1961).
4. We feel that this is what political theory excels at and that it should be at the heart of our enterprise.
5. On utilitarianism you might start with David Lyons, *Forms and Limits of Utilitarianism* (Oxford: Oxford University Press, 1965).
6. Aristotle, *The Politics*, which comes in many editions.

7. For the entire subject of current ecological thinking, see Roderick Nash, *The Right of Nature: A History of Environmental Ethics* (Madison: University of Wisconsin Press, 1989).

8. See Martin Luther King, Jr., *A Testament to Hope: The Essential Writings of Martin Luther King, Jr.*, ed. James Melvin Washington (San Francisco: Harper & Row, 1986).

9. T. D. Weldon, *The Vocabulary of Politics* (Baltimore: Penguin, 1960).

10. Don Herzog has both described this view well and argued it well. See his *Without Foundations: Justification in Political Theory* (Ithaca, N.Y.: Cornell University Press, 1985).

11. While he might not be entirely comfortable to be described as a contextualist, Charles Anderson is a very good one; see his *Pragmatic Liberalism* (Chicago: University of Chicago Press, 1990).

Chapter
2

The Individual and the Political Community

*H*uman beings are social and political animals. We customarily live in close proximity to each other and develop informal divisions of labor with great ease. Moreover, our historical pattern has been to build and empower formal political institutions, usually as means to expedite the public relationships we find so valuable and sometimes as tools used by leaders to extract goods and services from their followers.

Political relationships and institutions have apparently always been a part of our history. Undoubtedly, our ancient ancestors built some sort of political communities as means to deal with each other and nature as soon as environmental circumstances put groups in proximity. And as even the most primitive technology emerged, it is likely that some political arrangements were instrumental in its development, deployment, and control. This remains true in today's nuclear age.

Since circumstances motivate intellectual curiosity and questions among human beings, the ubiquity of political communities inspired a lot of speculation and analysis about the relationship of the individual and polity. In fact, these analyses are so extensive that they constitute one of the major currents of Western political thought. For example, the relationship between the individual and polity is what inspired Aristotle over two millennia ago to write that man is a political animal and that without a political community we can be either beasts or gods, but not men.[1] He felt that politics were as natural to people as breathing and that we become fully developed only as political (social) animals.[2] Rousseau also observed in his influential *Social Contract* and other essays that there is an inevitable intertwining of the arts and sciences, civilization, and politics.[3] Modern thinkers like Marx,[4] Freud,[5] Camus,[6] and most others have made evaluations of the same phenomena a

17

prominent part of their political theories. Each of them argued that the needs and prospects for humankind are best met within a political setting.

The prominence of analyses about citizen and polity in political theory does not mean that all thinkers agree on what kind of political institutions are best. Nor do they agree on how powerful they ought to be, who should be in charge of them, how much sway they ought to have over individual lives, how much the individual ought to appreciate and defend the political, and many similar questions. Such questions have been at the core of political theory for the twenty-six centuries since the conversations of Socrates and writings of Plato. Though many of these are discussed elsewhere in this volume, our present context focuses on the ideas and debates in political theory about humans as political animals.

HUMAN NATURE AND POLITICAL THEORY

The most enduring and contentious theme students of political theory encounter involves human nature. Virtually every major political thinker has wrestled with what human nature is and its relevance to political institutions and practices, whether explicitly or implicitly. The subject has always had the capacity to engender arguments and prescriptions with profound political consequences. The ideas of ancient theologians like Augustine and Aquinas,[7] contemporary Muslim theocracies where Sharia[8] controls the state and the laws, and the utopian and anarchist communities of the last two centuries[9] all depend on certain assumptions and visions of the nature of human beings. So did the very different social contract theories of Thomas Hobbes, John Locke, and Jean Jacques Rousseau.[10] The many political theories of socialism also envision a new socialist human being whose nature can be transformed from competitive to cooperative.[11]

Though human nature seems to be a straightforward and uncontroversial concept to many of us, to many of the social scientists and biologists who study it the idea of human nature is quite controversial. Statements like "All people are evil by nature," "Human beings are naturally aggressive," or "People are loving and cooperative until they are trained to be otherwise" conflict with the evidence of modern sociobiological research.[12] The chief debate among these scientists involves the respective roles of biology and culture in human behavior. This debate, popularly referred to as "nature versus nurture,"[13] is between claims that our actions are natural and universal and counterclaims that they are learned.

Most contemporary scientists recognize that each side is able to marshall some convincing but not definitive evidence. The ability of New Guinea tribe members to identify correctly and then describe photographs of Americans acting out anger, surprise, loathing, happiness, and fear and the ability of Americans to do the same for photographs of the New Guineans registering the same emotions in their own way suggest that there is some universal biology at work here.[14] Similarly, the existence of many different work ethics, sex roles, and concepts of the proper role of the state in family life in different societies (or the difference in language between New Guinea tribe members and Americans) suggests that culture affects our behavior too.

The controversy between how much nature and nurture contribute to human nature is far from settled among scientists. The current state of the research suggests that there is a genuine role for both in our sociobiological understanding of human nature, even though these roles have different political relevances. Unfortunately, science cannot tell us much more than this.

That leaves us in a troublesome position as political theorists because the substance as well as the extent of such a role has important implications for political theory. The question of whether or not there are innate human behaviors with political implications occupies the heart of our enterprise; whether people are X or Y, what X and Y are, and whether this "Xness" or "Yness" is learned or genetic is not philosophically neutral. If a person's behavior comes from nature, he or she cannot help it because of drives, reflexes, or temperaments. (Even if we do not have instincts, our drives, reflexes, and temperaments are channeled by learning despite their natural origins.) What is more, we are powerless to design a polity to change what is unchangeable. But if our behaviors are learned, we can change what is done through changes in our political institutions and policies. Since doing political theory forces us to design polities and policies and pursue political values that are based on such assumptions about the nature of people as citizens (whether we have definitive evidence for these assumptions or not), our advice is to tiptoe carefully through this dark and foreboding forest.

Whether people are by nature aggressive (as certain religions and political theories hold) or cooperative (as is maintained by other religions and political theories) has profound implications for our holding of values like freedom and equality. As a result, it has a great impact on what kind of political institutions we ought to build in the name of such values for the common good. For example, the familiar institutions and values of democracy depend on assumptions that human beings are bright enough to understand complex political issues and personalities, reasonable enough to evaluate them and make the right decisions for themselves, if not for the general good, and cooperative enough to be willing to play the game, no matter what its outcome.[15] Unless nature permits such "democratic" human characteristics, any and all democratic institutions are bound to fail and a great deal of contemporary political theory is rendered nonsense.

Similarly, if people are intrinsically selfish and passionate, their coexistence and competition for goods and services in a world with finite resources are likely to result in a "war of all against all which ceaseth only in death" and a life that is "poor, nasty, solitary, brutish, and short." Such a human-nature-dictated jungle may require powerful controls to keep the peace at almost any cost by imposing order for the common good.[16] It may require an authoritarian, nondemocratic political system.

The kind of polity we build and the extent to which it should incorporate the values necessary for democratic participation and governing depend on whether citizens are (or can be taught to be) cooperative or mean and aggressive by nature. If they are the latter, we must separate and police them for their own good. If they are the former, then more extensive individual liberal rights and more liberal political institutions make sense.

Issues of nature or nurture also have profound implications for the possibility of reform and change. Even if there was overwhelming evidence that people actually behave aggressively toward others in a given social setting, the case for an inevitable human nature that thwarts any political change is not made because of the matter of cause and effect. If the observed aggression results from learned behavior in a political system that rewards competition and punishes cooperation (inadvertently or not), it is possible to change what is learned by changing the structure of rewards and punishments within the polity. Thus, it is possible to change the perceived "nature of people" and adopt political values and institutions that depend on reason, cooperation, and social behavior.

For instance, democracy (especially participatory varieties) as envisioned by Western political theorists depends on citizens who are interested enough—or see some personal reward—in public policy to participate in and to agree to abide by the results of the process even if they find themselves on the losing side. This is so because the democratic process itself is judged to be legitimate and will allow losers to reorganize and enter the fray and win on another day and another issue.

On the other hand, if the perceived aggression or mean-spiritedness of people is caused by instinct or nature, then no amount of social conditioning or attempts to teach more cooperative behaviors will work. Natural instincts will prevail and people will compete and conflict ceaselessly. A democratic political system that depends on cooperation and give and take would not last long among such citizens. A veritable police state (on the order of Cuba or Chile under Pinochet) would be necessary for public harmony. Policies and institutions would need to be security oriented and prevent inherent aggressions from undermining the greatest good for the greatest number. Democracy in such a situation would only lead to what Plato called rule of the mob.[17] Such "mobocracy" would get in the way of enlightened leaders searching for a government dedicated to order and truth. It would place the smart in a position to lead the stupid.

Ultimately, ideas and facts of human nature (and whether the way we act is innate or learned) remain topics of investigation among social and natural scientists. It is not clear whether natural drives and temperaments (so-called instincts, to the extent that we have them) are complex enough or of a high enough order to be politically relevant. Perhaps much of the complex political behaviors and roles that undergird democracies, dictatorships, and other contemporary political systems are learned and/or customary—and can be unlearned or relearned in different ways. Since most of what we commonly think of as human nature is more properly labeled human culture, most political theory should probably concentrate on how desirable behaviors can be rewarded and/or undesirable behaviors can be discouraged.[18]

One view is that of anthropologist Matt Cartmill, who suggests that while we know that some very basic kind of human nature is there, we should not assume that it contains any discernable or predictable political patterns. He submits that it is prudent to build social and political institutions that allow for human possibilities and development through learning but which are, nevertheless, somewhat cautious because of our worst-case fears about human nature.[19] As political theorists, we can do this by providing some safeguards against individual abuse and aggression in our polities. This complements our optimism with prudent caution about human nature. Even if further research renders more pessimistic theorists of human nature[20] to be inaccurate, caution on the subject will do little harm. For the present, human nature is a subject about which we still know too little to proceed with no restraint.

POLITICAL THEORY AND THE ELUSIVE PUBLIC INTEREST

As we examine the relationship between the individual and society, another controversy occupying political theorists involves the public interest. Like human nature, this concept appears to the layman (especially journalists and politicians) to be straightforward until an exploration of its subtle meaning and impacts reveals otherwise. Actually, the parameters of an objective public interest are so important, diverse, and controversial that no political theory worthy of the name can afford to ignore them.

The public in public interest refers to our common life, the problems and possibilities of people sharing the same corner of the planet at the same time. Social proximity brings interaction and forces us to deal with each other in some way, whether peaceful or violent, accommodating or exploitative. The set of relationships, institutions, techniques, and values that the interactions develop constitute the public relationships of politics. These include such disparate current examples as the building of a united Western Europe or the civil violence that has accompanied the political realignments of Yugoslavia or Ethiopia. Such events contrast with relationships that are more private and less affect the general public. What we do with our families on a weekend afternoon or whether we watch television or read on a weeknight are typical examples.

Political theorists have always struggled with defining which public relationships, policies, and institutions are justified and which are not. The ones deemed just are what we know as the public interest. One political dictionary defines it in part as "an interest that concerns the community at large."[21] A current American government textbook presents a sampling of definitions that refer to it alternatively as "the common good"; the "common right, the public good, the universal law, in preference to all private and partial considerations" (John Adams); "what men would choose if they saw clearly, thought, rationally, acted disinterestedly and benevolently" (Walter Lippmann); or "the aggregate of common interests, including the common interest in seeing that there is fair play among private interests . . . not the mere sum of the special interests" (E. E. Schattschneider).[22]

These definitions of the public interest illustrate that there are things in the common good that transcend and go beyond merely aggregating private needs or interests. Such familiar values as liberty, equality, and justice have been commonly argued by political theorists to be in the public interest. So have institutions like democracy, fair tax policies resting on ability to pay, spending policies based on public need, and government interventions into the economy for the protection of the consumer.

There is considerable controversy surrounding specific definitions and components of the public interest. What is more, there is controversy as to whether there is an objective and enduring public interest at all, or whether there are just coincidental collections of private interests and needs that must be kept from conflicting in a good society. If the latter is true, the only valid role for government to pursue is night watchman. If there is a public interest, then the good polity should pursue it with all of its resources.

One approach is what has been called the political theory of public utility[23] because it envisions a role for government in providing utilities for the public. Because it is a powerful and serious institution, government is in the best position to supply basic needs directly or by encouraging/mandating other institutions to do so. In the contemporary West, basic utilities (taking technology and values into account) are national defense, abundant energy, public education, a fair economy, public safety, public communications and transportation, civil liberties, and participation in government. They stop short of any alleged rights that exploit others. Rights to pursue luxuries or private gain are recognized, but lie in the private realm and are not included in the public interest.

Thus, the public interest is government making certain that the basic needs of citizens are provided for (usually by the public and private sectors working in tandem) and that the values and institutions of the common good are protected from private manipulation. This theory of the public interest has room for both laissez-faire and social reform liberal concepts of government. Also, the theory is variable enough to shift as technology changes and public personalities and institutions perform differently. As a result, the theory's definition of basic needs, luxuries, and appropriate institutions and sectors to provide goods and services to the public is dynamic rather than fixed.

No matter what theory is used to define public interest, debates about its precise content are inevitable because the "real" public interest is difficult to define. Yet, it is a useful concept and its broad outlines need to be kept in mind when the proper relationship of the individual and society is contemplated in political theory.

A problem of any conception of the public interest involves which private interests should be preserved from public trespass. Political theorist Sheldon Wolin warns that "The most important developments in the last twenty-five years have been the closer intertwining of economic and political power structures. . . . Managerial skills, managerial attitudes, managerial ideology, are fundamental to both . . . an extension of power . . . from a combination of public and private powers . . . the result is a common network of control and surveillance pressing into the private lives of people."[24]

He counsels that the public interest may be served by limiting this kind of power through slow, deliberative, participatory forms of democracy. Public power so organized, he suggests, "comes down to people cooperating" and is a way to control both public and private power through a kind of public sector that will allow people to get along well together, in spite of differences.[25] Thus, to Wolin, the public interest is served by limiting its reach by limiting some public power through democracy. Such limits would prevent abuses of power—whether public, private, or cooperative—through serious attention to democratization of all of our institutions with political implications, whether they are officially governmental or not.

Other political thinkers (principally earlier liberals like John Locke and John Stuart Mill) have suggested that there is an important sphere of private rights and/or interests that must never be violated by any governments, even for the greatest good for the greatest number.[26] These include virtually absolute freedoms of speech, press, assembly, and all other political rights that allow a free marketplace of ideas in which minorities can attempt to become majorities by hawking their political wares. Functioning as limitations of the rights of majorities, these rights are commonly referred to and valued as minority rights within the liberal tradition.

Taking these perspectives together gives us a perspective on the public interest. It is defined by and requires an infrastructure of values and institutions that meets the legitimate needs of majorities and limits arbitrary and selfish power regardless of public or private origins. Interestingly, this view of the public interest is also consistent with the advice that Cartmill gave about dealing with human nature and politics.

RIGHTS AND RESPONSIBILITIES

Political rights are controversial concepts that involve important issues of debate about the proper relationship of the individual and society. The arguments about them focus on the newsworthy topic of human rights and the equally important relationship of political rights and responsibilities of citizenship and government.

Human rights have dominated headlines in recent decades so effectively that they have entered our popular vocabulary. Virtually every citizen recognizes the term, and news commentators and after-dinner speakers assume that human rights are a seamless whole with an objective definition that is understood and accepted by all. Unfortunately, that is not true, despite such widespread assumptions.

In principle, most knowledgeable observers agree that a human right is an inviolable moral claim that all human beings possess as a part of their humanity. By definition, such a right ought not to be denied by any individual or institution. Regardless, the same knowledgeable observers disagree on what specific rights are included and how extensive they are. The Nuremberg Tribunals (held after World War II by a victorious United States to prosecute Germans and Japanese for war crimes and crimes against humanity); the various Geneva Accords specifying the rights of civilians, noncombatants, and prisoners of war; the claims of such international human rights advocacy groups as British-based Amnesty International; and many general provisions of international law have done a lot to clarify the general outlines of human rights involving war between state combatants. Critical ambiguities remain, however. Furthermore, the human rights associated with civil conflicts (such as the Intifada by Palestinians against Israeli occupation of the West Bank of the Jordan River or various coups and revolutions around the world) are still very ambiguous. So are the alleged rights of terrorists and their victims. It is hotly debatable whether acts of terrorism are crimes or violations of human rights under any circumstances and whether innocent victims or governments have any rights against terrorists.

Also contested are just what rights there are. Are there human rights to a secure economic environment, a liveable natural environment, a democratic government, basic privileges of acting on conscience, fundamental civil liberties, and so on? Not only is there a substantial list of different rights advocated by different groups; there is also a major problem of enforcing rights once a consensus about them emerges, since the sovereignty of nation-states is frequently claimed to be a bulwark against any interference in the domestic politics of nation-states and groups that are alleged to deny human rights. There is also debate about whether human rights belong exclusively to nation-states on behalf of citizens, groups on behalf of members, or only to individuals, who (unfortunately) have no official legal standing in international law.

Therefore, while human rights is certainly a valid concept that is an important component of any sophisticated understanding of the proper relationship of the individual and the political system, it remains controversial and ambiguous within international and domestic law as well as political theory.[27]

POLITICAL ECONOMY, INDIVIDUALISM, AND POLITICS

Political economy encompasses a substantial area of individual interaction with politics and government that has barely been recognized, much less dealt with, by contemporary political theory. As technology has effectively shrunk the world, our economic interactions have more political impact than ever before. The reverse is true also. Political theory needs to perceive and deal with the new reality of a world of human interdependence. Global transportation, communications, money transfers, ecological impacts, wars, and political struggles are a reality. Major economic and political events anywhere on the planet create ripples that wash across the globe.

The failure of the wheat harvest in the former Soviet Union, for instance, has a major impact on the agriculture and the economy of North America. Farmers, food processors, freight haulers, and others are affected even though they may never have seen or known any residents of the affected countries. Similarly, a critical decline in the value of the stocks on the New York Stock Exchange causes virtually mirror reactions in financial markets in Zurich, London, Tokyo, and elsewhere; and the individuals, governments, and corporations who have a stake in those financial markets are affected substantially. Pollution dumped in the air in the Ohio valley is shown to harm Canadian forests through acid rain while Ohioans breathe air pollution spewed into the air from smokestacks far to their west. Furthermore, Europe is well along in the process of becoming one economy, and some so-far weak political institutions have emerged to manage it. Along the same lines, the General Agreements on Tariffs and Trade in Geneva, Switzerland, continues to sponsor negotiations (with some limited success to date) on lowering of trade barriers globally. Also, the International Monetary Fund has relieved some of the debt burden of South American governments, but with the strings of mandated economic reforms that have made life more difficult for individual Latin Americans at least in the short run.

Such events are part of the larger process of political economy that has enveloped not only the globe but virtually all of the individuals in it, no matter where they live or how much they are aware of these phenomena. Political economy concerns alternative economic and political systems. As such, it embraces our traditional ideas of both the polity and the economy. It views economics and politics as different ways of thinking about and organizing the same things—things that are not inevitably separate simply because we are taught to think about them that way. Used by political scientists and economists alike, political economy describes the public interactions that pertain to distribution and regulation of material goods and services.[28]

Political economy as a concept embraces both free and guided markets and a vast range of political and economic institutions and behaviors. Although both, it is probably more political than economic because most major economic decisions and allocations ultimately are made at least indirectly by governmental or quasi-governmental organizations. Consequently, they are political dominators of the values and facts of our material lives. The economic dimensions of politics, on the other hand, come from the reality that political decisions and governments cannot operate independently of the economy and resource patterns that they regulate. Economics has an important effect even on the politics that regulate them. We as individual citizens are affected by the whole constellation of structures, processes, and policies of the public sector, whether traditionally political or economic.

Political economy's evolution has been accompanied by a profusion of issues that modern political theory must sort out if it is to remain relevant. Fortunately for us, these questions are just manifestations in political economy of questions that have traditionally been among the central concerns of political theory. Thus, our literature of liberty, justice, and equality has many useful applications in our search for answers.

A major concern involves exploration of the legitimate public and private roles of individuals in the economy. How much economic liberty should an individual have? How much economic equality should he or she have? Does a person (or a group acting as a business firm) have the right to produce any products they wish, even those that will harm the environment or are dangerous? Do they have the right to lie to us about their products?

If we view these questions from the perspective of the desirable balance between liberty and equality, some general pathways and guidelines emerge. All other things being equal, human beings ought to have as much individual liberty as possible in order to develop and mature. However, ours is a world with finite resources, and our proximity to others produces an economic as well as a political interdependence. Consequently, we argue that we must limit the economic freedom of individuals and voluntary groups to the extent that their pursuit of individual economic liberty denies the same right in others. Thus, we have the right to any economic choices and priorities that our desires and means will allow, provided that we do not abuse, exploit, harm, or steal from others as we pursue them. Environmental degradation, fraud, theft, production of dangerous products, and so forth are clearly proscribed by this argument. Being wealthy, producing or owning luxuries and ostentation, and pursuing material instead of other priorities are fine as long as they meet our other criteria, however.

Equality falls into the equation here neatly. If we all have the same liberty to make economic choices that are only limited by others' same liberties, then the case is made for an equality of opportunity in political economy. From this perspective, each of us is not guaranteed an equality of wealth or outcome, but all of us have a right to market our talents fairly (labor, ideas, creativity, etc.) in a free marketplace of political economy. Discrimination because of sex, ethnicity, race; lack of access to quality minimums of education, nutrition, housing, and so forth are prohibited under this notion of equality. The bottom line is simple, though not easy. Our view is that liberty and equality work best in the sphere of political economy when they are balanced so that neither suppresses the other. Both flourish within limits. Of course, this theory of the best approach to political economy is debatable. Socialists may argue that we ought to have more individual equality and less liberty; laissez-faire liberals may argue the opposite; and social reform liberals may want strong controls on corporations. But overall, this approach to the individual and society in political economy makes sense to us because it is rooted in the traditional values of political theory.

A similar set of questions emerges regarding the legitimate private role of the public institutions in an economy. How much should the government regulate individual economic behavior? How much should the government influence corporate economic behavior? Here, too, the traditional values of political theory provide us with a great deal of insight. One widely accepted approach to these questions is advanced by laissez-faire economists who advocate a substantially free commercial marketplace.[29] Political economists like Adam Smith and John Stuart Mill have suggested that commercial goods and services as well as political ideas and ideologies ought to be dispensed in a free marketplace, where any merchant has a right to offer his wares to the public. But there are no guarantees of success: If the wares are attractive to the consumer and the price is competitive, then the merchant will ring up many sales. Entry into the marketplace is virtually by right. But success or failure in it is determined by the competitive realities of the marketplace. Equality can be harsh.

Under this approach, citizens are consumers as well as sellers, and private firms have a natural right to consume as well as offer their products for sale in a free marketplace. Government's task is to make certain that the marketplace remains free and that no firms, governments, or cabal of forces conspire to restrict entry into the marketplace, thereby destroying its freedom. Individuals and entrepreneurs are to be regulated by the forces of the market, not by external forces such as government. The faith of this position is that the public interest will be secured by the operation of the market and that fraudulent or unattractive products and practices will not sell. Thus, the profit incentive to produce them would not be present and they would not be produced or followed. Individuals would boycott firms that discriminate unfairly in hiring, and shoddy products would remain on the shelves if this form of market regulation worked perfectly.

In opposition to this perspective, other political economists[30]—such as John Stuart Mill in his later years, Karl Marx, and John Maynard Keynes— have suggested that unassisted markets do not work in the public interest. They argue that unregulated producers and sellers of goods mislead consumers about quality and suitability of products and produce them in socially harmful ways that exploit workers, pollute the environment, and serve little social purpose. And individuals either do not know about or care about unfair discrimination. Thus, they suggest that the government is the only social agent that represents all without favoritism and has the power to restrain giant and selfish corporations who violate the public good in their quest for profits. They argue that the public interest can only be served if government regulates the marketplace. Government, itself subject to public regulation through elections, has a duty to guarantee entry to the marketplace to all who maintain standards of production, product safety, truth in advertising, and competitive practices that are consistent with the public interest. Firms that violate these norms should be restrained and, if necessary, punished by laws and regulations that define and pursue the public interest through antitrust, environmental protection, regulation of advertising, product safety, and so on.

In principle, under this system the public interest is safeguarded by government while a large degree of operational individual and group freedom in the political economy is still maintained. Firms willing to comply with rules for the public good are still able to enter the marketplace, and individual consumers are entitled to pick the products and services they wish from an abundant menu of choices. We are persuaded by the history of free enterprise that this approach makes sense and ought to be pursued. Notwithstanding, it does not work as neatly or as fairly as its advocates suggest. Government regulation sometimes is ill-conceived or punitive or becomes obsolete as technology and conditions change. Moreover, private interests sometimes manipulate government for their own ends (thereby bypassing the public interest), and consumers can be persuaded by advertising to purchase products that are not as they seem. Nevertheless, despite defects and imperfections, we feel that the question of the desirable role of the government in the political economy is best answered by the approach to political economy and political theory that suggests that markets are the best regulators of economic behavior, provided that they are helped out by government intervention that aims toward the public interest and individual economic freedom. The values of liberty and equality seem to work out best in the marketplace under such an approach.

Because government at its best can have a major impact on how individuals live, its injection into our lives should not extend further than protection of the public interest and securing equal opportunity for all. Government has no place in telling us what our life-styles ought to be, how we should dress, think, and act, except for a moral obligation to restrain all behaviors that present a clear and present danger of harm to others. We suggest that the burden of proof ought to rest on government: Its intervention needs to be justified in the public interest, and individual freedom in the political economy (and other areas of public life) should remain unmolested unless a convincing case is made that it is a threat to the public good. Under those circumstances, government intervention that is only as extensive as is required to solve the problems at hand—and that restricts behaviors and not classes of people—is sensible and should serve as a guideline for the answers to the questions we have posed in this section.

PRIVACY

A special aspect of individual rights and the public interest concerns the right to privacy of individuals: their right to be free from snooping by public and private interests alike. Not necessarily obvious, this moral claim on the part of individuals has a long and well-established history in political theory. It is especially prevalent in the modern Western political theory that has accompanied the Industrial Revolution.

Today's information technology has provided a historically unprecedented ability to monitor the behavior and habits of people. Modern vehicles, workplaces, banks, shopping places, and homes are increasingly equipped with telephones, fax machines, computers hooked to on-line services, and similar devices. Government and even commercial groups have access to sophisticated satellites and other listening, measuring, and tracking technologies that can monitor all kinds of information while remaining unseen themselves. Therefore, seemingly innocent conveniences and devices make us vulnerable to those who can monitor our uses of telephones, credit cards, computers (even ones that are not thought of as freestanding computers, such as the ones in our telephones or cars). We are equally vulnerable to those governments and businesses that maintain files on us (individually or in the aggregate) in national and international data banks, with credit, pension, banking, traffic control, arms control and disarmament, and consumer purchase pattern information being added every time we use a credit card or an automatic teller machine, make a phone call, or perform other acts with hidden or undiscernible consequences.

High technology makes us more vulnerable than ever before to those who can and/or want to follow and monitor our activities for public or private, legitimate or illegitimate purposes. Surely, few of us would object if a regional transit planning authority used modern technology to study how many people drive from our suburb to downtown, when and with how many passengers in their vehicles, what they bought and carried back while downtown, if they made cellular phone calls along the way, and similar habits and patterns in order to plan a commuter rail line that might be heavily utilized and thereby contribute to the public interest. Most of us would accept this as a legitimate purpose for monitoring habits with information technology.

Yet the same or similar technology can be used for more sinister purposes that fewer of us would accept. A government trying to suppress civil liberties (freedom of speech, press, assembly) used by dissidents in opposing unpopular policies can track whom we go to see, who was with us, whom we called on the telephone, to whom we sent a fax, if we were away from our homes or offices during a given period, and so forth. A private corporation can measure what television channels we watch in order to test new markets for products or in order to decide whether we are interested in pornography or activities they deem subversive. Whether it is legitimate to track such information depends on who is using it and for what purpose. Thus an important task for contemporary political theory ought to be to fashion some guidelines for answering such questions. Thinkers who value personal liberty highly, such as John Stuart Mill,[31] maintain that individual rights of liberty and privacy are so important that they must not be violated by anyone, including governments. Such rights come from our very personhood and allow us the freedom and the space to develop our minds and live with dignity. Thus the proponents of personal freedom advocate such civil liberties as freedom of speech, press, assembly, and life-style choices and argue that not even democratically elected majorities can take such rights away. These rights allow minorities in a democracy a chance to become majorities and protect minorities who may be right about things even if the majority never agrees. They usually argue that basic rights include an unambiguous right of privacy. U.S. Constitutional law, for example, recognizes a right to privacy, and court decisions often restrict government actions by citing this right. As technology becomes more and more obtrusive, this right will become more and more precious.

Interestingly, the sole exception to a virtually absolute set of civil liberties and rights permitted by rights advocates like Mill involves exercises of such rights as they interfere with the right of others to use their rights. In other words, the concept of the public interest referred to earlier is used by these political theorists to specify the limits of all rights, including privacy. Relying on the value of equality, Mill makes a persuasive argument that the public interest incorporates the equal moral worth of all. My rights as a human being are identical to yours because you, too, are human. Both of us have rights to dignity under a politics justified by how well it serves its citizens individually and collectively and by how effectively it can reconcile the two if they are in conflict.

If that is true, it is sensible to argue that a person has a valid moral claim to all rights (including a right to privacy that follows from the individual's right to different choices in life-style and to one's integrity of personal worth) except when those rights are used in a manner or context to exploit, dominate, or otherwise infringe upon others. In practical terms, my right to listen to whatever music I desire on my stereo does not extend to listening to it in a manner that will disturb you in your home or space. Moreover, governments or corporations have a right to monitor only the public aspects of my life-style for statistical or planning purposes, but no right to monitor or evaluate what is largely private because it has no public impact on others and thus is none of others' business. Citizens and consumers ought to realize that technology is such that the privacy of cellular telephone conversations or credit card limits cannot be secured despite regulations that exist to protect them. Thus, in these matters, care is in order.

The AIDS epidemic has taught us that there is no purely private realm. Almost everything we do has some impact on others. We need to recognize degrees of impact as we apply labels and policies to decide what is private or public. We also need to acknowledge that there are natural-law or religious traditions that advocate limiting privacy even if little social damage is done by it. Some environmental activists and some fervent members of religious communities that emphasize community fall into this category, and their arguments should be viewed as interesting alternatives.

We are persuaded that a good political theory of privacy and the public interest ought to define and defend an extensive right of privacy based on prudent rights of individual worth. The intrinsic moral worth and choices of people ought to be protected and not be violated by public authorities except when such violations are limited to and by the public interest in extent and kind. Private research and data collection ought to be restricted to an essentially unlimited right to observe and record public behavior only. The boundaries of the home, office, and vehicle ought to be respected as parameters of privacy, and what goes on within them ought to be considered private.

The right of privacy is an extensive one and the burden of proof should rest on those who would deny such a right. A good case for exceptions to that right must be limited to the context and to the extent that violations of others' individual rights (including but not limited to the right to privacy) are a clear and present danger. Only then should these rights be subject to regulation on behalf of the public interest. A person's right to privacy cannot serve as a shield that protects the violation of the rights (including privacy) of others. Thus, the government or other agency is justified in snooping and collecting data on criminals, spies, and other willful violators of individual rights.

Like other civil liberties, however, this right on behalf of the public interest is not a general license. Prior restraint and censorship cannot be tolerated on the part of government, although government has a right to hold individuals responsible for the consequences of their behaviors if they can be proven to violate the public interest. Our right to privacy is so strong that the case for each and every violation of our right to privacy by government snooping must be made before duly constituted authority, and permission to snoop or otherwise violate the rights of privacy should only be granted by limited and specific warrant to ascertain specific information in a specific manner that follows carefully drawn guidelines. Violation of such warrants by information collectors should be criminal acts subject to prosecution of abusers just as is the case with police brutality.

CONCLUSION

Modern citizens are social and political animals who interact with others not by choice but by circumstances. Political relationships and interactions are an inevitable consequence of the fact that we are traveling on a crowded planet at the same time in history with other voyagers through time and space. Since the public context to such sharing is the subject matter of political theory, our discipline has a prominent place reserved for ideas and values about the proper relationships of the individual and society.

Politics and government are important enterprises that ought to be pursued and perfected to the best of people's abilities. At the same time, we must also respect the individual. People formed the first governments, and there would be no need for politics, government, or political theory without us. Consequently, the individual and his or her worth are at least as important as the collective interactions of individuals and perhaps even more so. For that reason, it is our position that public relationships and institutions must be instrumental to individual needs and moral claims. Politics and government are justified and honorable only to the extent to which they make individual interactions and relationships in the public realm more humane, meaningful, effective, or comfortable.

Our view of the proper relationship between individual and society comes from this perspective. It is the context of our whole approach to political theory. Our moral choices and the values we embrace about the public interest, human rights and responsibilities, political economy, and so forth define us as political theorists and human beings. Thus we have chosen values and institutions that place the rights of the individual first. But we are willing to define individual rights in ways that could limit those rights if so doing helps us to track the seemingly always elusive goal of equality. We feel that exceptions to the rights of individuals must be justified by a solid case for such exceptions rooted in equal rights. Even though political institutions are valuable, they overstep their authority when they violate individual human rights without a corresponding clear and present gain in an unambiguous public interest. Collectively, human beings can accomplish more than they can do alone. And political institutions and values play a proud and effective part in that collective heritage. Nevertheless, we want to ally our pride and support of political and governmental institutions with an idea of political values that recognizes and protects the linkage between individuals and their social environment. Political theory serves best when we remember that our political institutions ought to serve us as political animals and not vice versa.

GLOSSARY OF KEY TERMS

drives, instincts, reflexes, temperaments Various terms used by natural and social scientists to describe different aspects and degrees of allegedly innate human tendencies.

human nature Behavioral tendencies that humans are born with and cannot change.

human rights A set of moral claims that all people possess. They are held to be sacrosanct even above the claims of governments and are widely discussed in political theory and international politics. Many disagree about the specific content of them and how they ought to be enforced.

laissez-faire (French origin—literally, "let it be") A hands-off policy for government in the political economy.

nurture Term used by some anthropologists to signify the effect of the environment and conditioning on human behavior. It is usually contrasted with nature as a cause of behavior

political economy An integrated approach to public interactions that views them as involving both politics and economics. The study of alternative political and economic systems.

privacy right The moral claim that individuals have a right to go about their business (as long as it does not harm others) secure from snooping or interference from government or other groups.

public interest A term used to summarize institutions, policies, and so forth that are in the best interests of the public. For some it is more important than individual claims or needs.

SUGGESTIONS FOR FURTHER READING

Arnhart, Larry. *Political Questions*. New York: Macmillan Publishing Co., 1987.

Cartmill, Matt. "Four Legs Good, Two Legs Bad." *Natural History*, November 1983.

Dworkin, Ronald. *Taking Rights Seriously*. Cambridge, Mass.: Harvard University Press, 1977.

Flathman, Richard E. *Concepts in Social and Political Philosophy*. New York: Macmillan Publishing Co., 1973.

Hart, H. L. A. "Between Utility and Rights." *Columbia Law Review* 79 (1979): 828–846.

Hoover, Kenneth R. *Ideology and Political Life*. Monterey, Calif.: Brooks/Cole, 1987.

Phelps, Edmund. *Political Economy*. New York: W. W. Norton, 1985.

Sibley, Mulford. *Political Ideas and Ideologies*. New York: Harper & Row, 1970.

Spragens, Thomas A., Jr. *Understanding Political Theory*. New York: St. Martin's Press, 1976.

Stewart, Robert M., ed. *Readings in Social and Political Philosophy*. New York: Oxford University Press, 1986.

Wiser, James. *Political Theory: A Thematic Inquiry*. Chicago: Nelson-Hall, 1986.

NOTES

1. Aristotle, *Politics*, trans. Benjamin Jowett (New York: Modern Library, 1943), Book 1.
2. Mulford Sibley, *Political Ideas and Ideologies* (New York: Harper & Row, 1970), Chapter 5.
3. Jean Jacques Rousseau, *The Social Contract, Discourse on the Sciences and the Arts, Discourse on the Origins of Inequality*, in *The Social Contract and the Discourses*, trans. G. D. H. Cole (New York: E. P. Dutton, 1927).
4. Karl Marx's collected works are widely available. A good one-volume interpretation and explanation of them is Isaiah Berlin, *Karl Marx: His Life and Environment* (New York: Oxford University Press, 1963).
5. Sigmund Freud, *Civilization and Its Discontents*, trans. Joan Riviere (New York: Doubleday, 1958).
6. Albert Camus, *The Rebel* (New York: Vintage Books, 1956).
7. St. Augustine and St. Thomas Aquinas were theologians who advocated a political system that served the needs of God and dealt with the depraved or imperfect aspects of human nature.
8. Sharia is the practice of using Islamic law, as found in the Koran, the Muslim holy book, as the basis for state laws and policies. It often carries harsh penalties for violation.
9. Utopian communities (usually but not always socialist) of various kinds grew up based on the idea that free communal association among liberated human beings would lead to cooperation and justice.
10. Thomas Hobbes believed that humans are selfish and only partly reasonable. Thus they need the police to keep them in line and preserve peace. John Locke felt that human beings are a bit more benign and he advocated a democratic state

of the propertied that could enforce the peace through majority will. Jean Jacques Rousseau felt that people are potentially cooperative and that a participatory democracy could develop a general will that would substitute socialization for coercion. The extent to which each of these thinkers felt that people could participate in a free and open community depended on the extent to which he viewed humans as selfish or cooperative by nature.

11. Karl Marx is the most famous socialist theorist, but there are many other socialist thinkers who came before and after Marx and who had strong visions of what socialist man ought to be. See George Lichtheim, *Origins of Socialism* (New York: Praeger, 1969).

12. A good article that is representative of some of the controversies inherent in any objective analysis of human nature is Stephen Jay Gould, "Taxonomy as Politics: The Harm of False Classification," *Dissent* (Winter 1990): 73–78. Another interesting one is Boyce Rensberger, "The Nature-Nurture Debate II: The Steps Toward Human Nature Are Built of Culture and Genes," *Science* 4(1983): 38–46.

13. Rensberger, "The Nature-Nurture Debate II."

14. Ibid., p. 42.

15. The willingness to play the game is discussed in the context of democratic culture in Chapter 9.

16. These quotes and the idea of a strong sovereign are from Thomas Hobbes's *Leviathan*.

17. Plato in *The Republic* was an implacable foe of democracy because he felt that it would lead to pandering to the politics of the lowest common denominator and lead the polity away from virtue.

18. I am indebted to Professor John Harkness, Department of Sociology and Anthropology at Kent State University, for his patient counsel and suggestions for this section.

19. Matt Cartmill, "Four Legs Good, Two Legs Bad," *Natural History*, November 1983, pp. 65–79.

20. St. Augustine, for example, argues that we are flawed by nature by original sin and until we enter the City of God we are depraved and must be helped to live a good life.

21. From the definition of public interest law in *The Encyclopedic Dictionary of American Government*, 3d ed. (Sluice Dock, CT: Dushkin Publishing, 1986), p. 260.

22. William Keefe, Henry Abraham, William Flanigan, Charles Jones, Morris Ogul, and John Spanier, *American Democracy: Institutions, Politics, and Policies*, 3d ed. (New York: HarperCollins, 1990), p. 17.

23. See the longer discussion of this in Jeffrey Orenstein, *U.S. Rail Policy* (Chicago: Nelson-Hall, 1990), pp. 15–17.

24. Interview with Sheldon Wolin in Bill Moyers, *A World of Ideas*, ed. Betty Sue Flowers (New York: Doubleday, 1989), p. 100.

25. Ibid., pp. 100–103.

26. The so-called utility principle advanced by orthodox utilitarians in the nineteenth century, including John Stuart Mill's father, James, as well as Jeremy Bentham.

27. Rights are frequently alleged to be tied to political responsibilities. Usually the claims surrounding this issue are rooted in popular ideas of patriotism and "good" citizen behavior and are frequently endorsed by political leaders who stand to benefit from citizen acceptance of such principles. The argument is that while individuals have rights to various political behaviors, these rights contain a

concomitant responsibility to behave carefully and not "abuse" the rights. We raise this now only to point out that these issues are discussed at length in our chapters on obligation and patriotism.

28. Edmund Phelps, *Political Economy* (New York: W. W. Norton, 1985), and William K. Tabb, *The Political Economy of the Black Ghetto* (New York: W. W. Norton, 1970), are an economist and a political scientist who have used the term *political economy* recently. Marx, Rousseau, Locke, and Aristotle were prominent historical political theorists who used the term as well.

29. Joseph E. Stiglitz, *Economics of the Public Sector* (New York: W. W. Norton, 1986), p. 8.

30. John Stuart Mill, a prominent advocate of laissez-faire who later advocated strong government intervention into the economy on behalf of the public interest. See his *Principles of Political Economy.* Marx was the major advocate of socialism in the face of the Industrial Revolution in nineteenth-century Europe, and Keynes advocated an active role of government to cope with economic cycles in the twentieth century.

31. John Stuart Mill, "On Liberty," in *Essential Works of John Stuart Mill* (New York: Bantam, 1961), pp. 255–360.

Chapter
3

Community, Authority, and Leadership

Ours is an age of dethroned gods. Community, authority, and leadership often seem weak even as we frequently view them all with more than a little ambivalence. Authority more and more looks fallible and our leaders in many realms often stumble. Community can seem restrictive and freedom-denying. Perhaps it is no accident that divorce, crime, and sexual abuse sometimes appear to be more the story of our age than authority or community. In this age of the individual, many see themselves as the only legitimate authority or have decided that community is attractive only on their own individual terms. And there are few leaders who excite much trust or enthusiasm.

Yet these very conditions worry many citizens. There are many signs that people and institutions are often adrift without much sense of what or whom to follow. There are innumerable indications of social breakdown in terms of family and social collapse that are marks of the decline of a community in terms of shared meanings and lives for many people. It is no wonder that interest in effective leadership, legitimate authority beyond the self, and satisfying community remains strong. Thus there is plenty of cause in our age to explore community, authority, and leadership, to ask what we may learn from their present tattered conditions. And there is understandable anxiety about the situation regarding authority, leadership, and community for the future.

In this chapter we explore the concepts of authority, leadership, and community, a process that we continue in the next chapter as well, especially for authority and community. These three concepts are not the same, of course, nor are they necessarily linked. They do not have to go together, and certainly they do not in many people's political outlook. Moreover, by no

36

means are they always connected in our discussions. But they come to the fore in political theory today out of a common situation.

One way to start is to examine the situation that lies behind their weakened condition today. One view is that it results from a spiritual crisis: We are adrift in modernity without much in the way of spiritual or religious grounding for any values. In such a circumstance, we hardly expect to find dependable leadership, flourishing community, or strong authority, though we may very well find the conditions for the emergence of despotism.

Daniel Bell argues that the "real problem of *modernity* is the problem of belief . . . it is a spiritual crisis."[1] He is not alone. Other voices acknowledge the costs of widespread spiritual exhaustion and emptiness: "the workday world . . . has become empty and alienated, without a transcendent justification. . . . There are private escapes from this fate, such as the religion of sexuality. But these can hardly hold a community together."[2]

Others make the same point while avoiding religious language and assumptions. They agree that our world is very much without compass and it is no wonder that authority and community are not easy to achieve in such a world. In our situation we miss the "language of communal meaning," our absent "public ethic," and our lost "sense of shared responsibility."[3] As individuals we have, some argue, the same problem. We float with "no common object, no common good, no natural complementarity."[4]

This is obviously not fertile terrain for leadership or community. They require a foundation on which to exist and to grow. Some complain that the situation is made worse because it leads in very concrete ways to damaged lives and people separated from each other. Our society is now distinctly "loose-bounded," and its confusion and division about values and a basis for values enters into the home, the family, the neighborhood, and among friends. The result is the decline of tradition, culture, and institutions. They have all eroded, and authority and community with them. Many of us are left "alone and adrift in an often alien . . . universe."[5]

Much of the debate about leadership, authority, and community today proceeds from this assessment of the problem posed by what many take to be a crisis of values and value justification today. But much also proceeds from a related analysis, one that concentrates on individualism in modern society. One widely discussed approach is Robert Bellah's in his *Habits of the Heart*. Bellah and his associates describe the process of growing up in our culture as one that is self-focused, a process where each of us creates our own self. Moreover, Bellah and his associates argue that this process continues long after childhood. It governs our practice toward marriage and family, which our gods of today—individualism and personal freedom—indifferently support at best. Today to stand by such values as duty, obligation, or family is demanding and difficult. Many choose instead to hurry to a therapist who promotes a definition of family as each person doing what he or she wants ("needs") or the search for a new "career" that is (somehow) "fulfilling," whatever the consequences for the family community.[6]

One result may be people grasping for anything that may provide meaning or help them overcome their loneliness as individuals without ever helping them to gain much awareness of what community is—or authority either. This possibility only makes more urgent a serious exploration of both.

TOWARD DEFINITION

Understandings of what community means are all but innumerable. Moreover, community is a contested concept. Arguments abound over its meaning because the debate involves major issues of principle and policy that are implied by any definition of community. The picture is complicated but also interesting. We need to accept from the start that a completely shared definition of community does not exist.

Yet there remain common themes present in most discussions of community. It is an open concept, but that is not the same thing as one with no boundaries and no hope of definition. Most views of community do agree that at a minimum the concept implies commonality, sharing in common. We agree, and define community as the condition of being and experiencing together.

We also agree that community sharing must have an emotional dimension. Community is and must be a felt experience among humans. This fact does not mean that community or its advocates spurn reason. Most welcome both reason and feeling in community. One view puts it well: Community involves "fraternal sentiments" but it is also a communal "mode of self-understanding." At its richest, community goes into the heart but helps us understand ourselves and others in rational terms too.[7]

Finally, sharing must be serious for there to be a community. Students who attend the same class may be said to share something in common, but they would not necessarily constitute a community. They might if the course was an intense one that bound them together in some notable way. Ordinarily, though, they are not really a community. They are not to be compared to more likely community situations: a squad of frontline soldiers, a close family, or even a stable and friendly neighborhood. To be sure, it is always a matter of degree, but the more intense the bonding, the more valid the claim to be a community. In short, where there are relationships of sharing—serious, emotive sharing—there are communities.[8]

The meanings of authority and leadership are not self-evident either. Arguments over authority are inevitable. So much is at stake over issues of authority, when it exists and when it ought to exist, that there could hardly be an easy consensus over what authority is about.[9] Moreover, the very idea of authority, however understood, always attracts enemies. There are many—and perhaps there always should be many—who are eager to "question authority." For them, no one and no thing can or should limit individual autonomy and sovereignty. Their voices help authority and its meaning be encircled in clouds of controversy.[10]

Still, what authority means is less contested and controversial than the views as to when authority is legitimate, or if it ever is legitimate. By ordinary definition, authority means *legitimate power* to influence, direct, or guide. It suggests that one has the right to speak or act. Authority and power, therefore, are not the same thing. Power is about the ability to make people do what you want; it is not about right or wrong. On the other hand, authority is a moral term. Authority implies rightful, legitimate voice and action, and we consider authority that cannot meet this standard to be illegitimate, not really authority at all. If authority is misused, or falsely claimed, we think of it as wrong.

Another way this distinction has been put is to separate de jure authority, or legitimate authority—the kind we normally mean—from de facto authority, or what is not legitimate authority. A person or government that has power may force us to obey, but we recognize that this is far from what ought to be, far from real authority.[11]

Authority is like community in that it also implies a reciprocal relationship. A parent has human authority over a child only so long as they both accept that authority. A government may try and make parental authority last legally, but in real, emotional terms authority can never be forced. When one partner in any relationship renounces the legitimacy of the relationship, its authority is gone.

In more conventional political terms, authority brings us to the issue of leadership. Leaders are people who have authority, and one central reason why there often seem to be so few leaders is because authority is a concept in eclipse among us. To be a leader, as to have authority, requires followers. There is simply no possibility of leadership or authority in political life unless it is acknowledged, affirmed, or honored by citizens.

Authority and leaders must have legitimacy or they do not exist. As Augustine pointed out long ago, even a robber band has its bonds and leaders. They may not have authority in the rest of society, but within their own world they do and they must. Otherwise, sheer force or power will rule, a situation all too often true in the modern era.

Leadership and authority can be and sometimes are found in a multitude of settings. One of the great contributions of Max Weber's meditations on leadership and authority was his perception of this reality. A German scholar of a century ago, Max Weber suggested that there are three great bases of authority and three basic kinds of leadership. One type of leader emerges from the modern world of bureaucracy and law, with authority rooted in legal and rational structures and procedures. This kind of leader is constitutional, bureaucratic, and limited. A second variety is the version often present in traditional societies. There leadership and authority have little to do with modern institutions and laws and much to do with traditional roles assigned by religion and custom. A third type, which Weber perceptively realized lies just below the surface in the modern world, is authority derived from people's emotional needs and desires. These can result in what he termed charismatic leadership, inspiring and sometimes dangerous leadership that taps deep emotions.[12]

PUBLIC LEADERSHIP, AUTHORITY, AND COMMUNITY

As we proceed in this chapter and the following one, we explore leadership, authority, and community through discussion of concrete examples. Our hope is that by this means we can illustrate the challenges and dilemmas of these central concepts. We suspect that community best comes alive in examples of community and so do leadership and authority.

Our first step is to divide our discussion between the public and the private dimensions. We understand, of course, that this line is less real than some believe. What is private is rarely completely so, and what is public frequently reaches into the most private corners of life these days.

Yet we insist that the spheres are not quite the same. The public sphere still refers to what we have in common—in political terms, to common life and political decisions of the whole society. The private area refers to what is individual to us and our own world, apart from the larger society. Authority, leadership, and community are fundamental concepts in both realms, and here we begin by examining them in the context of public life, of politics as it is usually understood.

One model of public community which we know continues to attract interest is the participatory model.[13] For its devoted partisans it is not only the very model of community, but it is also enormously attractive because it promises a secure base for public authority. Still others celebrate it because they believe it will end the necessity and the danger of leadership.

There is no single definition of a participatory community. From one angle it is about face-to-face, direct self-governance. From another, it concerns citizens united by shared goals, mutual respect, common sympathies. From a third, it focuses on broad equality, equality of influence and the necessary political, economic, and social equality to make equal influence a reality. Every version agrees that this understanding of community involves small-group decision making in conditions of respect and equality.

Every model of community has a model of authority. In this case authority is overwhelmingly democratic. Legitimate power or authority comes from the people in their direct decision making. They are the source of authority and there are few or no others. Their authority is absolute.

Leaders should not really exist in this view. There may be a need for facilitators to carry out the wishes of the community or to make temporary decisions or to assist the community in practical business when community decisions are made. But the assumption of the participatory model of community and authority is that as leadership increases its role in a society, both community and democratic authority decrease. They have an inverse relationship with leadership. Thus leaders are something to be frightened of, and the goal is to reduce their antidemocratic influence as much as possible or even altogether.

Proponents argue that this kind of community is vital for individual self-development. It assists people's self-confidence. It raises their level of thinking. It nurtures their sense of community and concern for others. It promotes a communitarian, participatory person, who is the way we all are at our best. We are all then citizens, the preferred word for these communitarians, since their goal is an individual who is self-confident and community oriented, active and participatory in common self-government. We learn to depend on ourselves and the community and never on some leaders.[14]

Of course, there are those who think about community in this public, participatory sense who have their doubts in terms of realizing such a community. Few believe it is a kind of community that can be achieved on a national level. National communities may be possible as matters of national patriotism or cultural unity, but they are not what energizes participatory community supporters. Such "communities" seem remote to them. But national community in their sense is also elusive because there are so many different and conflicting interests and perspectives in an entire nation's life. Diversity dooms community at the nation-state level.

So does the sense that at least some leadership is required for coordination and for quick decisions that sometimes have to be made in the foreign policy realm. However, these factors simply make participatory community advocates all the less enthusiastic about the nation-state level of government—and all the more suspicious of it. At best it is, as are leaders, a necessary evil.

Such an analysis does not really apply, however, to local situations, as long as community in such settings does not eliminate conflict and mutual learning. One of the larger uncertainties, though, is the role of leadership even at the local level in this model of community. Leadership immediately invokes a number of issues, but one is certainly the question of authority. We should understand clearly that in the participatory community model there is plenty of authority, though that term is often avoided. The participatory community itself is the community's authority, perhaps an unusually powerful source of authority. On the other hand, we know that any understanding of authority in community that translates to welcoming leadership makes participatory enthusiasts wary.

This is why on the level of local community most participatory communitarians seek any and every way to avoid leaders and thus the hierarchical authority they dread. They are, to be sure, more sensitive to hierarchies of economic class or traditional political leadership than to those that a participatory community may unintentionally promote, such as elites based on verbal skills and education. And they encourage people to take the lead in offering ideas and proposals to the community. Yet their spirit is distinctly antileadership and antihierarchical, though the ancient question remains: can any community escape hierarchy and the practical necessity of leadership? Some ask whether participatory advocates would not do better to struggle with whatever kind of leadership might be compatible with their ideals rather than to chase the illusion that they can escape leadership altogether.[15]

Meditations on these concerns do not sit well with some advocates of participatory community. They fear that the heart of community may be eliminated by compromises as so-called practicality engenders the sacrifice of community. For them we must press ahead with the goal of community with confidence and optimism, if not naïveté.[16]

We commonly hear two other major reservations about participatory community as the ideal of community. Skeptics ask: will participatory community be too conformist? This is a serious query which reaches toward the core of community as an ideal. Its proponents, we know, believe in it in large part because it will, they hope, bring people together, help them live well together, and meanwhile develop each person. But the skeptic wants to know: how does it develop each person and what kind of a grouping does it promote?

First, the fear is that such small-group community may lead to conformity, the creation of an atmosphere where everyone is extra sensitive to and thus under the pressure of all others. The threat of tyranny of the majority seems possible in such an atmosphere of intense interaction. Political discussion could become stifled and political freedoms fade away, whether or not they are protected by being written into law. More broadly, the fear is that such a community will restrict freedom in general and thus human possibilities for individuals. Skeptics worry that the authority of a participatory community will simply be too strong and too overwhelming. What other authority would be honored by participatory advocates? What other sources of authority would be in a position to limit the community?

A related concern is the conviction that such a community (or a conformity) will produce a lifeless economy with no entrepreneurial energy or creativity. In such a community, how many people are willing to risk the enmity of the others, break from the pack, and try creative economic actions that in the long run will improve economic life for them—and for the community as a whole?

Second, participatory community faces the perpetual criticism that even if the ideal is laudatory, it is impossible. Practicality stands in the way. For example, skeptics are willing to bet that participatory community will always meet one of two fates: dull conformity or chaotic collapse. The questions raised are essential for political theory: How cooperative are people? How willing are they to work for the common good? How much will cooperative work fit individual desires for individual growth and freedom?

The issue is in part one of human nature. Some thinkers do not worry much about human selfishness nor assume it will doom community. Others—including all critics of participatory community—do worry about the effects of selfishness. Sympathetic skeptics recognize that the challenge is real: how to encourage human behavior that is community oriented and yet not so much so that it turns into stifling conformity. These are daunting tasks, but they cannot be grappled with unless they are acknowledged as challenges. Practical objections must be faced.

Many advocates of participatory community resist institutionalized checks such as, for example, courts modeled on our Supreme Court. Participatory advocates fear that such institutions will promote new elites and hierarchies. Yet abuse of power by a tyrannical majority cannot be ignored or pretended away in any ideal of community. To put it another way, the question is one of abuse of authority. How can a society that vigorously stresses community exercise restraint on the majority or encourage a kind of fruitful diversity that defeats dangerous conformity? It is a conundrum for every ideal of community, especially in such an intense and face-to-face version as participatory community.

Another example of the practical concerns, as we have suggested, turns around the leadership question. Is it really possible to avoid the practice of the past that in every situation some emerge as leaders with much more say over outcomes than most people have? Is it not true that some will have the energy and skills even in a participatory community to assume this role, while most people here as elsewhere will not want to spend the time and energy on communal, political life? In a variation on this age-old concern, will not many citizens conclude that participatory community takes too many nights, and let leaders emerge to do the job for them most of the time?

In the end, there is no escape from a return to human nature. We can and some do discuss at length what the data show about human experiences with community in the past and now, in this country and elsewhere, in the factory or in the political system. The data are all fine and often quite interesting, but they are also very much subject to alternative readings, just as is human nature and its potential. Few may believe that we are impressively cooperative and socially concerned beings today, ready to forgo leadership and rally to a public, political life, but the issue is our human potential. Can we become so? And, if so, how do we get from here to there?

Many of the most determined advocates of the participatory model of community insist that their ideal should exist in all areas of life, but they often are especially anxious that it obtain in work life. This version of community is sometimes called workers' control. For its proponents in every workplace—as elsewhere—all employees should be a community of self-governing equals. Moreover, they contend that workers' control in the economy is a prerequisite for any genuine community in the formal political system. Inequality in one place will soon chase out equality in any place.

Worker-control images of community immediately raise again the matter of practicality. Critics expect economic inefficiency and collapse. Won't the system become inefficient, with many loafers hiding behind the group, opposing all efforts to increase work or be innovative? Won't there also be disastrous problems of coordination in the larger community, complete with conflicts of authority without end? Can one seriously do complex work without an understood leadership of skill and authority?

Opinions differ here, too, of course. Some supporters maintain that productivity should increase in a setting where all count and all count equally because everybody will care. Others are much less sure, sensing some very wishful thinking. Either way, though, supporters argue that what they are interested in is not efficiency or increased productivity above all else. They want to expand community, a sense of participatory and equal sharing. Given the primacy of that goal, they will take their chances on the practical consequences in terms of the economy.[17]

Doubts have accelerated with the collapse of socialism in Eastern Europe, the Soviet Union, and the favorite country of worker-control supporters, Yugoslavia. Marxism talked of workers' control and participatory community, but the reality in these countries turned out to be very different. There was little workers' control or community or economic health. Yet, except for Yugoslavia—where there were steps toward participatory community (with no great success)—most of the Marxist mess did not stem from participatory community. Communist, top-down economies had nothing to do with participatory community. Thus one cannot conclude from that situation that participatory community is worthless in theory and practice. Some argue that the opposite is true: that Communist regimes were a lesson in the failures of a top-down approach to economic life, where "leadership" failed because it lost touch with the community and forfeited its authority.

Michael Walzer argues that the norm that a good community must include all of us and have responsibility for all of us (to at least some extent) is now accepted if not so widely practiced. One of the sources of that principle is in socialist and often worker-control ideas of community that can be distinguished from the Marxist societies that failed.[18]

THE GLOBAL COMMUNITY AND AUTHORITY

A second ideal of public community is the global model of community, now both popular and controversial in this age of environmentalism. We think it will provide a very different perspective on the questions of leadership, authority, and community. Moreover, we are convinced that in no arena in the long run will matters of community and leadership prove more important than those revolving around the global community and whatever authority it may come to wield. The issue is our future and perhaps our survival in the twenty-first century.

We all recognize the widespread concern over the global environment present today. And most of us are aware that in these terms we are all part of one threatened community, a threatened community of humankind, or—in another version—a community of all in nature. Innumerable theorists with agendas of incredible variety address the ecology of life on earth in such terms today.

Proponents of global community invariably begin with the assumption that the global community is in terrible crisis. To preserve it, they argue, only the most dramatic changes will help, for the crisis is real and life itself is at stake. Drastic change must come, though it will not be easy to implement or quick in its effects.[19]

Thus there is little that is passive in the approach of those who talk of the global community, no matter how pessimistic they often are in their analyses of present conditions. They burn with anxiety for vigorous action, convinced as they are that their community will be lost if they—and we—do not act. But globalists understand that action is very much dependent on awareness.

Thus globalists agree on the essential importance of instilling an ethic of worldwide community. This desire may seem strange in that it might imply that there is not yet such a community. Yet globalists never doubt that there is such a community within nature. Indeed, this assumption, among others, is something of a problem with their thought, because it is rarely argued. Globalists need to defend the idea that the earth is a community as well as their view that it is the community that is more important than any other. What does receive much argument is, who belongs to the community, with the most inclusive visions of nature steadily gaining strength in today's interpretations.

Those concerned with global community see that their major problem at this point is to gain recognition with others for the global community and its moral authority. For them, the community of nature is real, whereas human recognition of it lags far behind. They maintain that recognition of global community has great moral urgency because change to preserve it is so desperately needed. Thinking globally is essential, even if, in the cliché, one necessarily acts locally.

For those oriented to a global model of community such a community is fully appropriate. It is not that we are somehow stuck with global community. Rather, global community is a wonderful, rich, complex, interrelated community—our ecosystem—one where we as humans are one part of an amazing whole. Appreciation of this great, natural community is the crucial first step toward honoring the community. Attitude change must precede all else and will facilitate all else.

But what is the moral basis for such a community? What are the arguments which people offer for its authority? In terms of authority, the question is, what is the basis for claiming the global community as central? We know we have to ask such questions of every community and of every claim for the authority of every community. Yet there is an especial relevance of asking this question in this instance. The reason is that proponents of the global or natural community frequently do not ask it themselves. Still, there are arguments made and they are important. Sometimes the argument is largely religious. There are many within religious communities who insist that the global community must be integral to true and deep religious living. There is indeed something to the idea that a "Greening of Religion" has taken place within religious circles.[20] Within the Jewish and Christian context most arguments on behalf of the global community are variations of the idea that God created the earth and all that is on it. Thus it is special, and the natural,

God-given community that it is must be treated with deep respect. Some-times that respect treats all parts of God's creation as equal. Most often the analysis is that God placed the human in charge of God's creation and it is up to us to be good stewards of divine work.[21]

Not everyone, to say the least, is very sympathetic to this religious perspective, which locates ultimate authority with God as creator. Some place the blame for our present environmental problems and general global degradation on Western religions. Critics contend that the Bible is filled with passages which suggest that man (or the human being) is given some kind of dominion over nature for his own use. Such a view shocks and angers globalists. They insist that it is inherently hostile to the earth and to (their version of) egalitarian, interactive community. They also charge that it has wrought enormous damage to the fragile global community.[22]

Some globalists are interested in other religious traditions, which they take to be more devoted to nature and/or more "holistic." Taoism is popular in this context and so is Buddhism. Eco-feminism, a form of holistic spirituality stressing the closeness of the feminine to nature, has also drawn interest. Each of these perspectives has its strengths and limitations for the religion of nature, and each—along with others—may play a greater role as the search for authority for the sovereignty of the global model of community con-tinues.[23]

A second approach toward authority for the global community—one that is as familiar—is the celebration of nature. Indeed, it is the overwhelming response among globalists to the question of what is the proper basis for global community. For them, nature carries authority. They crown nature sovereign and affirm that on its strength must rest their community.

The goal is often a return to something seen as "true" nature, though exactly what nature is (and is not) is often not as clear as it might be. For them, nature is a reality in which the human is thoroughly integrated and in which all parts of nature are interrelated, respected, and protected. Frequent invocations to "harmony" and "holism" underline the insistence that humans and the rest of nature must self-consciously reconcile for nature's authority to be full.[24]

Questions arise quickly, however. Nature certainly exists and has the complexity and unity in which global community thinkers believe. But why does it follow that it is the moral grounding for some kind of global commu-nity? Where does its moral authority derive? In classical philosophical terms, how does one derive an "ought" from an "is"? Just because something exists does not make it moral or the proper foundation for morality.

Moreover, as we know, many of those who look to nature for the basis of global community also argue that many parts or every part of nature has rights within nature and must be respected as such. Affirmations of the rights of animals and pleas for "animal liberation" are routine today. Some would go much further and argue that flowers or trees have such rights in and from nature. Such arguments force us back again to ask: how does nature confer rights? And at the same time, we must also consider: where might we draw the line? If humans and dogs have rights, do stones? Does every object in nature? And how do we decide?[25]

Finally, and this is a serious challenge, how does an approach to nature that interprets nature as a provider of rights fit with community? We have seen already that many thinkers today who are reaching toward community are critical of what they perceive as the excessive individualism all around us. As a result, they are often reluctant to affirm rights except most cautiously. The concept of rights often directs us to particular individuals or groups and their claims against the whole community. It can point us away from the whole. How can focusing on the rights of part or all of nature vis-à-vis each other or human nature build community?

The most radical of those who look to nature as a source of justification for community in environmentalism are those who are concerned with "deep ecology," as this stance is sometimes termed. Among them are the activists of Earth First![26] This view is highly community oriented. Its vision is less one of rights than of nature as a whole, with each part on equal footing with every other. In fact, for them nature is greater than any of its parts, including the human being. Thus they urge the liberation of nature from human domination, an act which they are confident will yield a rebirth of community in the entire ecosphere. Here as elsewhere, exactly what nature means and includes is not always obvious, nor is the reason why it is the great source of moral authority. The interest in community is real, however.

While nature in some sense or other is the common source of legitimacy for community in environmentalist arguments, we know it is not the sole one. Yet another perspective is rooted in utilitarian perspectives. Here we encounter no rhapsodies to Nature or to nature's rights or the eco-community. Instead, the tone is one of fearful practicality and the guiding theme is survival. The claim is that we are in environmental crisis and survival is at stake. We must respond quickly and create community for the survival of us all.

Some of this writing is apocalyptic, talking in drastic terms, predicting an imminent collapse or even death of planet Earth if we do not act now for the common good of all. One famous example is Robert Heilbroner's *Inquiry into the Human Prospect*, which pursues global community on just such a premise. The book contends that all countries, rich and poor alike, need to work together to solve our global problems. Put in our terms, we need to begin to respect world community to ensure a surviving global community. If we do not, we will face wars over dwindling resources which will jeopardize survival. It is a matter of pragmatic utility.

To be sure, Heilbroner thinks of community more in terms of human order than of nature. In that he is similar to many survivalists. They are often anthropocentric, focused on human beings above all else. From the perspective of those who call on nature and nature's authority, this is not acceptable. Then, what *should* drive the concern for global community? That is the issue. Should it be practical utilitarianism or the authority of "nature" or the world as a sacred creation of God?

It is among the utilitarians and survivalists that tough questions about leadership arise. This is in contrast to many environmentalists and globalists. The general orientation of many globalists is to celebrate nature as an inter-dependent web and to attack the ancient hierarchy of human beings over the rest of nature. *Community* and *equal rights* are at the heart of their favorite vocabulary. Sometimes for them, the result is that concrete matters such as how change is going to be accomplished get lost.

In particular, environmentalists and globalists do not always face the matter of leadership. This situation is less true, however, among many of the utilitarians and survivalists. Often they are less passionate about nature than they are about survival. Perhaps as a result, they frequently focus directly on practical matters including the question of how to ensure survival. That in turn leads them to address the issue of leadership and democracy.

While many environmentalists are absolutely convinced that ecology and democracy—even participatory democracy—can and will go together, there are plenty of skeptics. Robert Heilbroner, for example, explores the question, wondering whether it really will be possible to resolve the difficult and conflicting positions within the international system without a good deal of very strong leadership, perhaps even strongly authoritarian leadership. This would certainly not be his choice, but the issue comes to this: what do you do if you face great division of opinion and of interest in a time of crisis? How much democracy can we afford in a world that seems to be growing more democratic, ironically, every week? Will the result be conflict, parochialism, confusion, and inaction?

To save the global community, we may ask, do we instead need world government under tough centralized leadership? Or, perhaps with more hope, can we settle for some combination of international leadership and popular input? The answer is not obvious, but addressing the question is absolutely essential for those concerned with the model of global community. Authority and leadership are matters that cannot be avoided if a global community is to be achieved or maintained. Issues of leadership do not and will not go away.[27]

CONCLUSION

The image of global community, the community of the earth—however it is defined and defended—is obviously a very different model from that of participatory community. One is vast in its reach; the other is small, the smaller the better. Yet both are ideals of public community. Both depend on authority and both raise problems of leadership. Each illustrates for us the conceptions and challenges of thinking about public community, authority, and leadership.

Both models also raise the question of the status of politics in community thinking of every sort. By politics we mean public conflict and agreement in the public realm—the ordinary pushing and pulling, arguing and compromising that make up politics around the world. For some, community is somehow intended to be grander than anything so mundane as the routine dimensions of public life and its ordinary disagreements and compromises. Advocates often see community as a special kind of bonding that builds refreshed people and a common life, whether in a small setting or a vast one. Where would ordinary politics—or usual leadership—fit in such an ideal?

This query is also relevant because of the impatience that many community advocates understandably express toward the pace of progress toward their goals. Why are we waiting around to argue about politics when the global community is threatened or when the chance to have individuals develop to their fullest beckons? The temptation to forget politics and embrace alternative, including authoritarian, leadership is strong. Yet does it make sense to talk of community unless all are heard and counted as part of the whole?

GLOSSARY OF KEY TERMS

existentialism A philosophy which holds that there is no certain truth and that people must choose values to define themselves and their communities.

family A source of authority with a shifting definition. Any group of persons of common ancestry or domicile.

freedom A political value stressing the absence of restraint or the ability to exercise social options.

fundamentalists Religious practitioners who insist on a literal reading of holy scriptures as a basis for authority.

justice A political value that emphasizes fairness and equity.

new age movement Holistic, loose, spiritually oriented affinity of people pursuing goals of uniting the person within and then the person with the larger universe.

religious community A principle of authority for real or potential community based on religious faith.

tradition A theory of authority that places legitimacy in precedent and historical custom.

SUGGESTIONS FOR FURTHER READING

Barber, Ben. *Strong Democracy: Participatory Democracy in a New Age.* Berkeley: University of California Press, 1984.

Bellah, Robert; Madsen, Richard; Sullivan, William; Swidler, Ann; and Tipton, Steven. *Habits of the Heart: Individualism and Commitment in American Life.* Berkeley: University of California Press, 1985.

Benn, S. I., and Peters, R. S. *Principles of Political Theory.*

Friedrich, Carl J., ed. *Authority.* New York: Liberal Arts Press, 1958.

Gerth, Hans, and Mills, C. W. *From Max Weber.* New York: Oxford University Press, 1958.

Heilbroner, Robert. *An Inquiry into the Human Prospect.* New York: Norton, 1974.

Mansbridge, Jane. *Beyond Adversary Democracy.* Chicago: University of Chicago Press, 1983.

Nash, Roderick. *The Rights of Nature: A History of Environmental Ethics.* Madison: University of Wisconsin Press, 1989.

Ophuls, William. *Ecology and the Politics of Scarcity: Prologue to a Political Theory of the Steady State.* San Francisco: W. H. Freeman, 1977.

Pateman, Carole. *Participation and Democratic Theory.* Cambridge: Cambridge University Press, 1970.

Santmire, Paul. *The Travail of Nature: The Ambiguous Ecological Promise of Christian Theology.* Philadelphia: Fortress Press, 1985.

White, Lynn. "The Historic Roots of Our Ecologic Crisis." *Science* 155 (1967): 1203–1207.

NOTES

1. Daniel Bell, *The Cultural Contradictions of Capitalism* (New York: Basic Books, 1978), p. 28.
2. Michael Harrington, *The Politics at God's Funeral: The Spiritual Crisis of Western Civilization* (New York: Penguin, 1985), p. 128.
3. Richard John Neuhaus, *The Naked Public Square: Religion and Democracy in America* (Grand Rapids: Eerdmans, 1984), pp. 21, 61, and 64.
4. Allan Bloom, *The Closing of the American Mind* (New York: Simon and Schuster, 1987), introduction and p. 125.
5. Richard Merelman, *Making Something of Ourselves* (Berkeley: University of California Press, 1984), pp. 1–2; also see Alan Wolfe, *Whose Keeper? Social Science and Moral Obligation* (Berkeley: University of California Press, 1989).
6. Robert Bellah, et al., *Habits of the Heart: Individualism and Commitment in American Life* (Berkeley: University of California Press, 1985).
7. Michael Sandel, *Liberalism and the Limits of Justice* (Cambridge: Cambridge University Press, 1982), p. 150.
8. See Robert Booth Fowler, *The Dance with Community: The Contemporary Debate in American Political Thought* (Lawrence: University Press of Kansas, 1991), a source for parts of the discussions of community herein.
9. A good place to start in thinking about authority continues to be C. J. Friedrich, ed., *Authority* (New York: Liberal Arts Press, 1958).
10. For example, Robert Paul Wolfe, *In Defense of Anarchism* (New York: Harper & Row, 1970).
11. Another good source on authority and power is R. S. Peters, "Authority," *Proceedings of the Aristotelian Society,* supplementary vol. 32 (1958), pp. 207–224.
12. Hans Gerth and C. W. Mills, eds, *From Max Weber* (New York: Oxford University Press, 1958), part 2, Power.
13. See Fowler, *The Dance with Community.*
14. Two classic advocates of participatory community are Carole Pateman, *Participation and Democratic Theory* (Cambridge: Cambridge University Press, 1970), and William M. Sullivan, *Reconstructing Public Philosophy* (Berkeley: University of California Press, 1982).

15. Benjamin Barber discusses many of the main issues in *Strong Democracy: Participatory Democracy in a New Age* (Berkeley: University of California Press, 1984).
16. For example, see Kirkpatrick Sale, *Human Scale* (New York: Coward, McCann, and Geoghegan, 1980).
17. A good discussion by advocates may be found in Samuel Bowles and Herbert Gintis, *Democracy and Capitalism: Property, Community, and the Contradictions of Modern Social Thought* (London: Routledge & Kegan Paul, 1986).
18. Michael Walzer, "Socialism Then and Now," *New Republic*, November 6, 1989, pp. 75–78.
19. For example, see Mihajlo Mesarovic and Edward Pesler, *Mankind at the Turning Point: The Second Report to the Club of Rome* (New York: Dutton, 1974); William Ophuls, *Ecology and the Politics of Scarcity: Prologue to a Political Theory of the Steady State* (San Francisco: W. H. Freeman, 1977); Lester Brown, *The Twenty-ninth Day: Accommodating Human Needs and Numbers to the Earth's Resources* (New York: Norton, 1978).
20. See Roderick Nash, *The Rights of Nature: A History of Environmental Ethics* (Madison: University of Wisconsin Press, 1989).
21. For a rich discussion see Paul Santmire, *The Travail of Nature: The Ambiguous Ecological Promise of Christian Theology* (Philadelphia: Fortress Press, 1985), and Tim Stafford, "Animal Lib," *Christianity Today*, June 18, 1990, pp. 19–23.
22. Lynn White, "The Historic Roots of Our Ecologic Crisis," *Science* 155 (1967): 1203–1207.
23. Charlene Spretnak, *The Spiritual Dimension of Green Politics* (Santa Fe: Bear and Co., 1986).
24. See, for instance, the arguments of Ophuls, *Ecology and the Politics of Scarcity*, and Brown, *The Twenty-ninth Day*.
25. See Nash, *The Rights of Nature*, for his discussion; Christopher Stone, *Should Trees Have Standing? Toward Legal Rights for Natural Objects* (Los Altos: William Kaufman, 1974); Tom Regan, *The Case for Animal Rights* (London: Routledge & Kegan Paul, 1983); Peter Singer, *Animal Liberation* (New York: Random House, 1975).
26. See Nash, *Rights of Nature*, Chapters 5 and 6, and J. Baird Callicott, *In Defense of the Land Ethic* (Albany: State University of New York Press, 1989).
27. See Robert Heilbroner, *An Inquiry into the Human Prospect* (New York: Norton, 1974).

Chapter
4

Religion, Community, and Authority

*T*wo of the most discussed kinds of community today are participatory community and the global community. Each has its characteristic image of authority: one, the assembled "people"; the other, Nature. Both are good illustrations of public images of community and authority. Yet these are, as we know, but two examples of many, not at all the full story. Another model—which has played a greater role over the course of human history in defining and directing both human community and authority—derives from religion.[1]

There is little doubt that religion is a powerful authority today in world life. Islam, Christianity, and Buddhism—among other world religions—flourish in many parts of the world. Predictions that religion will die should be viewed with great caution. It may have faded in a country such as Sweden, but its vigor and growth in many other regions of the world suggest that Sweden and the few similar places are more exceptions than harbingers of the immediate future.

More than any other conceptions of community, those that rely on religion often span the hazy line between public and private in our society. Some people self-consciously employ religion to fashion a community that will have impact on public policy, which raises complicated and challenging issues over the boundaries of church and state and religion and politics. Most, though, see religious community as an end in itself. It is an objective which has its origins in a spiritual authority that its followers find overwhelming. Consider some of the religious communities and communitarians in the United States. A famous example is the Orthodox Jewish communities, such as the Hasidim, who are found in parts of New York City and other large urban centers (as well as in Israel). These groups build their entire life around an intense communal sharing, living God's law and teachings as they understand them. For them, religion is the door to both tight community and unshakable authority.

There are numerous, similar Christian communities. The many orders of Catholic priests and sisters—from the Jesuits to the Sisters of Loretto—are examples in point. They constitute—and are formally known as—communities, and they have their own internal and larger church authority, which is ultimately spiritually based. They are private in the sense that their community exists apart from any political regime, any national government. Yet their members are citizens of one country or another, and the communities are often quite involved in the politics of various nations.

Protestant communities—such as the Sojourners fellowship in Washington, D.C.—are another example. They are dedicated to living out modern life in the New Testament model of the early Christians. Sojourners, a community set in a rough section of Washington, D.C., seeks both to embody Christian community and to minister to the fractured community around it. It is based very much on religious authority as seen in the Christian Bible.[2]

Some of these communities are committed to spreading their particular word as much as possible. Others, such as the famous Amish, are distinctly more inward-looking. What they all have in common is the ideal of community, a shared way of life, often quite a sharply defined one, and a belief that its legitimacy lies in religious truth.

While these communities are often small, whole societies see themselves as real or potential communities based on their religious faith. This perspective is now quite common in many Islamic countries, just as it was in much of the history of Western Europe from the fourth century through the Middle Ages. For such views, the idea of the separation of church and state, or religion and politics, usually makes very little sense. Why would one separate what they believe ought to be united in the good community under God? On the other hand, what if one does not share their beliefs? After all, community and authority are not automatically positive ideals. They can be dangerous to those who are seen—or who see themselves—as outsiders.

In much of our own history, many of the early colonies had official religions and churches, meant to provide or enforce a spiritually based community. While these communities eventually changed or disappeared, other similarly based groups followed in their place. Most famous among them, the Mormons in the later nineteenth century established in Utah their own Zion, a community whose basis was religious and whose openness was limited.

Our culture may be far too pluralistic for any religion to expect to collapse church-state boundaries and make our nation coterminous with their religious community. But there are many religious conceptions of community and authority in the United States that are far from conventional in terms of our history. The pluralistic richness is truly stunning.

One modern example of some interest is the New Age movement. This spiritual world is a loose-jointed affair, one that goes in many directions. But it is not small in numbers, though an actual count is impossible in so fluid a movement. Its best-known advocate is actress Shirley MacLaine, but she is just one figure among many. Today there are many signs of New Age prosperity: bookstores, magazines, radio programs, and music, of course.

New Age thinkers are clearly spiritual, celebrating a wide variety of religious authorities from goddesses to Eastern religions to spirits (reached through various means of "channeling"—communication with the spirits). In most cases, New Age spirituality stresses individual potential and powers in connection with the spirit(s). In that sense it emphasizes individual authority more than political or institutional authority within or without religion.

New Age individualism may seem to make it distant from community, but that is far from the case. Its spirituality is community oriented in almost all its forms. The community it speaks of is in part the universe. The spirit brings one into contact with that universe, and New Age participants hold that this is as it should be. It also can bring one in touch with all of oneself, which New Agers—like so many others today—believe is sadly lacking in our time and place. Thus "holism" is a major New Age goal, uniting the person within and then the person with the larger universe. What they call holism we have called community.

Notice, once again, that there is little room for politics in this vision of the good life, a fact that leaves no very good way for the larger, more pluralistic, community to relate with the New Age. To be sure, New Agers are associated with various liberal causes such as environmentalism or feminism. But the deeper orientation of the movement is apolitical. As may often happen with spiritual approaches, the implication is that politics is not really very important. It is not about community and it cannot provide authority.[3]

COMMUNITY, FAMILY, AND AUTHORITY

If religion often exemplifies the kind of authority and community that is at the public/private edge of our lives, the clearest example of the "private" community is the family. It is the most crucial arena in the conflict over community and authority today and as we look toward the twenty-first century. No setting is more important for us in illustrating authority and community and the debates that swirl around them.

Of course, it is in the family that everyone first experiences community, or its absence, and the same applies to authority. Here the first images are formed and reformed, the first yearnings expressed, and the earliest dreams formulated. No realm is more important for any of us in our development and thus none is more worth fighting over.

Private though family may seem, however, it is also a public institution, deeply interconnected with public life and laws, as we all understand. There is no clear public-private dichotomy, only a spectrum of degrees. From that perspective, the community and authority associated with family and ideas of family are more private than the participatory or globalist or other strongly public models.

The status of the family today is increasingly controversial. This is true both in terms of its authority and of its representation of community. From every side the family is now under attack. One charge is that in most of its expressions family has been a bad form of authority, destructive of human life and certainly of human community. Another is that family is more and more failing to provide for its members a stable and enduring authority structure.

The first charge usually involves outright hostility toward the family. It often proceeds on the assumption that the family is inevitably patriarchal and thus bad. That is, critics assert that family is or must be ruled by the father/male and is therefore unjust to its female and children members. From this perspective, there is little that should be done to "save" the family, most reform ideas rarely beginning to go far enough. At times this analysis assumes that men are evil, and especially so in their relations with women. It also reveals an inclination to reduce most human relationships to power struggles.[4]

For some, the community alternative is family organized as an egalitarian community with equal participation by its members, a kind of semiprivate participatory community. Others are more interested in a larger, public participatory community which goes beyond any single family. They hope it could replace the old family to a great extent. Still others propose to substitute a community of women or a community of lesbian women.[5] Many other critics reject these proposals for a variety of reasons, including their impracticality for most people. Some insist that there is no reason to attack the family as long as it is reconstituted toward a more egalitarian community with authority more diffused among its members.[6]

Many arguments are heard, on the other hand, for family. Often the argument is that it is an institution designed and defended by God. Sometimes the defense comes in terms of psychology, the point being that all of us need a place of community and regularized authority where love and companionship make us secure. Others stress family as a universal human institution (however various its forms) and doubt that we can exist without it, whatever the reasons, given the teachings of human history. Even among feminists, however, there is a good deal of support for family as a community. Rarely do feminists suggest that the family should be anything other than an egalitarian community at least among adults, but many maintain that family can be about community.[7]

The bottom line here is that arguments about community and family are deeply linked. Is family the ideal of community? If so, what kind of family should we have and what kinds can we have? How should it provide authority to its members? These are the questions that are raised in our time about the family.

There is little doubt that there is no more powerful image of community than the family. From many perspectives, the questions arise about the consequence of its weakening as an authority and as community. How much damage occurs to those who have found the end of such community and authority more a tale of alienation and confusion than of freedom and liberation? A lot of people are adrift in the United States, from the homeless to street youths to drug addicts and many others. How much are they witness to the danger of defective community (and weak authority structures) in the family?

The issue of authority is equally central to the entire debate over the family. Just as there is no consensus on the proper conception of community in relation to the family, there is also no agreement on the subject of authority and the family. We have noted the determined case for authority to be egalitarian, for which feminists and others argue so vigorously. But they do not have the field alone by any means.

There are plenty of arguments for the view that family ought to be understood as a traditional community, with men and women having different spheres of equal worth and the man's sphere to include headship of the family. Such a position insists that this is the only way that effective authority can exist in a family and that this authority in turn is the only means to a viable community in the family.

Proponents of this perspective insist that any other arrangement will deny community. It will leave women vulnerable—free in theory but in practice often abandoned—with children but neither husband nor much else. Protestant Fundamentalists, for example, argue as well from their reading of the Bible—where God's authority is supreme—that God teaches that the proper image of community is the traditional family.[8]

While most of the present argument concerns authority between husband and wife, another issue of authority concerns that between parents and children. Today there is great fear that such authority (and concurrently family community) has badly eroded, but there is also much debate over what kind of authority ought to exist between parents and children. How much authority should parents have? What authority should children have?

As with all family issues, some people may see this as a largely private matter, but it affects all of us and society as a whole, far more than most obviously public issues. The family remains our first and most unforgettable teacher about authority and community and in one form or another it frequently continues educating us in these demanding realms as the years go by.

TRADITION

Quite another approach to community and authority concentrates on tradition. There is little doubt that tradition as a source of authority and community exercises renewed vigor today. Sometimes defense of tradition as a source of community and authority takes the form of celebration of the value of tradition in itself, apart from any particular tradition. At other times, defense of a particular tradition, historical or intellectual, garners the plaudits as the model for community and authority.

Proponents of tradition in itself often make three arguments which they consider decisive. They argue that traditions are a wonderful basis for community or authority just because they are familiar; they are known, down-to-earth, concrete practices or ideas. There is nothing about them that is risky, whereas abstract, utopian (and untested) visions necessarily involve risk. Indeed, for some traditionalists the real struggle in political life lies between them and the abstract ideologues and moralists who constantly try to bend the world to their diverse dreams. Traditionalists insist that dreams and dreamers are dangerous. For them, human history is littered with the bones of those sacrificed to realize failed visions.[9]

A second major group of advocates for tradition as a good in itself contends that tradition presents a tested way for people to control themselves and others. Traditions from this view are models of community and authority that work to direct and guide us. These traditionalists maintain that we all need guides and guideposts in life. While it is fun to think that we are completely free to do as we wish, this is not what we really want over time. By analogy, we all understand that the first day of vacation is wonderful, but soon enough we grow bored and even confused if we do not have regular work and routines to engage us.

Third, some insist that traditions are absolutely vital to help us to define ourselves as individuals. They hold that we require traditions to help us form values and to help develop our characters. We are happiest and most fulfilled as persons when we are not simply blank checks on which we write whatever we wish. What we need are connections with others in life—communities and established authorities—and that is exactly what traditions provide.

Such traditions are in tune with people, therefore, and this is why many advocates of tradition insist that in honoring tradition they are really honoring people and their choices. After all, they contend, traditions that last do so with reason. They endure only if they have had the blessing of people over time. Traditional communities last only if they accord with real needs and preferences, and the same is true regarding any authority. Whether anyone has voted on them formally is irrelevant. Traditional images of community and authority abound. One obvious example is the American patriotic tradition. For many citizens of the United States, patriotism is the proper standard for our collective life—a basis of community and a powerful authority. Sometimes it is grounded in worship of such symbols as the flag; or documents such as the Declaration of Independence or the Constitution; or celebration of events in our collective history, such as the Revolutionary War or the Civil War. These traditionalists underline the importance of such symbolic items or events with greater and greater vigor today as the United States grows more diverse. They fear that no basis for national community will soon exist otherwise.

Other kinds of tradition focus more on intellectual traditions, alive less in history than in the human mind. One example that has stirred much controversy in the modern university is the proper role of the tradition of Western culture and thought. Its proponents praise that complex tradition of thought about authority and community first fashioned in fifth- and fourth-century-B.C. Athens and what has followed over the past twenty-five centuries. They are convinced that those who are able should have exposure to this tradition.[10]

Adherents of this view—among many other traditionalists—believe that it is no accident that authority and community are in decline in the contemporary United States. That is a disease to be expected in a culture which they perceive does not honor tradition or community or authority but only respects the individual. Often such analysts diagnose the greatest problem as the decline of the family as the major agency for passing on traditions of all sorts. If it is declining, they doubt that there is hope for much else. Traditionalists declare that we cannot expect authority or community to endure if children learn at home that authority and community do not matter.

For traditionalists, little better comes these days from education. They add their voices to the general critique of American public education. They note that it rarely respects traditions of any sort—religious, historical, cultural, or intellectual. More to the point of our example, education increasingly does not respect the intellectual legacy of the West. All of that is spurned in the name of diversity, multiculturalism, relevance, and educational fun and games. The result is the usual. People are left uneducated and without any meaning or morality.

Resistance to approaching community or authority from the world(s) of tradition is plentiful. Critics do not agree that simply because a practice, belief, or idea has been around for a long time, somehow that makes it good. To them that is silly. Traditions require rational defense and justification—each tradition specifically—and anything else is not acceptable. Moreover, they maintain that traditions inevitably give some ideas and some groups more political power than others and sometimes argue that dominant traditions have a way of justifying the values and rule of dominant groups.

A skeptic need not deny that there are—or may be—some good traditions, but there may be at least as many bad ones. Thus just because a community is traditional should count for nothing. Similarly, an authority established by great age has little inherent moral significance. Age does not automatically equal wisdom and who could think otherwise?

Nor should one take seriously the smooth assertion that just because a structure of authority or community has lasted in practice or as an idea, it must meet human needs and somehow, therefore, be democratic. It is true that every tradition puts somebody (or some group) in power and it is in this person's or group's interest to preserve that tradition according to the most unsparing, tough-minded political analysis. Thus traditions can be less about democracy and more about elite manipulation. Yet no one can dismiss this basis of community and authority too quickly. It endures now as in the past. This alone suggests its power and its compatibility with human beings. What is always necessary before invoking any form of this basis of authority and community—as with all others—is an argument for its legitimacy.

EXISTENTIAL COMMUNITY AND AUTHORITY

We may approach community and/or authority from innumerable directions. Our goal is to give you some examples of how people think about them but not to exhaust all the ways in which they address them. With that modest goal in mind, we believe a last interesting example is worth examining. This we call the existential perspective.

We noted in Chapter 1 that for existentialists, there is no certain ground of truth in politics or in anything else. The same necessarily applies for any authority or community. Thus their perspective quickly raises the issue that confronts a great many of us today. We live in a world in which we have to make choices in terms of politics, community, and authority, and yet many believe that we lack a basis to choose and to act.

Existentialists propose that we must rely on ourselves. We have to choose, with awareness and with reflection, but choose we must. No one can choose for us and no one should. There is no one who has authority over us in the sense of knowing the truth or the correct tradition or whatever. We are on our own and we must do the best we can.

This judgment, which is so familiar—if not always so comfortable for many of us in this modern age—does not mean that existentialists resolve the question of authority by denying there can ever be any. To be sure, most existentialists have little use for religious or traditional authority or—for that matter—the authority of law, the charismatic leader, or the democratic majority. Existentialists label most claims for authority as implausible and unsubstantiated, and they routinely advise skepticism and caution.

Although they sometimes do defend the value of authority, the kind of authority they accept derives its value from the act of choice made by the individual. Choice is the only existential source of authority. If, for example, one chooses to believe in a religion, then that religion has authority for you. Yet from an existentialist perspective, such authority is not inherent in the alleged religious truth but rather in the existential choice that affirms such a truth.

Nevertheless, existentialists are not temperamentally at ease with authority. Authority implies truths that they suspect are elusive at best and more likely nonexistent. Discussions of community are much more congenial in the existential framework. Despite existentialism's focus on individual choice, it is closely identified with community. There is no inherently logical reason why this is so, but perhaps it flows from the existential sense that we are so alone in a world without truth. In such a situation, we need others and need to share with others in community, and thus community is an ideal of considerable prominence in existential thinking.[11]

Existential images of community include all kinds of communities: large and small, public and private, family and national or global. What they all have in common is the absence of any absolute basis for their existence. They are never the True community. Nor do existentialists visualize them as guaranteed or even likely in actual human experience. The existential world is one, after all, of contingency in terms of truth, life, and any matter of life. Nothing is certain; nothing is guaranteed.

Moreover, there is often a good deal of existential distaste for most "true" models of community. For existentialists, these often sound utopian, whether they are local or global. They seem to build from self-confidence about truth and proceed to self-confidence about realization. Neither step is wise, from an existential slant, and neither has much basis in reality. What existentialists often fear, however, is that such ideas of community promise many deaths as their proponents lunge forward in fruitless effort to recreate the world to fit their fantasies of community. As has happened in the past, the process will turn ugly once the human spirit and human history provide their inevitable resistance to utopian dreams of community.

Supporters of most conceptions of authority—and of community, too— find the existential perspective pretty weak. Authority disappears in existential thinking. At most it is the authority of the individual grounded in nothing. And they ask how such a view can fit in with community. What means do existentialists have to build community? What would hold an existential-based community together if their only authority is individual choices . . . or whims? No wonder most supporters of other images of community find it hard to take existentialist community seriously, and advocates of the value and/or necessity of authority often describe existentialism as anarchism.

For existentialists, life is about paradox. For example, community is something everyone sometimes yearns for with all his or her being. Yet community always proves disappointing and elusive. We are beings inevitably alone in a world that conspires to keep us that way. We are right to try to reach for community as long as we do not try too hard and create oppression and terrorism instead of community. Thus the future is important and there is work to be done to edge toward community. But in the future we must also be realistic about ourselves and about others. Community is an agenda, not a reality, and so it will always be.

The main problem is human limitation. Some call it sin, others selfishness or the inherent separation of one from another that is part of life. For all, this sense of being alone cannot disappear and stands as an implacable impediment toward community. As a result, existential thinkers as they approach community often think less of achieving community in terms of structures and more of the kind of person—in or out of community—who continues to seek good community through a sequence of positive choices. They talk of character, recognizing that to succeed—or even to begin to succeed—community must be grounded in people of the right sort. As they discuss character, they give us quite another perspective on the idea of community and politics.[12]

Existential political thinkers vary, of course, in the particular traits of character that they seek, but the idea remains constant. They hold fast to the notion that forming character is the appropriate means toward community as well as toward crafting an authority structure that is deeply connected with us. The only community that can be fully realized is the community in us, and to that task one must be devoted. In the process, they contend, much may be accomplished toward building the community among men and women.

CONCLUSION

As the existential model surely demonstrates, understandings of community and authority come in almost every imaginable form. We have gotten a sense of that variety through our examples. Yet there must be a close examination of every idea of community, of what it promises and whether it can deliver on those promises. Community frequently looks great and its proponents sometimes surround it with romance and excitement. But nothing should distract us from probing the worth of any form of community's goals and asking whether there is much reason to believe that they may be achieved.

Integrally related is the question of how community, in whatever form, fits with other values we may wish to achieve. Community does not somehow fulfill all human needs. No community does or could do that. For example, there is the matter of human freedom. As Michael Walzer has argued, this is a serious matter worthy of the closest discussion. Indeed, nothing, he insists, should be more important to those committed to community than matters of freedom, diversity, agreement and disagreement, choice and boundaries.[13]

Of course, we need not assume that freedom and community are always opposites, or even mortal enemies. That is not a matter for assumptions but for the test of experience. But supporters of community must make clear how much community and what kinds of freedom they want. They must ask where freedom and community might conflict and what they will do to make sure that, as much as possible, both goals are promoted by the arrangements of society or there is a clear-sighted adjustment of those goals. Proclaiming that all will be well or that we can worry about such problems later is dangerous foolishness.

One must expect, too, that any version of community address questions of justice. A community is, among other things, an arrangement among people, an arrangement that is somehow just. As our chapter on justice suggests, there are, of course, different conceptions of justice, and more than one such concept may be present in every community. What we can't do is pretend that our idea of community is just and think no more about it, nor can we avoid thinking about justice and community altogether.

It is a fairly common charge, in fact, that too many theorists of community do skirt justice.[14] The argument sometimes flows from an advocate of one or another theory of justice who believes that a kind of participatory or religious or global community rejects his or her version of justice. But often the point is broader and more important. Often the argument is that where justice is not addressed, community will fail. For community is not a god but a pattern of shared life. The nature of those patterns—their justice—and their defense are central to any conception of community—and will be central to its success or failure.

Such warnings do not imply that we should not take seriously those who seek one or more communities. Far from it. They also do not mean that we are sympathetic to those who may dismiss concern with community as a kind of nostalgia, a wishing for another time and place in which there was, or there might have been, community in one garb or another. We recognize that nostalgia sometimes plays a role in the communities people envision. We also appreciate that nostalgia creates no actual community, just as we appreciate that community in this age is not easy to accomplish. But whether one is working toward global community or toward the smallest participatory community, the degree of nostalgia that one may feel about community is neither an argument for or against it. There are arguments to be made for and against every ideal of community, and they are what must be addressed.

At the same time, we must also address matters of authority contained within visions of community and everywhere else. Many modern thinkers are uncomfortable with the matter of authority. Some would prefer to concentrate on freedom, others on community or equality. But there is no escape from authority. It is a constant in human affairs. The real issue is not how to escape it, but how to have a kind of authority that one believes is morally right and practically sound.

And it follows that this in turns involves us in the matter of obligations, including political obligations. Authority and the terms of one's relationship with authority are the subjects of obligation, for authority and obligation are in fact closely related to each other. That is one reason why we have a separate chapter on obligation. It is too important to ignore, just as authority itself is.

Authority, as we have seen, requires a clear argument about its basis. It does not and should not exist in thin air. It must have a foundation, and that grounding must be defended. But, equally, it must have its reach and its limits securely defined and defended. Authority without justification like authority without limits is a formula for tyranny, as human history has too often illustrated.

GLOSSARY OF KEY TERMS

alienation The state of being estranged from society, organizations, or people.

anthropocentrism Focusing on human beings above all else.

authority Legitimate power to influence, direct, or guide. An attribute of legitimate governments.

charisma A power or virtue, attributed to a person or office, culminating in special powers of leadership.

community An open concept of shared experiences and obligations involving both feeling and reason.

"deep ecology" environmentalism An ideology of radical activists who urge the liberation of nature from human domination as a source of community.

eco-feminism A form of holistic spirituality stressing the closeness of feminism to nature.

ecosystem A scientific term describing the interrelationships of organisms within the natural environment.

environmental utilitarianism A source of community rooted in the greatest good for the greatest number defined as environmental survival.

global community model An approach to community that assumes an ethic of a transnational human community.

holistic Emphasizing the organic or functional relation between parts and wholes. A form of community theory.

participatory community model An approach to community that assumes a democratic ethic of legitimate power coming from people through their direct decision making.

value justification The process of using logic and argument to demonstrate the validity of value positions.

SUGGESTIONS FOR FURTHER READING

Bloom, Allan. *The Closing of the American Mind.* New York: Simon & Schuster, 1987.

Camus, Albert. *The Plague.* New York: Vintage, 1972.

Cochran, Clarke. *Character, Community, and Politics.* University: University of Alabama Press, 1982.

———. "The Thin Theory of Community: The Communitarians and Their Politics." *Political Studies* 37, no. 3 (1989): 422–435.

Eisenstein, Zillah. *Feminism and Sexual Equality: Crisis in Liberal America.* New York: Monthly Review Press, 1984.

Elshtain, Jean. "Feminists Against the Family." *The Nation,* November 17, 1989, pp. 1, 497–500.

LaHaye, Beverly. *I Am a Woman By God's Design.* Old Tappan, N.J.: Revell, 1980.

Oakeshott, Michael. *Rationalism in Politics and Other Essays.* New York: Basic Books, 1962.

Okin, Susan. *Justice, Gender, and the Family.* New York: Basic Books, 1989.

Wallis, Jim. *The Call to Conversion.* New York: Harper & Row, 1981.

Walzer, Michael. *Spheres of Justice: A Defense of Pluralism and Equality.* New York: Basic Books, 1983.

NOTES

1. Some of the discussion of religion, family, tradition, and existentialism that follows is based on the fuller discussion in Robert Booth Fowler, *The Dance with Community: The Contemporary Debate in American Political Thought* (Lawrence: University Press of Kansas, 1991).
2. On Christian communities of this sort, see Jim Wallis, *The Call to Conversion* (New York: Harper & Row, 1981); Parker Palmer, *The Company of Strangers: Christians and the Renewal of America's Public Life* (New York: Crossroad, 1981).
3. For the New Age see Shirley MacLaine, *Out on a Limb* (New York: Bantam Books, 1983); Marilyn Ferguson, *The Aquarian Conspiracy* (Los Angeles: Tar-

cher, 1980); for a negative view, Richard Blow, "Moronic Convergence: The Moral and Spiritual Emptiness of the New Age," *The New Republic*, January 25, 1988, pp. 24 and 26.

4. Jean Elshtain, "Feminists Against the Family," *The Nation*, November 17, 1989, pp. 1, 497–500.

5. Some relevant works: Zillah Eisenstein, *Feminism and Sexual Equality: Crisis in Liberal America* (New York: Monthly Review Press, 1984); Susan Griffin, *Women and Nature: The Roaring Inside Her* (New York: Harper, 1978); Jean Grimshaw, *Philosophy and Feminist Thinking* (Minneapolis: University of Minnesota Press, 1986).

6. Susan Okin, *Justice, Gender, and the Family* (New York: Basic Books, 1989).

7. Grimshaw, *Philosophy and Feminist Thinking*, Chapter 2.

8. Beverly LaHaye, *I Am a Woman by God's Design* (Old Tappan, N.J.: Revell, 1980); Phyllis Schlafly, *The Power of the Christian Woman* (Cincinnati: Standard, 1981); George Gilder, *Naked Nomads: Unmarried Men in America* (New York: Quadrangle, 1974).

9. Michael Oakeshott, *Rationalism in Politics and Other Essays* (New York: Basic Books, 1962).

10. Allan Bloom, *The Closing of the American Mind* (New York: Simon & Schuster, 1987).

11. Albert Camus, *The Plague* (New York: Vintage, 1972); Clarke Cochran, *Character, Community, and Politics* (University: University of Alabama Press, 1982).

12. A good example of this kind of thinking may be found in Cochran, *Character, Community, and Politics*.

13. Michael Walzer, *Spheres of Justice: A Defense of Pluralism and Equality* (New York: Basic Books, 1983).

14. Clarke Cochran, "The Thin Theory of Community: The Communitarians and Their Politics," *Political Studies* 37, no. 3 (1989):422–435.

Chapter
5

Justice

The cry of the prophets in the ancient Jewish Scriptures (the Old Testament) was for God's justice. It was the cry of Jeremiah, of Micah, and Ezekial. They sought justice for the poor, the suffering, the widows and orphans. They yearned for justice for the Jews—and for the enemies of Israel and Judah. The philosophers in ancient Greece speculated and argued about justice. They sought it just as intensely, though by different routes. Both the Hebraic and the Greek traditions constitute the earliest records in the West of sophisticated philosophical/religious concern with justice, though there seems little doubt that all human societies have had standards of justice.

Today justice is front and center in the realm of philosophy and even more in the events and crises of everyday life. Desire for justice continues to exercise an unmistakable, formidable sway over the human mind and heart. We all want justice, and our desire for justice is as much a part of our era as of those of the ancient Greeks and Hebrews.

Roman Catholic liberation theologians and the local, political communities they inspire are one example in which some third world peoples in Latin America and elsewhere echo the age-old desire. They represent an influential combination of two of the most justice-oriented outlooks of human history, the Judeo-Christian religion and the philosophy of Karl Marx.[1]

All over the world, racial and ethnic groups from South Africa to the Soviet Union speak in the language of justice, in demanding their place in the sun. So do numerous other political, economic, and social movements today in the United States and elsewhere. Feminists invoke justice on their behalf. Recently men's groups are speaking up, demanding their justice regarding child custody and rights. Gay rights organizations demand justice; so do workers, teachers, the disabled. The list is endless. Justice is the master political word of the age.

Who would dare say as we peer uncertainly into the future that this situation will change? The particular occasions for debating justice may change; indeed they will change. But we can expect the cry for justice to continue undiminished. All we need to do is to look at the environmental movements now more and more active in the United States and around the world and we will expect justice to continue to be the cry of the future. With increasing frequency, justice is a crucial concept for environmentalists: just treatment for animals, for the nonsmoker, for the globe. Survival is not the only word in the environmental vocabulary. More and more it is justice for the "rights" of nature.[2]

Yet it is not only the realm of great issues that brings justice into our consciousness. Justice is not only out there, far away. Its greatest presence is in the realm of the ordinary, daily life. It is then for all of us that justice (or its equivalent, "fairness") comes up most frequently. Justice is, in fact, people's most common political topic—always. After all, everyone wants to be treated fairly or with justice and most of us want the same for others.

So often do matters of justice arise in practical life that we don't necessarily notice how much justice and fairness are integral to our day-to-day vocabulary. We routinely invoke justice and fairness regarding rules, grades, pay; in relations with lovers, family, and friends; concerning the courts, bureaucratic decisions, tax burdens. Declaring our views on justice or—more often—injustice is thus a basic part of human existence.

Moreover, we have no reason to expect that a day will come when "justice" will somehow disappear as a factor in ordinary life. All that we know of human history suggests that people have always been concerned with justice in their daily existence. The future should be no different. How we are treated is not likely to cease to exist as a chief concern even if the forms and the focus of justice may change over time. We have no reason to think that men and women will not continue to be justice-seeking creatures.

Utopians of all ages have dreamed otherwise. They have visualized a world where (their) justice is realized at last. The allure of this ancient hope also appears to be eternal in human affairs. It is premised on the assumptions that we could ever agree on what justice ought to be and, second, that we could ever discover how to realize it in practical life. Neither has much foundation, for better or for worse, in the light of the long history of human discourse and disagreement about justice.

Some of us may find this prospect discomforting or discouraging. We may ask, what is the point then? We think that the point is that we all want justice and will continue to do so even though there is little chance that some shared perfect justice will be realized. Given that fact, we are required as citizens and ethical people to come to grips with what justice is and ought to be. We must know the alternative conceptions of justice and the arguments among them, for different ideas and arguments will govern this disputed concept everywhere it is employed. Because justice and disputes will be part of our lives and our society's, we must face it as a contested concept, understand the grounds of disputes, and ultimately make our own choices.

Our discussion of justice in this chapter concentrates on two central issues. First we ask, what is justice, what do all understandings of justice share, and where do they differ from each other? Second, we explore whether or not justice is really what people want. Or, to put it another way, we pose the issue of the relative importance of achieving justice (however it is defined). Though justice and fairness are often on our lips, they are not self-evidently the most important human values or even important to everyone. There are other candidates for this honor. In noting them and their appeals, we simultaneously observe the limitations of thinking about the world in terms of "justice."

The first great written record we have of serious philosophical consideration of justice comes from Plato's work in fourth-century-B.C. Athens. His discussion in *The Republic* is stunning in its originality and brilliant in its argument. Plato has the memorable Socrates consider a range of answers to the question, "What is justice?" In the process, Plato begins the journey on which we still continue, the fascinating investigation of the multiple answers to this classic question.

Justice can mean doing one's traditional duties, as Plato's character, Cephalus, suggests to Socrates. Or it can mean being good to one's friends and hostile to one's enemies, as Polemarchus proposes. Or, perhaps, it is nothing more than the triumph of the stronger, as the cynical Thrasymachus observes. Plato's own view is that justice is each person in his or her proper place in society, where each deserves to be, based on their innate ability.[3]

Thrasymachus really suggests that "justice" discussions and politics concerned with justice are something of a hoax. For cynics in all ages, people who pursue justice are naive at best and evil at worst. They either don't know there is no justice or they do know it and use grand phrases about justice as a cover for their own effort to seize power. Either way, the argument is that justice is a phantom in any principled sense. It cannot be found in theory and it is never, in any case, followed in practice.[4]

For Plato and most others since, such pessimism is unworthy. It denies human ability to discern some kind of truth about justice or to develop wisdom about it and to struggle toward its realization. Undoubtedly Plato's broadest insight into what the concept of justice concerns is on target. As he understood it, justice is about what is due to a person, what each deserves. From Plato's time to ours, when people talk of justice, they are almost always speaking as he would. They are speaking of justice as people getting their rightful due.

This idea is clear, but what remains very much contested is, What is a person's due? That is, the debate over justice is not on the meaning of the general concept but about the specific standards to be employed in assessing what people deserve. What ought people receive as their due? This question is the focus of all justice talk. It calls us to address what principles we should use to decide what a person deserves in any given situation.

There is now, as in the past, no shortage of competing answers regarding what should be the standard or substance of justice. Our discussion that follows explores the case for and against a number of these standards, all of which are familiar to us when we think about them. As we do so, we will also consider that in alternative situations or aspects of life, it may be that contrasting notions of justice apply. What is due to us in one area of life may be quite different from what ought to happen in another of its dimensions. Justice in the courtroom and justice in an economic system are not necessarily the same thing.

JUSTICE AS EQUAL OPPORTUNITY

It is obvious that for many citizens justice is intimately connected with equal opportunity. If we have received equal opportunity, the view goes, then we have obtained justice. Certainly in our age the air is filled with demands for equal opportunity and charges that it has not been afforded to one group or another, to one individual or another, which underlines how integral the concept is in justice thinking.

In politics it is common for citizens to speak the language of equal opportunity and to watch carefully to see that, if they want it, they have equal opportunity to influence the political process. Whenever the almost constant charges arise of too much special interest influence or of Political Action Committee (PAC) money having entered the political process, implicit is the ideal of justice as equal opportunity and injustice as the denial of equal opportunity. The same is true in the sometimes bitter disputes over affirmative action for various minorities, differentials in school financing resources, or struggles about whom or what should be considered in school curricula. Over and over in our politics, the issue is equal opportunity, its importance, and how to achieve it.

However, equal opportunity is, in fact, rarely anyone's final definition of justice. Almost always those who favor equal opportunity do so as part of a larger vision of justice. It is usually a means rather than an end value. For example, those who define justice as rewarding people according to their achievements must and often do include equal opportunity as an integral part of their system. They appreciate that varying outcomes based on achievement—for example, varying incomes—would be fair only if people have a roughly equal start in the competition. That is, they must have equal opportunity at the start or the expected pattern of unequal outcomes at the end is suspect. Few think that it is fair for the poor to be poor unless they have had a chance and have not succeeded. Fewer are impressed with the justice of the achievement of the successful if they have simply inherited their position or otherwise have had far more than equal opportunity in life.

We need to ask why equal opportunity is a part of justice or fairness for most of us. The reason is that justice for most people involves respect for every person. Justice must honor each of us in some basic (perhaps we may say equal) fashion; it must honor our moral worth and our very personhood. Why we think this way receives alternative defenses, but the assumption itself is pervasive. Of course, this does not mean that justice must therefore be properly defined as equality in all matters. That is one, but only one, view. It is one thing to argue that justice involves equality of respect as one element and quite another to hold that equality is all that justice is about.

Despite the popularity of equal opportunity's close connection with justice, the critics of this connection very much exist. They can be harsh as they stress their conviction that equal opportunity is scarcely alluring once we go beneath its shiny surface. In particular, they may argue that attention to equal opportunity in matters of justice leads in the end to injustice. Perhaps it even encourages injustice.

This complaint sometimes comes especially from those dissatisfied by inequalities in one dimension or another of existence. After all, equal opportunity is a process view of justice. The process—that of providing equal opportunity—is what counts, not the outcome. Thus if equal opportunity were the only principle of justice (as it rarely is), then it could justify every outcome of inequality (if all started roughly equally). It could legitimize rule by a few, or unchecked wealth accumulation by a few, or whatever.[5]

Other arguments might be made—and more often are—to the opposite point, that equal opportunity tends to be congruent with a system of justice which opens things up for more people. Equality of opportunity may not be about substantive equality, but it is directed to equal respect because it is built on the equal respect that equal opportunity advocates.

In every case, however, the arguments wend their way back to how to achieve equal opportunity. Here the problems and disagreements are sometimes staggering. For instance, does equal opportunity require special advantages to individuals or groups which are now way behind in the assorted competitions of life? This query is about "affirmative action," the divisive and controversial policy dilemma so much a feature of life now in the United States. It is a part of the larger public policy issue that forces us to ask if we can increase opportunity for everyone at the same time. Aren't painful choices inevitable among people and opportunities, given limited jobs, modest resources, and the existential constraints in every life? There are troubling practical challenges here, and how to meet them is no light matter. They reemphasize the point that politics is not only about principle but also practice, and no political theory is worth much if it does not connect with practice.

Moreover, almost all efforts to realize equal opportunity in the various arenas of life require government action, laws, rules, taxes, and public officials. How much do we want to commit to this task? And where is the line (in economic life, for example) beyond which the pursuit of equal opportunity becomes absurd, when government regulation and taxes are so great that equal opportunity to succeed becomes worthless in practice?

DESERT OR MERIT

If equal opportunity is a frequent starting juncture in reflections on justice, the desert or merit standard is a familiar ending point. From this perspective, justice is giving all their due as defined by their respective and varying merits (or deserts).

While there is no unanimous agreement on what a merit or desert test should look like, the most frequent version defines merit in terms of productivity.[6] It holds that rewards should be given on the basis of what one achieves. This conception of justice underlies all merit pay schemes, the usual practice in the private sector and sometimes in the public sector as well. Higher pay for better work is the principle.

Another version is more committed to merit defined in terms of character rather than achievement. What counts here is not what one does but what one is. Such a mode of thinking is not especially dominant today, but the philosophers in ancient Greek civilization argued that the just person was one who had proper character, above all else. The ancient Hebrews connected righteousness (proper being and living) with justice just as tightly. In our own time, character may be undergoing a revival among political theorists and among citizens, too, as recent discussions of our presidential candidates have shown.[7]

In merit discussions of justice, however, achievement is the usual standard. Proponents make two points. First, they argue that people should be rewarded for what they actually do in life. Mere existence is nothing special in an overpopulated world, and it deserves no particular honor or recognition. Rewarding people for what they do, on the other hand, is honoring people for what they as individuals accomplish, what they put their stamp on. In this fashion, merit philosophers insist that they are respecting the individual. They celebrate each for what he or she does (or doesn't) do and assume that people are responsible for much of what they do or fail to do. In the process, they insist that they respect people not as some abstraction called human beings but as living persons who do what they do and must accept responsibility for it.

To be sure, most merit theorists have their limits. They favor desert as a principle in questions of income, job promotion, or academic grades, but not in matters such as free speech rights, degree of religious liberty, or the right to vote. Here they are much more inclined to understand justice in egalitarian terms. However, even in largely political realms, they judge outcomes acceptable only if they respect merit. The candidates with greater achievement records—they often argue—deserve to win, and those with lesser records do not.

A second advantage merit theorists cite for their view of justice is that it tremendously benefits society. They contend that merit provides incentive for people to work and to work hard and fruitfully. Those who do in a merit society will benefit personally and so will society as a whole. The classic pie of production will expand this way and the benefits will be broad.

Moreover, desert advocates suggest, a society governed in its economy by the merit system will encourage and reward the talented and creative. These people will tend to get ahead, and their accomplishments in science, technology, the arts and entertainment, business and finance will redound to the common good. No society can flourish without such people. The United States has attracted such individuals from all over the world and continues to do so. Why? merit thinkers ask. For them the answer is that income in the United States is sometimes distributed according to merit, and it is only natural that the creative want to go where they are freer, including freer to obtain very concrete rewards.

A complete merit theory also stresses that all should have roughly equal opportunity to participate or compete. A good way to tell if a merit theorist is serious is whether or not he or she makes efforts for equal opportunity that go beyond mere rhetoric. Some merit thinkers do not, but all must. Otherwise the inequalities that the merit system necessarily generates cannot be justified.

There is one other proviso that may be found in merit systems, though it is not always self-conscious. That is an insistence on a kind of utilitarian qualification. Merit thinkers believe merit should be rewarded only if it does in fact benefit society as a whole. They hold that the achievement that merits approval is what the market rewards, but they do not propose to reward the successful robber or rapist or flimflam artist. Merit theory honors individuals and their particular achievements, but it also recognizes that we live in a society. Thus they are also utilitarians who agree that society and its standards must and will help shape which achievements we judge are admirable and deserve reward.

One special version of a merit test of justice employs the criterion of effort. This standard is familiar to every student who complains that he or she should have done better on the hour exam because of having worked hard. The standard is that effort merits reward. It is natural to us to think this way, and we all do it. Yet few merit supporters are enthusiastic about the effort test. The reason is that they fear the social consequences. If effort alone is what we take into account, then we may end up with a society of drudges or drones, plodding along. Such a society will not reward creativity or striking achievement. It will turn stagnant, dull, and unproductive.

On the other hand, effort is definitely a kind of achievement. All merit theorists favor effort in life. The issue is how much it should weigh in comparison with achievement in determining reward, especially in the economic system. The same with grades: should the highest grade go to the best answer, regardless of the effort put into it? Merit theorists would generally say yes. At the same time, they might pass the poor student who tried as opposed to the poor student who did not.

There are, of course, many skeptics of the merit conception of justice. They often complain about the kind of society that they fear a merit system encourages. They think it will result in a social order with too much competition and too little community. In merit societies they see too many individuals devoted to themselves or their families pushing to get ahead and too few people who have concern for others or society itself. They also worry about those who lose in the merit competition. And there are losers, of course. Romantic notions aside, where there are winners there must be losers.

Skeptics are also suspicious about how much equality of opportunity merit advocates really favor. Are merit people serious about equal educational opportunity, for example? How do they feel regarding tough inheritance laws? Critics suspect that often merit theory is little more than a justification for those on top to stay on top.

EQUALITY OR NEED

Many critics of the merit advocates have a preference for some form of egalitarian justice. Certainly no ideal of justice has resonated more widely nor caused more revolutions in the twentieth century. None has so transformed the modern world.

Chapter 7 discusses equality in considerable detail. For our purposes here, we approach it specifically as the context for a theory of justice. We might start with the idea that justice as equality means giving each the same—the same vote, the same wage, the same grade. However, if we think about it we realize that to get to actual, substantive equality, we must often give unequal amounts of things. This insight lies behind Karl Marx's famous proclamation, "to each according to his needs."[8]

Egalitarians like Marx sought equality in all dimensions of life but knew that to reach this goal the reality of differing needs had to be addressed. For example, if our objective is equal income and you have three children and I have none, we cannot both get the same income. You will have to receive more. If our goal is equal health care and you are healthy and I am not, we cannot both receive equal medical care payments. I will need more. In short, we sometimes have to have inequality to achieve real equality.

The argument of egalitarians for equality as justice is straightforward. It is almost always an argument that concentrates on the claim that each of us is a person of great and equal worth, regardless of our ability or background. Given this assumption of equal human dignity or worth, they insist it follows that justice requires people be treated equally. People of equal worth should have equal political power, equal financial status, and equal justice in the courts. They should see their high and equal dignity affirmed everywhere.[9]

One recent effort to reason about equality as justice that makes a somewhat different argument is John Rawls's *Theory of Justice*.[10] Rawls contends that equality must be the basic principle of justice in the political and economic realms of society, with equal opportunity central for jobs. The reason he gives has to do with an implicit natural law. He suggests that people who have a normal amount of interest in their success and yet also have concern for others—and *who do not know their future in life*—will agree on a basically egalitarian conception of justice.

In his famous formulation, Rawls maintains that when we are in such a (necessarily imaginary) situation, what he calls the Original Position, we would choose equality. We would do so because we would calculate that we need protection in political and economic existence and that equality in both would ensure this to us. From Rawls's analysis, we are cautious as humans and thus will take a bird in the hand over the risk of losing big in a merit system in the future *as long as we do not know that future*.

While Rawls may seem to argue for equality on the basis of consent (we would choose equality in the Original Position), in fact he grounds equality in natural law. For what he says comes down to the idea that humans are a certain way by nature, which would come out if we did not know what is particular about us (our future), and which should govern us morally.[11] By nature we would choose equality, and that must be our stance for a good society.

Rawls goes on to recognize that economic equality cannot be fully achieved. All we can do is work toward it by undertaking to close the gap between the poorest and the rest. We are to concentrate on the least well off and do what we can even if it means allowing some to benefit unequally *if* they help close the gap between the least well off and society in general. The goal is always equality, and Rawls believes it can be best approached by expanding the pie and helping the poor into the system rather than by promoting drastic redistributions of wealth or income.

Another place where today there is considerable sympathy for equality as justice is in gender studies, the study of relations between men and women. Consider, for instance, Susan Moller Okin's argument for equality for women.[12] It is Okin's position that many discussions of justice are embarrassingly silent on the proper relations between men and women and always have been. Where they have not been silent, they have too often celebrated traditional patriarchy, inequality in which men rule.

Okin wants to change this approach to justice and raises the issue in terms of gender and the family in particular. She is convinced that when we do, we must opt for justice as equality in these areas of mutual existence, between men and women and within the family. She calls her system "humanist" justice, underlining her equal respect stance. Much of her argument rests on a more or less implicit utilitarianism. Equality is good for everyone, and failing to provide it for women—or anyone else presumably—makes them vulnerable and denies them the chance to grow and choose as human beings.

The line which Okin walks is a narrow one between favoring equality of opportunity and favoring substantive equality. Women and men, according to her, must have equal roles in such vital arenas as the family or politics. On the other hand, Okin tilts toward equal opportunity in terms of jobs and, to some degree, toward merit in terms of income. She takes for granted that not everyone can have the same or as good a job as everyone else, but she insists they can all have generous equal opportunity.

While there are numerous other arguments regarding equality and justice in the context of the family and elsewhere, we need to have an awareness—with this form of justice as with all others—of what the opposing perspectives look like. One frequent complaint is that egalitarians misunderstand what honoring people is about. It is, say critics, about respecting people as individuals and acknowledging their unmistakable differences. Only a theory of justice (such as merit) which builds from such an obvious truth can be valid.

Another frequent objection is practical. In each form it points in the same direction and protests that equality is simply a theory that will not work. Equality doesn't work—skeptics protest—in politics, even when we try to make it do so, and it certainly won't do so in economics. People regularly seek to get ahead of each other (even if they deny it), and pretty sentiments about equality cannot change the way the world is. Why—critics may ask—promote a theory of justice, especially in the economic realm, that contradicts human nature and in the process will lead to a giant, freedom-denying bureaucracy that will endeavor to force people to be what they are not?

UTILITARIANISM

Quite another pathway to justice is cut by utilitarians. They agree that justice is what is due to us, but to decide what is due to us, they argue that we must look at the common good or the greatest good for the largest number. Justice for them is not so much an individual as a social or community concept. We have justice, by this view, when the general community sees its due as met.

Most utilitarians of this sort, those we call social utilitarians, leave open what people may consider their due or their needs or their pleasure. They know that views will vary among individuals, societies, and over time. What counts for them is not some hallmarks of justice—neither an established set of needs nor a fixed means to distribute income or political power. Merit or equality or effort is not the answer. The answer is what society decides should hold sway in one or all aspects of the community.

Most utilitarians are interested in the process by which this decision is made. They are generally democrats, though there is nothing inherently democratic about utilitarianism. At the least, some utilitarians have maintained that the greatest good could be determined better by experts or a wise leader. However, most utilitarians favor some means by which popular judgment may be brought to bear to reach a social decision. Majority rule, with minority political rights, is the norm and thus the mechanism by which the substance of justice is established.

Skeptics of utilitarianism have plenty of doubts. There are doubts about whether majority rule is much of a guide to people's sentiments. How much does simply counting noses tell us about the intensity of people's feelings? And always with utilitarianism there is the dilemma of minorities. The greatest good for the greatest number is a formula which could be and has been interpreted to justify evils such as enslaving a minority or, indeed, their genocide. Justice defined by a majority—no matter how grand the phrases surrounding it—can be only as impressive as the majority that gives it definition.

Safeguards can and would be incorporated by most modern utilitarians to ensure equal political opportunity for everyone (as part of the common good). The larger issue, though, is whether there really is any substantive theory of justice in utilitarianism. To the classic query, "What is justice?" utilitarians have no particular answer. It depends on what the community (or its leaders) decide. To skeptics this is their weakness. Yet to utilitarians it is a strength. It reflects a flexible and democratic view of justice of which they are proud.[13]

OTHER PERSPECTIVES

While the views outlined in the preceding sections are among the most famous candidates for what justice ought to be and mean, there are also many more. This proliferation occurs because the concept of justice is so important in human lives. It matters and so we can expect that there will be many alternative conceptions of justice. One of the most influential in human history has been—and continues to be—the idea that justice is what God says it is. For the devout Muslim, for example, there can be no other definition. This is true, indeed, for the committed of any religion. For all of them the final standard of justice is God's will.

That this norm often differs from religion to religion is true, despite optimistic claims that all world religions are essentially the same. But that there are sometimes disagreements about what God teaches is justice does not mean all versions are false. When they disagree, they cannot all be right, obviously, but one view or another may be. And for the devout, there can little doubt as to what view that would be.[14]

Similarly, the appeal to nature as the guide to justice is popular in our nation. Founded with appeals to natural rights in our Declaration of Independence, the United States has always had many who look to nature as the source of justice. Such an approach tends to stress individual freedom and individual protection for the enjoyment of freedom as essential to any conception of justice and to emphasize that these rights are absolute.

More recently, environmentalists have begun to define justice in terms of nature as they understand it. No longer is the model Jefferson's nature in the Declaration of Independence, but now it is nature conceived as an integrated whole, where animals and all elements of nature have rights within the ecospace of planet Earth as part of nature. In such a world of holistic nature, justice is often seen as equality requiring us to concentrate less on the human and more on the rest of nature. This form of justice as nature will be heard more and more in the future, for better or worse, as environmental and ecological concerns advance.[15]

Citing nature as the norm of justice has its limitations, too, of course. Even if one can show that something is natural, why does it follow that it ought to be the norm for our life? Nature may or may not have an understanding of justice. Yet that does not automatically mean it should be ours. Nor is there any more agreement about the teachings of nature than there is about the commands of God. Both need to be argued, long and hard. What does characterize conceptions of justice that call on God or nature is their absoluteness. These standards are about truth with a capital T or, more accurately, about conflicting truths each with a capital T.

Far away from this world is another perspective, that which looks at justice in terms of procedures. The idea here is that justice is about rules of the game, or procedures, not about outcomes, such as merit or need, or definitions based on the common good or absolute truths of God or nature.

This point of view is found among some legal systems and among those who are enamored of a legalistic justice. Some contend that justice means such things as giving all people a fair trial or due process, ensuring that they have available a set of procedures which allow them a chance to defend themselves. What it does not mean is a certain resolution of the trial or a certain distribution of goods and services in society at large. Instead it is about life as a fair trial, about getting due process, whether in the courtroom or in society.[16]

Most people do agree that justice must include a fair shake in the procedures of the courts and beyond. But in defining what a fair shake means, we are led beyond procedures to a more substantive sense of justice. What is fairness? It is more than procedures because *which* procedures we will want will depend on what our substantive theory of justice is. Is it about procedures designed to guarantee equality? Is it about procedures ordained by God?

Moreover, while we want a fair criminal trial, for example, we want more than that, if we are innocent. We also want to be found not guilty. Justice for us also involves a fair outcome. It includes our getting—in the end as well as along the way—what is due to us. So we value procedural justice, and we should, but this alone still leaves us hungering for more than procedural satisfaction.

THE PLURALIST MODEL

Whatever path we travel in pursuit of justice, few of us will use the same definition in every aspect of life. People may not have thought it all out, but they generally have a complex justice theory which employs different criteria in different arenas. In the courts, one may see justice in terms of procedures (a fair trial); in economics as merit (to each according to his or her achievement); in politics as equality and equality of opportunity (one person one vote and everyone should be able to run for office); or in personal morality as following God's teachings ("Thou shall not commit adultery").

Aware of this reality, those who describe justice in a pluralist fashion argue that we must not seek *the* principle of justice but rather always to consider the context in which we ask, "What is justice?" Michael Walzer is the contemporary theorist who has developed this approach most fully. He argues that we are and we should be justice pluralists. We should honor a wide variety of conceptions of justice—recognizing that different ones may be appropriate—depending on the part of life we may be considering.

Walzer has in mind what justice should mean in a variety of areas and he argues his views vigorously. But his larger point is that there is no single answer to justice questions. There are many answers, not just in the sense that people disagree, but also in the sense that in any one person's life a range of answers fit and, in fact, are used by most of us.[17]

Walzer invites us to explore justice not as a single problem with a single answer, but as different things to each of us in various spheres of our existence. This may seem a big challenge, but Walzer knows that he is merely asking us to do what we already do. He just wants us to be self-conscious about it and to argue what we conclude.

CONCLUSION

Justice can be an overwhelming concept. It is hard to think of an ideal which has affected so many people and for which so many have in fact sacrificed their lives. The "pyramids of sacrifice" formed by those who died or were killed in causes and revolutions in pursuit of justice have often, too often, been staggering in size. Even as the legitimate debate rages over what justice ought to look like, perhaps we should step back and wonder if there are not alternative ways to think about human interaction.

There are those who warn us to beware of the voices who cry for justice. They ask, Do such proponents of "justice" promise what we really want in society and in our own lives? This is not a matter of disputing one or another claim about justice. It is about justice thinking as a whole. It is about whether the idea of "giving each person his or her due" is what we want to be about.

How, for example, would we rate justice as a goal as against love or mercy? How would we rank it as against friendship? Such values may well point in different directions than justice. They point to union and community, whereas justice points to truth and may lead to social conflict in search of justice. Consider marriage. Is this a world we should think about in terms of justice? Surely it is about love, friendship, and forgiveness more than about justice. Perhaps we may say that justice and its questionable servants— lawyers and the police—arrive when marriages or societies are in decline, when human relationships have deteriorated.

We don't seek a just friend or a just spouse particularly, do we? Why would we stress a just society, particularly a just society above all else? Perhaps some of us would rather have Epicurus's ancient model of the good society, the society of friends.[18] Or perhaps it is a society based on love that we would want, as not a few of the world's major religions have proposed. How would justice stand in such a society? How would those who put (their versions of) justice first stand in such a society?

The alternatives to justice as the master organizing principle of society are all but endless. Each has value, though, in stimulating us to wonder about justice in society and for us. Each asks us to consider how much we want to try to erect a society devoted to rendering to each what is his or her due. Whatever our answer, issues of justice will continue to be important in every society. And the age-old search for justice will go on, as it should. In our grappling with justice, if not in our conclusions, we can be sure Plato would be pleased with us.

GLOSSARY OF KEY TERMS

due What is owed to people by right or custom in justice theory.

egalitarians Term describing people who believe strongly in equality.

equal opportunity Giving each person the same chance to succeed or fail, usually in the economic and educational spheres of life. A public policy designed to remove racial, sexual, social, or similar impediments to equal competition.

equality or need A standard of justice that says people ought to be rewarded proportionally to their needs. Alternatively, that all people ought to be equally rewarded.

desert or merit A standard of justice that says people ought to be rewarded proportionally to what they produce or accomplish. An achievement standard.

humanistic justice A standard of justice that argues that men and women must be equal.

natural law The immutable principles of the universe that some hold ought to be the inspiration for human values and laws.

pluralist justice Places justice in a sociopolitical context. Honors a wide variety of conceptions of justice because each may be appropriate in a different area of life.

process view of justice A theory that holds that processes (especially exhaustive and fair processes) determine justice, as opposed to outcomes or principles.

Roman Catholic liberation theology A combination of Judeo-Christian religion and Marxism that advocates a more just social and political order for the third world.

utilitarian justice The standard that holds that justice is avoiding pain and pleasure for individuals and for the greatest number possible.

utopians People who yearn for and/or work toward an ideal future that embodies pure justice.

SUGGESTIONS FOR FURTHER READING

Aristotle. *The Politics.*

Benn, S. I., and Peters, R. S. *The Principles of Political Thought.* New York: Macmillan, 1965.

Bentham, Jeremy, "Principles of Morals and Legislation." In *An Introduction to the Utilitarians.* Garden City, N.Y.: Doubleday, 1961.

Friedman, Milton. *Capitalism and Freedom.* Chicago: University of Chicago Press, 1962.

Friedrich, Carl J., and Chapman, John W., eds. *Justice*. Nomos VI. New York: Atherton, 1963.

Fuller, Lon. *The Morality of Law*. New Haven: Yale University Press, 1965.

Gutierrez, Gustavo. *A Theology of Liberation*. Maryknoll, N.Y.: Orbis, 1973.

Marx, Karl. "The Critique of the Gotha Program." In *The Marx-Engels Reader*, edited by Robert Tucker. New York: Norton, 1978.

Nash, Roderick. *The Rights of Nature: A History of Environmental Ethics*. Madison: University of Wisconsin Press, 1989.

Okin, Susan. *Justice, Gender, and the Family*. New York: Basic Books, 1989.

Plato. *The Republic*.

Rawls, John. *A Theory of Justice*. Cambridge: Harvard University Press, 1971.

Walzer, Michael. *Spheres of Justice: A Defense of Pluralism and Equality*. New York: Basic Books, 1983.

NOTES

1. See the classic: Gustavo Gutierrez, *A Theology of Liberation* (Maryknoll, N.Y.: Orbis Books, 1973).
2. See Roderick Nash, *The Rights of Nature: A History of Environmental Ethics* (Madison: University of Wisconsin-Madison Press, 1989).
3. Plato, *"The Republic,"* in *The Portable Plato* (New York: Viking, 1960), chapters 1 and 2.
4. Ibid.
5. John H. Schaar, "Equality of Opportunity, and Beyond," in *Equality*, ed. J. Roland Pennock and John W. Chapman (New York: Atherton, 1967), pp. 228–249.
6. See, for example, Milton Friedman, *Capitalism and Freedom* (Chicago: University of Chicago Press, 1962).
7. See these examples of the character and community movement: Clarke Cochran, *Character, Community, and Politics* (University: University of Alabama Press, 1982); or Stanley Hauerwas, *A Community of Character: Toward A Constructive Christian Social Ethic* (Notre Dame, Ind.: University of Notre Dame Press, 1981).
8. Karl Marx, "Critique of the Gotha Program," in *The Marx-Engels Reader*, ed. Robert Tucker (New York: W. W. Norton, 1978), pp. 525–541.
9. See S. I. Benn and R. S. Peters, *The Principles of Political Thought* (New York: Macmillan, 1965), chapters 5–7, for a discussion of justice and equality arguments.
10. John Rawls, *A Theory of Justice* (Cambridge: Harvard University Press, 1971).
11. Of late, Rawls has taken to saying that he is speaking only of those in liberal cultures; he thus seems to be moving toward a cultural rather than natural law argument.
12. Susan Moller Okin, *Justice, Gender, and the Family* (New York: Basic Books, 1989).
13. On Utilitarianism, inspect three classic discussions: Jeremy Bentham, "Principles of Morals and Legislation," in *An Introduction to the Utilitarians* (Garden City, N.Y.: Doubleday, 1961); John Stuart Mill, *Utilitarianism* (New York: Dutton, 1951); Rawls, *Justice*.

14. For example, both the Bible and the Koran are, among other things, works on justice, works which, in fact, have had more influence on human thinking and practice of justice than has any philosopher.
15. One can look in a lot of places from Henry David Thoreau, *Walden and Civil Disobedience* (New York: Norton, 1966), to animal rights advocates, well-discussed in Nash, *The Rights of Nature*.
16. See, for example, the classic exposition in the legal setting of Lon Fuller, *The Morality of Law* (New Haven: Yale University Press, 1965).
17. Michael Walzer. *Spheres of Justice: A Defense of Pluralism and Equality* (New York: Basic Books, 1983).
18. Epicurus, *Letters, Principal Doctrines, and Vatican Sayings* (New York: Bobbs-Merrill, 1964).

Chapter
6

Freedom

No word or concept is more familiar to us than freedom. Few are as treasured. We all want to be free and we all care about our liberty. But despite Thomas Jefferson's proclamation to the contrary in the Declaration of Independence in 1776, there is nothing self-evident about liberty or the right to liberty. What freedom means and the cases for and against freedom generate great controversy and deserve close exploration. This chapter first examines definitions of liberty and some of its alternative expressions. It then considers the major arguments for and against freedom as a value: What is the case for and against liberty in general—and in specific cases? We conclude with our reflections on liberty in our age and toward the twenty-first century.

CONCEPTIONS OF FREEDOM

One approach to freedom is straightforward. It defines freedom or liberty to mean choice. You have freedom if you have choice. I have liberty if I have choice, if I have options and if I am able to select among them. This is the common understanding of freedom and it is a good one. It tells us that freedom or liberty is a matter of particular circumstances, of the choices we have and can make at any given point or place.

Talk of freedom often gives the impression it is a quantity, a thing, that you or I have so much or so little of altogether. But this is not the way freedom works. Freedom is always particular, not general, and it is particular in at least two senses. Freedom is situation specific. You have freedom here and now (or you do not) about whether or not to buy an ice cream cone; or, you do (or do not) have the freedom to vote in a particular election. Second, freedom is always a particular freedom. It is the liberty to participate politically or the freedom to practice one's religion. In short, there is no "freedom" as a general thing, only individual freedoms in specific circumstances.

Thus here we talk mostly of particular freedoms in particular circumstances. We reflect on what people mostly mean when they discuss liberty: that they favor or oppose one or another freedom in one or another setting. This is why we discuss liberty and the arguments that swirl around it determined to separate the concept into the basic kinds of liberty, as people actually do in their lives, and consider each in turn.

Our kinds or categories of freedom are not set in stone—others would draw different lines, perhaps better ones. But the idea is to appreciate that there are several kinds of liberty and to think about freedom in the plural as freedoms. We identify four varieties of freedom and begin with what we term political freedom, the liberty to participate in the governance of one's political community. This includes the opportunity to enjoy such political liberties as free speech and free press and the right to organize politically. A second freedom is what we might call civil liberty, the right to have the freedom as a person to be treated with respect as a citizen, with equal application of the laws and room for pursuing one's life with family and friends. A third is liberty for self-development, freedom to pursue personal growth and personal moral life within the limits of social existence. Lastly, there is economic liberty, the freedom to pursue broad economic choices and advancement.

We appreciate that this is far from an exhaustive list. There are other freedoms, but this list points us in the right direction, toward a sense of freedom as a many sided concept that we cannot blithely argue for or against in the abstract. This becomes apparent when we think about the fact these freedoms may, and sometimes do, conflict with each other—that economic freedom may conflict with political liberty, that each kind of freedom may conflict with other values, that freedom for self-development may conflict with social order.

Another approach to freedom, indeed a most famous one in philosophy, is that articulated by Isaiah Berlin, a British political theorist. In his influential work, "Two Concepts of Liberty," and later essays, Berlin argues that expressions of freedom have one of two characters, either negative freedom or positive freedom. Negative freedom is when there is an absence of control or restriction.[1] It is freedom from things or people. We think in terms of negative freedom when we talk about freedom as liberation—liberation from foreign rule or parental rule or professors' rule. The implication of negative freedom is that individuals and groups regularly face threats from people who seek to control them against their will. Freedom in this light requires a constant struggle. This kind of thinking about freedom is routine in our culture. From the Declaration of Independence in 1776 to now, American politics resounds to proclamations of rights and freedoms for this or that person or group, each implying that all sorts of forces exist determined to deny the sacredness of self- or group-direction.

Positive freedom is quite another conception of freedom. It is the idea that freedom is more about the realization of objectives than the warding off of threats. Proponents of positive liberty maintain that we can be free only if we achieve our goals or certain specific goals. We are not free if we can do whatever we want or if every force or pressure leaves us alone. That is a negative view. Positive freedom, according to its advocates, has much more to offer. It is about participation in or realization of the proper or moral or true life. It is about cooperation and connection, not loneliness and drift.

Examples illustrate different views of positive freedom. Some see positive freedom as living in touch with a higher, often religious, truth. Such a life is true freedom, they contend. Others stress union with one (or another) community, as in Karl Marx's final stage of history, "communism." Here one is freed from history and all that stands in the way of possible human development.[2] Still others see it as being part of one or another nation, as do many zealous nationalists. For them, the nation is everything and unity with it is true freedom.

The origins of positive freedom are rooted in both the ancient Greek and the Christian traditions of thought. In the classic Athenian conception of citizenship in the Greek city-state, freedom in one aspect meant active participation in the assembly and other parts of self-government, which was the center of the community life. Those—such as all the slaves—who were not citizens were not allowed to participate and thus were not free. In the Christian tradition, as in many other religious outlooks, true freedom meant acceptance of the religion and its transcendent truths. The Christian Gospel says: "You shall know the truth and the truth shall make you free."[3]

Much of Western political thought in recent centuries has been closer to negative liberty, as Berlin understands it, than to positive liberty. While the state has grown, it is widely feared as a force that may limit our (negative) freedom. There is a similar fear of other institutions and, indeed, other people. The reigning disposition is that power is dangerous and so is anything that might constrict us or circumscribe us. Indeed, the very weakness of many institutions in our day, including marriage and family, is a sign of the power of the negative liberty idea in our time. Everybody wants to be free today, and when we say that, we mean free in a negative liberty sense, able to do what we want when we want.

Of course there have been exceptions in the relatively recent Western tradition of thought. One of the more famous, Jean Jacques Rousseau, argues in the eighteenth century that true freedom is unity with what he terms "the general will." We can only be free, he insists, when we unite with the truth that we help create through participation together in self-governance.[4] But such a declaration, quite lofty in tone, has attracted little interest from the people. It is decidedly not from the tradition of negative freedom.

Thinking about freedom through the negative/positive dichotomy is a valuable approach. It assists us in identifying different emphases in discussions about freedom and liberty. At the same time, it can be misleading. Gerald MacCallum deftly makes this point when he argues that every time we use the word freedom we are invoking both its negative and positive freedom meanings. That is, whenever we say we seek one freedom or another, we implicitly recognize that to achieve it we must break away from whatever stands in the way and blocks it (negative freedom); yet we also want that liberty in order to reach some purpose (positive freedom). Negative and positive liberty are simply two faces of one concept of freedom.[5]

For example, if we try to obtain religious freedom in a given place, we instinctively understand that we have to confront the forces that interfere with that liberty. We must necessarily campaign for negative freedom, for space from repressive forces. At the same time, the freedom we want is for a definite purpose, religious practice or worship, not just for itself in some pointless fashion. Thus we also campaign for positive freedom. Similarly, if we seek freedom to participate with others in self-government (positive freedom), we must try to eliminate whatever prevents the realization of our goal (we must pursue negative freedom). In short, while it is worthwhile to understand separately the negative and positive side of liberty, together they form the whole of all definitions of freedom.

A third—and similarly crucial—slant on freedom concentrates on *if* and *when* there is freedom. This approach turns first to the most fundamental issue for any discussion of human liberty—whether any freedom is ever possible—and then to when and where freedoms can flourish.

Arguments over free will continue among humans, and we suspect they will always ponder whether we can ever do other than we do. Intelligent and thoughtful things can be said about this topic. But while it is a matter that inevitably spurs curiosity and reflection, we suspect that in the end, it is a realm beyond human knowledge. We doubt that any of us will ever really know if there is, or is not, free will. A choice has to be made. We elect to believe there is free will. We contend that the world is a better place when we make the judgment that individuals have some freedom (and thus responsibility for their actions) even as we grant that we cannot prove our belief to be true or false.

We are more interested in the matter of how much freedom humans have in given circumstances. Perhaps such a determination is relevant for assigning moral responsibility, though Marion Smiley has argued that our judgments of moral responsibility have less to do with the facts about who caused *x* or *y* than with our society's cultural, social, and political assumptions about moral responsibility, regardless of the "facts."[6]

Yet the facts are certainly relevant for our simple but essential judgments of when freedom exists in a situation, for only then, of course, can we discuss freedom at all. In the proverbial example, we have scant freedom if someone places a gun at our head and tells us to do something. Yet a person in that circumstance has more freedom than someone who cannot walk but is told he or she is "free to walk home." Freedom is very much a matter of degree and circumstance.

In every situation we must examine the circumstances of freedom. How much actual choice is present? How much may we do differently than we do? Such issues are serious and raise fascinating and sometimes troubling questions. Freedom often turns out to involve a lot more than the conditions of the universe or the amount of overt coercion we face. Sometimes what matters is whether we have more than one choice. At others the problem may be to have so many choices that a kind of paralysis seizes us. Sometimes what is decisive is our life conditions. Money makes a difference, of course, but so do education, our psychological strengths and weaknesses, our upbringing, and the immediate circumstances of life and choice. How they work varies. Sometimes they limit one choice or another. At other points they make choices possible.[7]

Another circumstance of freedom is our perception of how much and what kinds of freedom we have or that others have. Freedom is not just a matter of perceptions, but it is partly that. If I think I am free I am freer than if I think I am not free, though I am not free to fly to the moon or free to win the lottery. Other attitudes matter as well. An obvious one is our attitude toward risk. We are freer if we dare to risk; freer to jump higher distances, freer to make human contacts, freer to stretch ourselves in many ways, mostly good ones, some not so good. Again, there are limits that attitudes cannot change, but limits are only part of the story of freedom.

For example, when do you or I have political freedom? When are we free to express our opinions about politics and policy and who should make decisions in politics? We can't be free here unless there are alternative ideas and policies to choose from, of course. Then we have to be able to choose among the alternatives without serious negative consequences. This standard becomes crucial. What is a negative consequence? How much pressure and conflict is a legitimate part of politics and how much is intimidating and denies freedom? Some of us frighten more easily than others and can be frightened from freedom more easily than others. But our point is that our attitudes here make a tremendous difference in how free we are.

While circumstances and attitudes are vital, they too are only one portion of the entire picture. Do we have political freedom if we do not exercise it? And can we exercise it if we lack the educational or psychological confidence to do so? And are we free politically if we are alienated from politics? Such questions cannot be ignored in calculations regarding political freedom.

Consider economic liberty. If we mean by economic liberty the ability to undertake to do or to try what we want in terms of economic life, then clearly many variables affect the degree of freedom we have. We can be freer economically the more we have resources, of course, and that is the same whether we are considering starting a business or choosing among new clothes to buy. But, equally, we are affected by the range of choices and opportunities that the real world offers in economic terms. We are also creatures of our self-confidence, our education, our ambition, and very much of our background in these matters. Always matters of freedom are situational and personal. Generalizations are risky, if inevitable.

ARGUING OVER FREEDOM(S)

Reflections on how to approach freedom are important, but they are not the same thing as indispensable normative arguments for and against liberty. In the United States we tend to celebrate freedom without enough thought. Yet we have no business assuming that all freedoms are good—or bad. The same applies to any specific freedom. There are arguments to be made.

There have been three great arguments for freedom. Many Americans may think first of the natural rights claim embodied in our Revolutionary War rhetoric and so much of our daily political language. The heart of this argument is that freedom is good because it is natural; it is right for us as humans; it is part of us, part of our nature, part of our very being. To deny us (at least some) freedoms would be to deny us ourselves and to repudiate our nature.

This view sometimes cites the naturalness of freedom as legitimate because we are the creations of God, or because of an inherent sacredness of nature, or simply through the practical claim that we are what we are—in this case natural, freedom-seeking people—and we should affirm it. But whatever the basis for the natural ground for freedom—what many term the natural right to freedom—the power and influence of this idea in our culture is formidable. It is a perspective that is as natural as apple pie.[8]

Of course, proclaiming that we have a natural right to freedom does not sweep away all the problems that this view possesses, beginning with the legitimacy of such a rights claim. It does not, for instance, tell us how to decide which of the innumerable "freedoms" proposed as rights today are truly natural rights. Do they include the right to free speech, the right to private property, or the right to do whatever one wants? Nor does it tell us how much of any natural right/liberty we should have in society. For example, parents may have the natural right to worship freely, but how does that freedom fit with other freedoms, such as the right of a child's life if parents do not allow medical treatments due to their exercise of what they see as their religious liberty?

A second great argument for freedom talks less of its foundation and more of freedom's benefit for the individual. If some classic thinkers such as John Locke or Thomas Jefferson write about freedom in terms of natural rights, others have done so more in the language of individual and social benefits. Perhaps the classic example here is in John Stuart Mill's memorable essay *On Liberty*. There the British nineteenth-century philosopher does not maintain that such things as natural rights even exist. But he has little doubt that freedom is a good thing for people and society as a whole. Given this conclusion, Mill holds that liberty ought to be restricted only where one person's freedom interferes with others'. No wonder that in *On Liberty* Mill is greatly sympathetic to human freedoms, only reluctantly conceding that government can have modest functions protecting people from the abuse of others. This remains a popular view today among those who are enamored of freedom above all other human values.[9]

Those attracted to this perspective on liberty identify three ways in which liberty can promote individual benefit, understanding that there are exceptions and necessary limitations. One theme has long been that political liberty in particular helps the individual. It ensures the individual a role in controlling his or her life as it provides a chance to consent (or not), to influence, or even to control one's government. Political liberty, the argument goes, immensely honors each of us as individual people. It says we are important; sometimes it even makes us important, depending on how much say we actually have. The consequence of this emphasis is that we are likely to be happier people.[10]

Another benefit of freedom that proponents often cite is that liberty helps development. From this view, we "grow" as human beings when we live in an environment that lets us develop, and we can do that when we are widely free. Cramped and repressed people are not open nor able to expand in life. They cannot discover, experience, or learn as much as free souls can. At its most enthusiastic, this view asserts that any check on human freedoms is harmful to development. In most cases, though, the analysis is more restrained. The principle cited is, again, often John Stuart Mill's: we need checks on freedom when our exercise of liberties ranges too far and damages others' chances to develop.

What is too often missing, however, is a specific discussion of exactly in what directions freedom promotes growth and human development. Freedom can allow a lot of things, some better than others. There is often more than a touch of naïveté in uncritical affirmations of the goodness of freedom for our "growth." Often a taste for anarchism or an affection for superficial pop psychologies infects this approach. Yet there is a core argument here that we all know makes some sense. Freedom in many circumstances is necessary for human growth. Smothering, overcontrolling, dominating—these and all similar behaviors ultimately lead to desiccated rather than healthy lives. In the right amounts and in the correct settings, freedom can be fertile soil for our human development.

Still others contend that freedom encourages the individual to flourish because freedom leads to happiness. We have no proof that living a life of broad freedoms correlates with happiness, but the belief that happy people are free people is common. The idea is that free people are more able to live in accord with their own wishes than those who are not free. In this straightforward sense, they can respond to their personal desires and wills—as we all like to do—and, of course, will be happier than those who must continually say no to themselves.[11]

Few advocates fail to add that they do not mean that freedom guarantees happiness, nor do they assume that happiness is simply a reflex of how many selfish desires we are able to fulfill. Neither proposition is true because both are far too simple to be true. Happiness is a highly personal condition and its constituents vary tremendously from individual to individual. Yet many enthusiasts of liberty assert that we are myopic if we do not see that freedom and happiness are connected, as they surely are.

A third argument for freedom identifies social benefits as the chief fruit of freedom. By this view, freedoms generate real social benefits and an atmosphere of broad freedoms is a situation in which societies normally benefit. Defenders of liberty cite numerous examples. Some celebrate economic freedom as the means to socially beneficial economic growth and higher living standards.[12] Others argue that intellectual freedom promotes new knowledge, movement toward truth, and human creativity in society.[13] Still others laud political freedoms as the means for humans to control and direct the power of human government with immense social gain for all of us.[14]

Yet the social benefits of broad freedoms are not quite so smooth and obvious as this position may make it seem. Some freedoms are not obviously beneficial to society as a whole. Indeed, their impact may be terrible for society. Thus for some citizens, pornography is an offspring of freedom that is distinctly unconnected with the social good. For them it corrupts society and/ or degrades women. Some citizens contend that substantial economic freedom is equally pernicious in its social effects. They see it leading to destructive inequalities among people, promoting a competitive society, and damaging the environment. Some argue that the freedom to have an abortion also has deleterious social affects, sanctioning an ethic of selfishness. The list could go on a long time and, obviously, each entry on the list is controversial and debated.

The larger point, though, is that claims for the social benefit of freedom, or of one freedom or another, require discussion and argument over what the general public benefit is. Announcing social benefits is not the same thing as arguing to show those benefits. That freedom has effects is not the issue; the issue is which of its effects do promote social benefit. The social value of the effects may never be taken for granted but must be argued and reargued with evidence.

Those who savor freedom on the basis of its naturalness or its promotion of individual benefit do not necessarily like the social benefit argument (and vice versa). There are, as we know, the usual reservations about the utilitarian defense of freedom as with any value. There is always the recognition that among utilitarians social benefit comes first and freedom or any other norm will be accepted as good only so long as it can be shown to facilitate "the public good." If freedom, or any particular freedom, runs afoul of the greatest good (however defined), it can expect short shrift. Thus to critics of utilitarianism, freedom rests on sand when it builds its case from social benefit arguments. To defenders this is no problem. They are confident that generous amounts of freedom are in the interest of any social community.

These arguments take place within the realm of those enthusiastic about liberty. They are arguments over how to uphold liberty as a good. Yet we should not forget that there are other, less warm, dispositions toward liberty. The celebration of liberty does not attract everyone, at least not in every case nor with the same degree of confidence. There is a host of objections to freedom. The first and most general—one that is joined by many lovers of liberty—is the attack on anarchism. Anarchism in this sense is total freedom, the absence of restraint or obligations of any sort. But for most defenders of liberty, the price of freedom is a surrender of a certain amount of freedom. This is the classic paradox of freedom. Those who accept restrictions contend that only then can freedom exist in reality. Total freedom is a fantasy and anarchist aspirations toward it soon degenerate into chaos or worse, a condition that denies in practice much of any liberty.

Such a belief underlies the entire tradition of the social contract defined in classic fashion by John Locke in seventeenth-century England. The social contract idea is that society is an agreement among people that they will abide by certain rules and procedures for the benefit of all. Put in terms of freedom, it is an agreement that the freedom of all will be protected from the antisocial few by setting up a protecting society and government. What is at issue is not whether a social contract is the actual foundation of any society or government in historical terms. What matters is the view that a kind of implicit social control is what a society assumes and that in mutually agreeing to limit freedom one acts to secure freedom.[15]

Anarchists and many of their critics are alike as freedom lovers. They disagree over how to ensure the safety and growth of liberty, but neither count as genuine skeptics of freedom. There are plenty of skeptics, however, who point us in quite different directions. Freedoms' enemies are those who suspect that liberty in theory or practice is wrong or promises troubling problems. For example, there are those who insist that in practice liberty is often nothing more than a force for destruction, something hardly worth praising in the axiomatic fashion that is usually the case. While some laud freedom as a source of new ideas, art, or cosmologies, others are uneasy or opposed to freedom for just this reason. For them, the acid freedom brings is more relevant than anything else. Liberty challenges, disrupts, redirects, breaks down, and ultimately destroys. It undermines the familiar, the regular, the expected, the comfortable, the conservative. Critics ask, Who wants this in their lives and—more to the point—what society prospers when liberty constantly tears and rips at the shared values and practices that are the sure foundation of a happy society?

On the one hand, few of us dare brush aside this reservation. Some types of freedom are powerfully destructive. The freedom to murder or to rape is obviously so and it has few defenders if too many practitioners. On the other hand, others hail much of the so-called acidic side of freedom as part of progress. New thinking, challenges, experiments, release from safe moorings, and change we may define as progress or the necessary condition for progress in every aspect of life.

Consider the role of economic freedom, especially of economic development and developers. Long ago, Karl Marx argued that capitalist freedom wields a tremendous force. It can and does transform accepted ways and longtime institutions with a speed and thoroughness that is awesome. Few can resist the power of the engine of economically driven social change.[16] Thus it is no surprise today that practitioners of economic freedom often clash with those who fear its change-making consequences. Opponents come in many forms, as environmentalists, historic preservationists, or planners. Again and again, those who seek to exercise the freedom to follow their economic goals clash with those who fear the results of such a freedom.

Another common example lies in the area of societal morality. Advocates of liberty for personal self-expression constantly come up against those who resist aspects of such freedom as destructive of social morality. Those who want to produce or enjoy pornography are a case in point. While critics now include two very different perspectives, both traditional moralists and some contemporary feminists are alike in denigrating this freedom, contending that it fosters social and individual degeneration.

This reservation, rooted in the destructive side of (some) freedoms, leads to a second. Critics charge that freedom simply does not always fit well with the value of community, of close affective relations among people. The reason that community is the subject of several chapters in this book is the tremendous interest in this norm now, as often in the past. Many, many citizens feel that our society is coming apart because the only god we worship is individual freedom. As interest in community has blossomed, once again there have been tough questions raised about liberty as an unqualified good.

The issue is not quite the same as the matter of the relationship between freedom and basic social morality. Every society has this tension. After all, every social order has a social morality of sorts as well as some freedoms. In each the balance is what is constantly in contention. But the issue of community is something else. Community involves a far more self-conscious goal and implies a more distinct closeness among its participants than does a society. It involves restrictions and limits through closeness. That closeness promises possible tensions along many axes with various freedoms.

An apt and sometimes painful illustration is the self-conscious community movement on many American college campuses. According to its ethic, there is a great need for sensitivity toward diverse groups and opinions on campus. Advocates proclaim that honoring this norm will lead to a happier and closer community on campus, building bridges of trust and harmony among groups. Maybe it will and maybe it won't. In the process of encouraging the sensitive community it is inevitable that those who are not interested in such a community will experience freedom-restricting pressures. And in some instances already, their freedom of speech has been curtailed.

Thoroughgoing communitarians, of course, have no ambivalence about such events. They are consequences that should be cheerfully paid for (by others).[17] Today political, religious, or ecological community advocates are sometimes quite explicit in attacking a wide range of freedoms as damaging to their community. They identify and critique freedoms that can damage their goals and undermine the spirit of unity on which all communities depend and thrive. Some ecologists, for example, frankly attack many dimensions of economic liberty in the name of endangered species or all species. The resulting tensions and conflicts are real and we can expect them to become uglier in the future. The struggle will be intense in our freedom-loving culture, but there is no doubt it is underway now.

A third frequent objection to freedom as the great goal in life—or even as a central goal—is that it is really a process value, not an end value. That is, we may ask, Who wants freedom, including any particular freedom, just for itself? Isn't freedom something that we seek for what we can accomplish through it or because of it? Freedom lacks an objective or a purpose and is distinct from the good community or happiness or political representation or economic equality. They are often ends in themselves and we value them according to how we respect them as part of our life plan. But freedom is something else. Skeptics perceive that it is about process and thus can only be evaluated in terms of the objectives it advances. Critics conclude that no one should endorse freedom in principle, but only one or another freedom that would encourage particular values we want.

CONCLUSION

Most of us, at least in our culture, resist skepticism about liberty. We assume that it is a good and hear its praises around us—and inside us—over and over. Yet such negativity has its worth. It can make us careful about freedom and arguments for freedom. When we assess the case for freedom in any instance, it guides us toward taking into account a tough, clear-sighted evaluation of (1) the amount of any freedom urged and (2) the particular freedoms affirmed in any context.

Of course it matters how much freedom one urges in any given circumstance. No one but anarchists lauds full freedom in all circumstances. Even more, the case for any particular freedom must be argued and argued again and never assumed. Thus it is a fact that some of us favor a broad freedom to divorce while others contend that such a freedom hurts children and society as a whole. Or some of us treasure unlimited artistic liberty as the prerequisite to creativity while others worry that such freedom damages the larger community and the moral fabric on which all communities must and do rest.

In short, most of the argument over freedom has to take place in terms of specific discussions over particular claims for and against individual liberties. There are points to be made for and against freedom in general. We have seen that and explored several. But we come back, as we have had to do, to the dimension of specific cases and circumstances. In arguing about freedom, it is true that we argue about x freedom or y liberty in this instance or that instance.

Such a process takes us out of the world of grand theorizing and brings us back to actual politics and particular policy choices. It pulls political theory down to earth. It also illustrates that so much of political theory applied to concrete cases will be about choices among values. So much of the conversation about liberty cannot be about declaring liberty bad or good, but of weighing liberty against justice or obligation or community.

There may be some people who find that a frustrating reality. It would be so much simpler to declare that we are for or against liberty in general, regardless of context, regardless of trade-offs. But that is not reality. Thus good arguments about liberty must reach toward actual human practice and actual lives and choices. Arguments that address hard choices and real alternatives in specific contexts are what the political theory of freedom is all about. Slogans are no substitute and freedom is too valuable to rest on them.

GLOSSARY OF KEY TERMS

anarchism A political theory advocating total freedom. It champions participatory communities with little or no government.

ecology The science of the interrelationship of living organisms and their environment. Also a political ideology and movement that advocates policies supporting protection of the natural environment.

economic freedom The liberty to pursue economic choices and to participate in politics and policy.

feminism A movement that advocates the rights and social and economic claims of women as a group.

freedom Choice or absence of restraint. Always situation-specific. Synonymous with liberty.

general will A concept of Jean Jacques Rousseau that equates the public interest developed through democratic participation with liberty. Similar to but stronger than positive freedom.

negative freedom Absence of restraint. A term used by British political theorist Isaiah Berlin.

political freedoms The liberty to express opinions and to participate in politics and public policy.

positive freedom A concept of liberty involving realization of objectives as freedom. Also a term from Isaiah Berlin.

SUGGESTIONS FOR FURTHER READING

Berlin, Sir Isaiah. *Four Essays on Liberty*. London: Oxford University Press, 1969.

Friedman, Milton. *Capitalism and Freedom*. New York: Bantam Books, 1982.

Jefferson, Thomas. *Basic Writings of Thomas Jefferson*. Edited by Philip Foner. New York: Wiley, 1944.

Locke, John. *Second Treatise*. Edited by Peter Laslett. Cambridge: Cambridge University Press, 1960.

MacCallum, Gerald. "Negative and Positive Freedom." *The Philosophical Review* 76 (1967):312–334.

Mill, John Stuart. *Three Essays: On Liberty, Representative Government, The Subjection of Women*. Edited by Richard Wollheim. New York: Oxford University Press, 1975.

Smiley, Marion. *Moral Responsibility and the Boundaries of Community*. Chicago: University of Chicago Press, 1992.

NOTES

1. Sir Isaiah Berlin, *Four Essays on Liberty* (London: Oxford University Press, 1969).
2. Karl Marx, "Critique of the Gotha Program," in *The Marx-Engels Reader*, ed. Robert C. Tucker (New York: W.W. Norton, 1978), pp. 525–541.
3. Gospel according to John, 8:32.
4. Jean Jacques Rousseau, "The Social Contract," in *Political Writings*, ed. Frederick Watkins (New York: Nelson, 1953).
5. Gerald MacCallum, "Negative and Positive Freedom," *The Philosophical Review* 76 (1967):312–334.
6. On free will and moral responsibility, see Marion Smiley, *Moral Responsibility and the Boundaries of Community* (Chicago: University of Chicago Press, 1992).
7. This is a complex and fascinating subject on which many have had much to say. But the person who first got us started seriously exploring this area is Alan Wertheimer. See his *Coercion* (Princeton, N.J.: Princeton University Press, 1987).
8. Thomas Jefferson, *Basic Writings of Thomas Jefferson*, ed. Philip Foner (New York: Wiley, 1944); John Locke, *Second Treatise*, ed. Peter Laslett (Cambridge: Cambridge University Press, 1960).
9. John Stuart Mill, *Three Essays: on Liberty, Representative Government, The Subjection of Women*, ed. Richard Wollheim (New York: Oxford University Press, 1975).
10. From Pericles in his "Funeral Oration" in fifth-century Athens to a participatory democrat such as Carole Pateman, this theme gets special attention. See Pateman, for example: *Participation and Democratic Theory* (Cambridge: Cambridge University Press, 1970).
11. There does, indeed, seem to be more than a bit of often unself-conscious Freudianism in such an analysis. See Sigmund Freud, *Civilization and Its Discontents*, ed. James Strachey (New York: W. W. Norton, 1962).
12. Milton Friedman, *Capitalism and Freedom* (Chicago: University of Chicago Press, 1962).
13. The great case is made by Mill, *On Liberty*.
14. The position of the authors of *The Federalist Papers*. See Garry Wills, ed., *The Federalist Papers: Alexander Hamilton, James Madison, and John Jay* (New York: Bantam, 1982).
15. For an able presentation of classic social contract theories, see Patrick Riley, *Will and Legitimacy: A Critical Exposition of Social Contract Theory in Hobbes, Locke, Rousseau, Kant, and Hegel* (Cambridge: Harvard University Press, 1982).
16. See Karl Marx, *Capital*, ed. Friedrich Engels (New York: International Publishers, 1967).
17. Jean Jacques Rousseau.

Chapter
7

Equality

*E*quality is about equivalence. People or things are equal when they are equivalent to each other. The idea is simple but the power of the idea is enormous in human history. The kinds of equality citizens have sought differ greatly, yet attraction to equality in the modern world is strong. We expect that attraction to continue and thus a book on political theory must consider equality.

The origin of human moral equality as an ideal in Western thought lies in two influential traditions. The first is the Greek and Roman tradition of Stoicism, which flourished at different points in ancient Athens and imperial Rome. It is among the most important of classical systems of thought. Among its most prominent thinkers are the slave philosopher, Epictetus (A.D. 50–138), and the Roman emperor, Marcus Aurelius (A.D. 121–180). While the Stoics' perspective is neither simple nor uniform, they share one central belief: the moral equality of all people. Whether slave or ruler, every person is of equivalent worth in God's universe.[1]

The other major source for the idea of human equality is the Christian religion, as expressed in both the Gospels (especially the Gospel of Luke) and in the writings of Paul. The Christian gospels portray Jesus as one who brings his truth to everyone equally—regardless of their origins or history or condition—and insists that each is equal before him, before God. Paul's letters to early Christian churches often make the same point and affirm, as Paul states in Galatians, that "there is neither Jew nor Greek, free nor slave, man nor woman, but all are one in Christ." All that matters is the essential unity of people as moral beings created by God.[2]

These ideas of equality do not necessarily imply any connection with social or political equality in actual life. They certainly did not in ancient

Roman and Greek society, which were far from equal by any imaginable measure. And they did not much in Christian society either, though the very earliest Christians, as the Book of Acts describes them, did practice a decided equality: "They had all things in common."[3] However, over time more and more developments took place which led some in the West to begin to make connections with egalitarian ideas of Western thought and the concrete world of living human beings. Especially in the eighteenth century, some theorists began calling for drastic consideration of equality. Among these was the influential French theorist, Jean Jacques Rousseau. By the time of the American Revolution in 1776, equality was no longer solely a theological and religious idea. Voices had begun demanding that it come down to earth and be a standard for this world.

This was the motivation, for example, of Thomas Jefferson in our Declaration of Independence in 1776. For Jefferson all (men) had equal rights and specifically they had an equal right to life, liberty, and the pursuit of happiness. The religious roots remained present. When Jefferson declares after all, that "all men are created equal," he puts it that "they are endowed by their Creator with certain inalienable rights . . . life, liberty, and the pursuit of happiness." Similarly, in the growing British antislavery movement of the eighteenth century, religious equality was used as a principal argument for why slavery had to end. The idea of equality had suddenly arrived in earthly politics.

An equality understood in more secular terms fueled the French Revolution for a period in the same era. There is also no doubt that its hopes and energies drove revolution after revolution in nineteenth-century Europe and revolution after revolution throughout the world in our own century. It has provided the spirit as well for many of the revolutions in our time—as in Eastern Europe—often made against those who praised equality but practiced something very different.

What is true today is that everywhere we look, in the United States or elsewhere in the world, we see that much of politics concerns equality and opposition to equality. Arguments over equality are always on the agenda in almost every area of government and policy. Demands for equal treatment or equal rights come from almost every conceivable group—the disabled, African-Americans, single mothers, senior citizens, divorced fathers, gays. Everyone seems to speak the language of equality, granted that they speak it with their own particular meanings. For some the focus is on equality of opportunity; for others it is on economic equality or greater economic equality; for others it is about affirmative action; for still others it is about political equality. The policies proposed vary with the idea of equality and the group promoting it. What does not vary is recourse to the rallying cry of equality.

Controversy abounds because equality is not just a concept with alternative, disputed meanings. It is also a value with enemies, many enemies. Some don't like one form or another of equality and argue strenuously against it, because it denies human freedom or the human individual, or because it is impractical. Others reject any type of equality as a denial of values they seek or because every kind is a futile pipe dream, not worth the human effort to undertake to achieve it.

In the future we can expect that concerns about equality will only expand. As communications technology spreads the ideal, more and more groups over the globe will awake to its attractions. More and more will demand equality— political, social, and economic equality and policies that they believe will somehow accomplish such ends. Moreover, we can expect that we will hear a concept of equality affirmed in the future that reaches beyond humans and demands that all of nature be included as equal with humankind. Equality seems destined to be a watchword of the politics and policy in the twenty-first century, as it has been in our own. Less clear is what it means, what the case for it is, and what the objections to equality are. They are the political theory of equality and they are the substance of this chapter.

DEFINITIONS OF EQUALITY

What does equality mean? We know that to get a secure definition of equality or any other key concept in political theory is not easy. The concept of equality, as with other concepts, is too important and too controversial for that. Among the issues are whether there is a core meaning to the word equality and what variations of meaning of equality there are. Later we must ask when and if equality is a good; what kind of equality (equalities) we care most about; how equality ranks as a value in comparison with obligation, democracy or, above all, freedom; and finally, How much equality can actually be achieved in the real world?

We have already stated that as we understand equality, it is about the idea of "equivalent to." To be equal to Sarah is to be equivalent to Sarah. It is vital to understand from the beginning that to be equivalent to does not necessarily mean being the same as Sarah. This distinction is crucial. You and Sarah may have equal political power, but that does not mean you have power in the same ways or power composed of the same elements. All it means is that the power you both exercise is equivalent. You may have power through your charm and Sarah have it through money, but if you exercise the same amount of power you are equal in power. Alternatively, you and Tom may be equal economically even though you have quite different incomes. As we saw in the chapter on Justice, the point is that if you have no children and Tom has three, you both can have equal incomes only if Tom receives a much higher income than you do. Again, equivalency is what matters when we consider equality.

This central point helps us deal with one group of thinkers who would brush aside any discussions of equality. Those we have in mind insist that equality is always a worthless subject because it is in profound conflict with the realities of the universe. People, this argument goes, are just plain different from each other. Who can deny this fact, when it is daily on display in the great human variations regarding strength, size, mental capacities, personalities, or looks? Moreover, each of us has his or her own history that we cannot ignore and which has stamped us uniquely in terms of character and attitudes. Critics conclude that in the face of such permanent differences, arguments for equality make no sense. They are silly. There is no such thing as equality and urging it amounts to pathetic flailing against the universe.

In one way such doubters are correct. It is obvious—or it should be—that people are not the same and cannot be made the same (though some fanatics have tried to make them so). There are natural variations among humans that no egalitarian, however earnest, can abolish. Yet it is less obvious that we cannot be equal in many realms of life. We can live in a world in which many of its inequalities are reduced as long as we define equality as equivalence rather than the abolition of differences.

To be sure, skeptics contest this claim also. They contend that background and heredity stand as barriers to much of the impetus toward greater equality defined as equivalence. Yet there are as many arenas where equality as equivalence is not so impossible. Surely equality defined as equivalence is much more possible in such policy areas as health care or income or educational quality—or even human respect—than is current human practice or than some skeptics believe. Perfection is unattainable and equality cannot ignore nature's limits. Yet practical objections cannot decide the entire issue of equality. We have to confront the essential moral question too: How much equality do we want in life?

We need to appreciate the practical challenges about reaching equality, however defined. But that becomes relevant only if we first face the question: should we seek equality? Thus while equality is best understood as being about equivalence, it is not just an empirical idea. It may or may not be possible in practice, yet the concept draws attention, energy, and debate because it is fundamentally normative. It is a moral or ethical concept. It is so significant in our age because it is something dreamed of as an ideal by millions and cursed as a nightmare by other millions. Therefore, we must be concerned with whether we ought to have equality and to that argument we now turn.

KINDS OF EQUALITY

To approach the normative issue of equality we first have to be analytic and break equality into its parts, into the kinds of equality that people support. In effect then, like freedom, equality has meaning only in reference to specific conditions or situations. There are few people who are complete egalitarians, citizens ready to defend the principle of equality in every and any circumstance. Even the most devoted egalitarian usually balks at the view that everyone should be equal to everyone else in all things, or that every inherited inequality be eliminated by state or society or magic. And, of course, those who are less devoted to or interested in egalitarianism definitely restrict what kinds of equality, if any, they may favor. Our mission now becomes how to distinguish one kind of equality from another in principle and in practice.

First, the concept of equality we are most familiar with is political equality. It is the idea that underlies all democratic politics and all democratic political systems. It stresses the great importance of providing for equal rights to participate for all citizens: the right to vote, the right to express one's opinions, the right to organize for political goals, and the right to run for office.[4] Today most countries in the world claim that they offer broad political rights. While this is often much truer in theory than in reality, it testifies to the popularity of this kind of equality.

A second familiar concept is equality of opportunity. It is a widely treasured value in the United States (though the degree of opportunity actually available is controversial). Its supporters hold that everyone should have a roughly equal chance to succeed in life, especially economic life. The frequent analogy of the horse race applies here. Equal opportunity holds that everyone should leave the starting gate in a roughly equal fashion. It takes for granted that the results will vary depending on health, drive, ability, luck, or heredity, of course. Equal opportunity is not really about equal outcomes but about equal chances.[5]

How to encourage or maintain equal opportunity is a formidable challenge in any situation. Part of the reason is that there are many more of us who say we support the idea than actually do. After all, it can easily conflict with our self-interest or with our desires for our children. How to use government to open doors toward equal opportunity is no simple matter either. Plans and programs have a distressing way of failing. Moreover, to speed one person's opportunity may conflict with someone else's. Eventually, too many programs and taxes for programs to support people struggling to get ahead can have the effect of eliminating the incentives for those who are seeking opportunity.

Economic equality is a third kind of equality that others seek. They see economics as the central aspect of life and the key to most others. What the goal of economic equality means is roughly equal incomes or approximately equal entitlements: equal educational opportunities or health care services. How economic equality will work out in society will vary according to how intent its advocates are on their objective and on what policies and institutions are their chosen instruments. Some expect to have socialism; others stress workers' control of industries; still others propose to proceed through tax policies; there are many ideas.[6]

A fourth perspective directs us to a broader concept of equality, the ideal of equal respect for all human beings. Other conceptions of equality draw on this view in part, at least in a portion of their justifications for equality. But an approach to equality that speaks first in terms of equality as respect is less about political or economic equality than it is about humane or spiritual values and relationships, no matter what form they may take. This outlook on equality self-consciously focuses on each individual as a whole person and his or her relationship with others. To promote equal respect there may need to be political and economic equality—or at least equality in terms of some significant economic entitlements. That is and will continue to be a matter of argument. But for these egalitarians, such pieces of equality are not enough or not quite the point. Equality is about something much larger, much more important, and much less amenable to laws and rules.

Equal respect must include how we are treated by others in human terms—how, for example, bureaucrats or businesspeople or friends or neighbors treat us. Again, the goal is less equal amounts of things—of influence or money—and more a spirit of equality. What policies or amounts of things might be needed to encourage and facilitate equal respect will vary according to circumstances. The test for any policy will be whether it reinforces equal respect for persons.[7]

The list of kinds of equality is lengthy and the four we have outlined are only illustrations, though they receive and have received the most discussion. In the future, in the next century, the twenty-sixth of Western political theory, we believe they will be joined by a fifth. It will speak the language of nature and define equality as equality within nature for all living things. There is no doubt that as animal rights advocates, enthusiasts for rights of wilderness, and more radical environmentalists grow in number, they will more and more place on our agenda the claims that all in nature are equal (equivalent) and that this view is the very foundation for what equality must be about.[8]

Supporters of these various ideas of equality do not necessarily separate them neatly as we have. They often argue that any aspect of equality is intertwined with others. For example, many economic egalitarians believe that economic equality will assist the achievement of political equality in a society. They insist that where large variations in income and wealth exist among us, political equality will be badly undermined and rule by the rich is likely. On the other hand, many of those who favor political equality do not support economic equality. For them economic equality is not worth the cost in terms of sacrifice of other values such as equality of opportunity or human freedom. They endorse other means—such as in campaign financing—to restrict the influence of the rich in politics.[9]

THE ARGUMENT OVER EQUALITY

Why do people favor equality in one or another situation? This is our central question. What is the case for equality in one arena or another after all the explanations and distinctions are made and in place? The answer is that there are many reasons for and against equality, a rich and fierce argument that has been going on—and will continue to do so—for as long as men and women have been on earth.

As we could predict, one argument that resounds loudly now and will do so more in the future is the argument for equality based on nature. According to this view, everyone is fundamentally equal as natural beings or has equal rights as natural beings. A variant expands natural equality to include all or many of the sentient creatures who share nature with us, an argument that we know contends that nature is holistic and integral within the whole. Such arguments take nature as the obvious standard for truth. If we (however the "we" is defined) are equal in nature, then we ought to have equal (equivalent) rights and protections in nature. The implications could be vast and will be vast, especially if equal rights in nature comes to include all living creatures. Yet the assumption that nature is the standard for morality requires a vigorous defense. It is far from self-evident.[10]

Another argument for equality is spiritual, present in most of the world's major religions. It holds that all humans are equal through our creation by God or because of God's presence within us. For those who take this approach it often follows that political, economic, and social practices must reflect God's norms and advance equality among people. Others who accept equality as a premise of God's creation are less sure of what follows in terms of earthly practices. They are aware that the world is always far from a godly ideal and skeptical that spiritual equality necessarily should be translated into earthly goals. They are not so sure that the heavenly city and the earthly city can be the same, or should be the same. In every instance, this approach appeals only to those who start with the religious premises on which it is so tightly founded.[11]

Other equality perspectives focus on "respect for persons." The argument is that if we truly honor each person, we would treat each person equally . . . and equally well. Such an outlook is often linked, of course, with such religious ideas as Jesus' proclamation, "Do unto others as you would have them do unto you," or Kant's famed maxim, "Act as if your action would be made universal." It has connections with many traditions, in fact, and this is partly why it is the most common basis for arguments for equality today. Why should we have political equality or economic equality or racial equality? Time and again the answer is the claim that these sustain respect for all human persons.[12] That is not, however, an explanation for why we ought to have respect for persons, nor why respect for persons can best be expressed as equality. Both assumptions are made routinely, but they must be argued, since they, too, are far from self-evident.

Nor is it obvious just how any of these three approaches would work in practice. They are about principle and not policy, which can be a problem. Vague principles do not necessarily help us all that much when we get down to the business of living together. In this matter, therefore, some argue that a more utilitarian understanding of equality would be better. It would concentrate more on specific policies and consequences of policies in regard to equality. Utilitarians agree that in every instance equality can be defended only when it benefits the whole, only when it results in more pleasure than pain or helps us achieve the greatest good for the greatest number in society.

Thus utilitarians who favor equality of opportunity speak in terms of how they believe it benefits the larger society; it opens doors for citizens, which may result in happier people and a creative, flourishing society. Those utilitarians who favor economic equality do so in the language of the common good. They contend that the common good will prosper from economic equality because the human respect they contend it will encourage leads in turn to happier and more satisfied people. They also maintain that economic equality will slash competition among people and reduce the jealousies and envy that cause so much human unhappiness.

Such utilitarian arguments make nonutilitarian advocates of egalitarianism uncomfortable. Critics of utilitarians know that for utilitarians equality is always a second rank value. The first value is the greatest common good and happiness. If equality (or a specific form of equality) promotes that goal, then utilitarians will rally to it. But if it does not, then equality will get short shrift. For example, if it turns out that economic equality results in a smaller GNP, a poorer economy, most utilitarians will not be very interested in economic equality. For the greatest good for the greatest number would not, by their lights, be helped by economic equality in this instance.[13]

This is why most arguments for equality have a way of getting back to respect for persons, whether grounded in nature or God or simply that norm as a chosen first principle. Utilitarian perspectives often play a role, but they rarely travel alone. Equality and respect for the individual and for every individual go together today.

ARGUMENTS AGAINST EQUALITY

Of course the ideal of equality in general as with any particular kind of equality has plenty of opponents. No normative idea can expect, or should expect, an unscathed existence. Each must be tested and each is tested. Regarding equality the arguments are most intense over the worth of economic equality. It is always the most controversial form of equality. It has never been more so than in this day, when much of the world has shaken off a Marxism that its zealots said they instituted in service of economic equality.

First and foremost, as we know, many critics argue that equality is always an illusion. It has nothing to do with the world as it is. Some scoff at the norm of political equality just as much as economic equality on these grounds. Where, they ask, does real political equality exist? Power and influence are always shared unequally, they assert, and they always will be. All pious proclamations to the contrary cannot alter reality. One nation varies from another only (if importantly) in the degree of political inequality among citizens, never in the fact of inequality.

An identical situation pertains to economic life. Governments can try as they might to legislate economic equality among people, but they will fail. These schemes simply run against the grain of people's desire to get ahead. People will always invent clever ways to escape the demands of egalitarianism. Black markets, payments in kind, tax avoidance—these and others represent the many strategies citizens employ to avoid the dictates of economic egalitarianism.

Critics suggest that what this kind of avoidance behavior tells us is that people don't want to be equal with others if equality goes beyond a general respect for persons and starts taking on concrete consequences, especially in economics. Citizens may vote for equality in one situation or another, but that does not mean they have a serious commitment to it beyond a vague respect for all people.

Skeptics ask, Who would expect it? People do not measure themselves in any of life's dimensions by whether or not others are their equal—unless they are striving to rise to a place where they are equal. Behavior tell us this story even if people sometimes pretend to deny it. Not too many citizens want to have the same salaries as everybody else or the same looks or to be just as good a dancer or soccer player. People want to succeed and that, they assume, means to be better than other people, quite frankly. While not everybody may like this reality, skeptics insist that egalitarians must come to terms with it and take their heads out of the clouds.

From another perspective, critics charge that egalitarians just misunderstand what society is about. It is not about equality (equivalence) on one or any dimension of life. This is simplistic reductionism. People in the complex world have contrasting yet intertwined roles, places, and experiences that just cannot be reduced to equality. Life is more about complexity, differences, and interaction than equality. Thus arguments consumed with the good of equality are artificial, endeavoring to cut people off from the diverse, changing, interactive world in which we all dwell.[14]

Not all the objections to equality assert its impracticality or its misunderstanding of people and society. Many do, but they are not the only arguments. Others decry equality because they believe it is morally wrong. While one rarely meets this argument about political equality, it is common about economic equality and about a society which seeks equality in a sweeping fashion, prepared to install it in every corner of society. The most frequent objection is that accentuating equality is to deny the good of individualism. It is to view people not as individual persons, but as some homogeneous whole, a mass into which the individual will disappear.

Critics argue that we may be willing to take that chance in order to honor people in providing political equality, but not in economic affairs. There, they argue, respecting individuals must mean, to some extent, letting us take the consequences of different accomplishments and varying amounts of effort. Citizens will then have varying incomes and sometimes that will be perfectly fair, a matter of rewarding us as individuals for what we have each done and not done in life. Why should everyone get the same income when some have not worked equally hard or not done equally good work?

From a utilitarian point of view, the consequences of such economic equality will be to manipulate people to act as members of the mass, not as individuals. People will not strive to get ahead, to work hard, or to be creative, because they will realize it will get them nowhere. As their individuality or individual efforts disappear, society will suffer a loss of productive capacity as has been so sadly demonstrated in the former Soviet Union.

The overall point of critics is that egalitarians don't like human differences and that in that attitude they dishonor people and our manifest desire to escape being just the same as others. Egalitarians say they favor respect for persons, but opponents of equality insist that to respect us is to respect us in our unique selves and for our particular accomplishments and personal life choices. They also charge that an egalitarian society will be a poor and unproductive one, hardly benefitting the common and individual good of anyone. Thus respect for persons is the most common reason for supporting equality, but it is also the most important reason for opposing equality, except for equality of political and civil rights.

Many of the arguments over equality are in good part arguments about justice, a subject we have considered in broader perspective already in this book. Equality and many of the types of equality we have examined are forms of justice. Yet equality is not the only kind of justice. Far from it as our justice chapter suggests. Moreover, arguments for equality need not be expressed only in terms of "justice," as this chapter has demonstrated. Equality may or may not be just in any circumstance, but for those who love it and those who hate it, equality or the denial of equality is almost always about respect or disrespect for persons.

EQUALITY AND OTHER VALUES

Objections to equality also arise from those who place other values higher than equality. Many who are not especially committed to equality beyond the political realm fear that most egalitarians are prepared to sacrifice too many other values in a determined effort to reach equality in many realms of life. Of course, even the most thoroughgoing egalitarian appreciates that there are competing values and choices to be made in any universe. Equality has to be placed in some sort of priority with other goals and values, a process which may involve painful choices, which is what politics is all about. Thus to know that someone favors equality in a specific area of life does not tell us all that much. We also have to know how they rank equality with the other values that may be in competition.

In our previous chapter we considered freedom. Let us consider, then, the possible trade-offs that may exist between liberty and equality. Let's look at policies designed to increase equality of opportunity for groups neglected in a given economic or political system. It is all well and good to support equal opportunity in such circumstances, but what might the costs of such policies be? There are always costs in any policy choice and only the naive or dishonest do not accept this stern fact of life. In this case, we may ask, How much liberty will some citizens need to give up? If we are prepared to curtail such liberty, then how would we do so? Would we go on and support affirmative action policies, policies that give some groups a substantially greater opportunity than that afforded others?

The point is not that we should necessarily reject equality of opportunity. The point is that we cannot just glibly announce that we favor both liberty for all and equality of opportunity and then go home satisfied. Things don't work that way. Choices have to be made about values. There are going to be costs for gains and in this instance as in others, we have to decide how highly we rank equality (or any other value) and how much of other values we are prepared to sacrifice. It is not an easy business and it cannot be made an easy business.

The same difficulties arise if we favor income equality. Once again the liberty of some—or many—citizens may in part be sacrificed. Income equality cannot be approached without a major commitment to government action. People's pursuit of individual self-advancement in economic terms would have to be sharply restricted. Rich businesspeople—and also small farmers and small businesspeople, among others—would see what they consider their economic freedom shrink. Similarly, we could expect an attack on the freedom to provide for one's family through inheritance, since this is a major way in which economic inequality is perpetuated. Again, tough decisions would have to be made. All values cannot be maximized at the same time.

Skeptics delight in dwelling on these kinds of trade-offs, but to be aware of them does not necessarily mean we will be, or should be, hostile to any or every form of equality. It is an argument against failing to be self-conscious of the necessity of choices. But if we cannot have all values or all goods at the same time in life, on the other hand we should recognize that equality and, for example, liberty are not always in conflict. To think otherwise constitutes an illusion of another sort. Critics stress conflicts, real or potential, but this is rarely the full story and often it is only a small part of it. Values do not always conflict; often they work together.

The fact is, for instance, that people who lack basic economic resources in life will have little political liberty. They may not need to have strict economic equality, but how can political freedom be equal where economic inequality is rife? Thus more economic equality for some citizens will increase their political liberty. It does not guarantee such a result, but it may make it possible. Moreover, serious economic opportunity is essential for poor citizens who want to begin to achieve and flourish in economic life. If we do not provide this kind of equality, then economic freedom for most citizens will be small or nonexistent. Once again, equality and liberty can work together, depending on the kinds of equality and liberty we are talking about.

There is simply no formula for when equality and liberty (or whatever value) work together or clash with each other. This is a matter theory cannot settle alone. Practice must also be our guide. We need to know how policies work in actual life. We can assume little and we must explore everything. We can imagine areas of value conflict and areas where equality and other norms will complement each other, but experience will tell us what the reality is. All that we can do is be alert to the possibilities and not merrily pass by the subject. Always we must assume that equality of any sort will neither automatically fit nor conflict with other values.

Thus, every argument for equality must take into account its relationship in theory and practice with other values. We must develop as much as we can a sense of the hierarchy of values among equality and other norms that are important. Without it we cannot have a good understanding of what version of equality we may favor, nor of how much we favor it. Priorities matter in politics and political theory just as they do everywhere else.

CONCLUSION

All over the world we see the signs that suggest what the twenty-first century will have to say about equality. More and more people want to be treated equally, want to have equal respect. There is no end of disagreement about how that should be expressed in terms of particular forms of equality, nor about the danger and drawbacks of most types of equality. Nor is there any agreement on what is the priority of equality next to competing values. But the signs of the times and the signs toward the future suggest that equality will hold its own and maybe grow in importance in our personal political theories. We can predict it will be much on the agenda of our common future and for that reason we urge each of you to grapple with its fascinating and important dimensions. We all will have to have arguments about equality.

GLOSSARY OF KEY TERMS

equal opportunity A value or prescription for public policies that mandates for all an equal opportunity to compete regardless of social or natural impediments. Often couched in terms of economic and educational opportunity.

equal respect A social value that mandates treating all people with equal honor and dignity. Often couched in giving each a fair hearing or opportunity in life and government.

equal rights A value that holds that each person has the same moral claims and right to equal opportunity. Sometimes used to describe public policies redressing past inequities.

equivalence A standard of human interchangeability. Presumes all people have the same moral worth, especially in politics.

liberty The political value of freedom (absence of restraint). Often conflicts with equality, but many political theories have found ways to balance liberty and equality.

political equality A democratic value of equal rights of political participation and decision making for all citizens.

reductionism The reasoning error that reduces complex ideas and values to overly simple ideas and principles, especially in relation to cause and effect.

stoicism A philosophy dating back to the Greek and Roman eras that emphasized moral equality.

value trade-offs Recognition that some values tend to conflict and that accommodating one value to another involves balancing desirable traits and goals of values.

SUGGESTIONS FOR FURTHER READING

Aristotle. *The Politics.*

Bible. Both New Testament and Old Testament.

Charvet, John. "The Idea of Equality as a Substantive Principle of Society." *Political Studies* 17 (1969):1–13.

Lakoff, Sanford A. *Equality in Political Philosophy.* Cambridge: Harvard University Press, 1964.

Pennock, J. Roland, and Chapman, John W., eds. *Equality.* "Nomos IX," New York: Atherton, 1967.

Rae, Douglas. *Equalities.* Cambridge: Harvard University Press, 1981.

Rawls, John. *A Theory of Justice.* Cambridge: Harvard University Press, 1971.

Verba, Sidney, and Orren, Gary R. *Equality in America.* Cambridge: Harvard University Press, 1982.

Waligorski, Conrad. *The Political Theory of Conservative Economists.* Lawrence: University Press of Kansas, 1989.

NOTES

1. See Whitney J. Oates, ed, *The Stoic and Epicurean Philosophers* (New York: Random House, 1940).
2. Galatians 3:26–28.
3. Acts 4:32.
4. A classic political egalitarian is Thomas Jefferson. See Philip S. Foner, ed, *Basic Writings of Thomas Jefferson* (New York: Wiley Book Co., 1944).
5. For another look at equal opportunity, see our chapter on justice.
6. For an economic egalitarian who reflects on many of the issues, we recommend Carole Pateman, *Participation and Democratic Theory* (Cambridge: Cambridge University Press, 1970); more generally, we recommend a look at our chapter on political theory and public policy.
7. See S. I. Benn and R. S. Peters, *The Principles of Political Thought* (New York: Free Press, 1959).
8. For a partisan but interesting discussion, see Roderick Nash, *The Rights of Nature* (Madison: University of Wisconsin Press, 1989).
9. For a nice discussion of many of these issues, see Robert A. Dahl, *Democracy and Its Critics* (New Haven: Yale University Press, 1989).
10. See Nash, *Rights of Nature.*
11. Would it be appropriate to contrast the Jesus of the Gospels with the Augustine of *The City of God?*
12. See Benn and Peters, *The Principles of Political Thought,* chapter 5.
13. On utilitarian ideas about equality, see Douglas Rae, *Equalities,* for a modern discussion; a classic exposition is Jeremy Bentham, "The Principles of Morals and Legislation," in *The Utilitarians* (Garden City: Doubleday, 1961).
14. This is a point well made by John Charvet, "The Idea of Equality as a Substantive Principle of Society," *Political Studies* 17 (1969):1–13.

Chapter
8

Political Obligation

Obligation is about what we owe each other in moral terms. It is about duties and responsibilities and what must be done whether we like it or not. It is a concept of enormous importance in ethical life, including political relations. As people struggle with what citizenship means today—what is their obligation to the state, to the planet, or to their family, perhaps in tension to their government—the significance of obligation and political obligation in particular come to the fore.

We need to study obligation in a political context because such obligations must exist. Political obligation is needed by every nation. It is required as an outward sign of the legitimacy of a regime, affirming that citizens may be rightly expected to obey under certain circumstances. It is also required as a way to check a regime. When one is obligated to obey and when one is obligated to disobey are *both* central questions of political obligation. Without a system of political obligation, including its limits, politics can concern power and interest alone, neither dependable nor moral. As Plato remarked long ago, it becomes only the story of the triumph of the stronger.[1]

Perhaps, too, as we look toward the future, we may think that we need political obligations that go beyond the usual, the conventional, to point us to a more developed moral future. There are those who insist we need an obligation to all of humanity, to the global community; others identify obligations to the world of nature, whether they have in mind whales, trees, or even mosquitoes. Still others call us to particular human groups, such as to the least well-off. In every case, obligation is proclaimed not just as fact but also as aspiration. They argue that we should be bound to obligations that take us away from a primary focus on the national state.

Obligation is a tough word, often a frightening one, especially in our culture, where it runs against the grain of our culture's individualism. To be sure, we can encounter a good deal of pious affirmation of the importance of obligations in our culture, even on the value of political obligation. Our chapter on patriotism and rebellion discusses this further, but we practice much less than we preach when it comes to obligation. Obligations are often worn lightly, as high divorce statistics hint. Political obligation to our country is honored in theory, but most Americans avoid its toughest demands in practice. We have carefully put away the draft, and universal military service is inconceivable in our society. American culture and obligation are just not a natural pair and there is no reason to think they will become so in the foreseeable future.

Is the resistance to obligation in our culture a good thing? It can be argued that we have turned over to such forces as the market and the government what we ought to do ourselves: take responsibility for each other. The results of these decisions may explain in part the decline of commitment and citizenship in society, the high crime rate, the incidence of divorce, and the other visible signs of individual will's triumph over all else. Obligations are not in fashion—and their absence shows.[2]

Contemporary Americans, particularly, prefer other concepts. First and foremost, we want and celebrate liberty. Freedom is what Americans love; every survey shows it, and there is a reluctance to part with it that is as strong now as ever. Obligation easily seems to be a concept which denies freedom, even is designed to deny freedom. Thus it is not likely to be a topic or a reality with which we are comfortable. All those jokes about slavery and marriage or the military are not exactly jokes in our mind.[3]

But our love for freedom and our suspicion of obligation are not the entire story. As a culture we also prefer both the romantic and the pragmatic to the dutiful or obligatory. Romantic and pragmatic are hardly the same. Perhaps they are even opposites, but they are alike in being different from obligation. All three are about bases of human interaction, but contrasting bases. For those of us who look to love as the basis for relationships, the alternative of obligation is somehow cold, unfeeling, and irrelevant. What has obligation to do with it? we may ask. Love and loyalty are vastly different and more valuable things.

Similarly, pragmatists are often not attracted by relationships of obligation. To them, obligations are too formal and too philosophical. They are also too rigid and inflexible for those who are interested in practice, policy, and pragmatic action. Pragmatists want a clear playing field for policy contests and their resolution. Matters such as duty or commitment have a fusty air about them which is rarely relevant to pragmatists, busy as they are with "practical" matters.[4]

Obligation won't go away quite this easily, though. In fact, it won't go away at all, which is why we must address this key concept. We may not necessarily welcome obligations, especially political obligation. Yet they are integral to life. They are everywhere, not just among people in their political or marriage relationships, but in other formal and informal interactions among people. They don't have to be written on paper or established by a law. They can be as binding or as powerful when they are simply understood, as among old friends who know not only that they can depend on each other but that they are bound to each other, deeply obligated.

The pervasive reality of obligation relations depends on the way we are and think. As humans we behave as obligation-forming and acknowledging creatures. We may have contrasting ideas of obligations, but living life in part on the basis of obligation is involved in what it means to be a human person. Someone who cannot form obligations is at best a stunted person, at worst deeply incapacitated. Obligations are "forms of life," involved in a basic way in what it is to be human.

DEFINITION AND ISSUES

There are no simple definitions of obligation and certainly no agreed definition of political obligation. But in ordinary use, obligation suggests a series of ideas or implications that taken together edge us toward a satisfactory definition. The first without doubt is that obligation implies that we must, we are required to. It implies duty, necessity, requirement. This is the aspect, as we have noted, that makes so many of us uneasy about the word.

Obligation also implies morally legitimate. The word carries a moral connotation. It is an ethical or normative word. If one has an obligation to fight in a war, one is morally required to fight in one. If one has an obligation to humanity, one is morally required to help humanity. Our personal preference is ordinarily not the issue. Obligation may sometimes have its roots in choices we have made, but if we have an obligation, the assumption is that we must fulfill that obligation.

Obligation is also a relational concept. It is about relationships between or among two or more persons or among one or more people and other entities ranging from God to nature. In the case of political obligation, it is among citizens or citizens and a government of other citizens. Thus obligation is about what we owe and must try to fulfill to others. In short, we define political obligation as the duties we owe to the political community.[5]

Our definition is a crucial start, but it leaves much unresolved, matters at the heart of the incredibly rich and eternally interesting disputes over obligation. They are the meat of all obligation conflicts from ancient Athens to modern America. They are the substance of this chapter cast in terms of the issues of political obligation. One issue concerns whether or not we can ever be obligated politically. If so, what determines when we are obligated and when we are not? Put another way, what are the grounds and limits of political obligation?

Then we must explore who is the politically relevant group. To whom are we obligated? Is it the larger political community, the government, all of humanity? To this question, the usual answer is the national political community. But the question for the twenty-first century is whether this is any longer acceptable. Communications and transportation technologies grow daily and so do concerns over the ecological future of our planet. Finally there is the question, How does political obligation fit with other obligations, those one may judge to be less political?

These questions frame the agenda for this chapter. What are the many obligations besides political obligation that may or should exist, including those specifically relevant toward our global future? What is the basis, if any, for political obligation and how should it fit with our other, multiple obligations?

A WORLD OF OBLIGATIONS

Political obligation is rarely the only obligation we have. In fact, almost all of us live in a world of many obligations. We are not islands. We are quite the opposite in most instances, enmeshed as we are in complex sets of human relationships—family, friends, work associates, neighborhoods, bowling leagues, churches, and the rest. Each of these relationships likely generates obligations. Moreover, many of us believe we also have obligations to humanity or God or planet Earth.

These obligations have serious implications for any political obligation, perhaps reinforcing it, perhaps challenging it. For example, if you are close to your family and are drafted by the military and your family urges you to serve, you likely will. One obligation may reinforce another. But if your family insists that your obligation to them requires you to reject military service, a serious conflict of obligations may be expected. Obviously the same situation can happen if political obligations conflict with your religion, your obligation to your friends, or whatever. The possibilities are numerous, and conflict is no rare thing in the real world of multiple roles and relationships.

Our first job is to formulate a clear sense of what other obligations we may have. They are the setting in which we must define, defend, and delimit political obligation. What multiple obligations we have will differ person to person. Thus it is valuable to explore some common types and probe how valid they may be. For instance, we may ask, is there an obligation to humanity in general, as many claim today? That this sentiment is popular hardly determines its moral validity.

Some argue that a person's declarations that he or she is obligated to humanity establishes the obligation's legitimacy. The idea is that an obligation exists when people consent to it. No doubt consent is one of the great and enduring approaches to obligation, but skepticism seems appropriate in this instance. How can anyone seriously choose to be obligated with people all over the world, individuals one has never seen nor even imagined? Obligation and consent involve relations with people. Where are these relations with billions of people, most of whom live far away?

Possibly there is consent defined as a kind of participation. We are human beings, participating in our species' life on the earth, and in that attenuated sense we have all chosen our form of life and may be seen as committed to one another as fellow participants. Yet surely this would be a weak, indirect sense of consent. Moreover, in the face of the record of wars, and many other experiences of conflicts over the globe, there is scant evidence that people accept this form of consent when we get down to reality.

If the test for an obligation to humanity is utilitarian, that is, it is for the benefit of the general community, we would need to have standards for what is the common good or the public interest. There is no such agreement today. The only exception might be a worldwide recognition that we all want to survive and that because we do, some things such as nuclear war may be immoral. Thus the obligation to humanity arranged through utilitarian analysis has possibilities, but as yet we do not know how much it does or can operate.

Another approach to an obligation to humanity argues that what counts is the nature of the community in which we dwell. It must be the point of origin for our obligations, political and otherwise. Citizens' intentions within that community will matter decisively. If they support expanding who counts as part of the community, then the potential for a genuine obligation to humanity may exist. Again, what will matter is whom people choose locally to include.[6] This is a kind of democratic theory of obligation and also a consent version.

The democratic consent theory offends those who do not want humanity and our moral commitments determined by choice or votes. Most often, those who favor an obligation to humanity cite natural or divine law. Some who proclaim this basis simply announce that we are all one because nature is holistic or because God created us that way. Others know well that this view must be argued in theory and practice, but they also argue that if done well, it could provide the securest of foundations.

Thus while the desire to establish or recognize an obligation to humanity is strong—and growing—the issue of how to argue it remains contested. Many of the most earnestly sincere efforts to address the need for this (or any other) obligation are finally unable to make an argument that is very robust or plausible. We know that good intentions and a good argument are simply not the same thing.[7]

If there is an obligation to humanity, what are the implications for political obligation? They could be great. Proponents of an obligation of humanity declare it is superior to any political obligation, but few nations and few rulers have ever agreed. The potential for conflict is real here, even if as yet few have invoked an obligation to humanity to challenge their nation's political obligation.

Obligation to humanity is only one example of the claimed multiple obligations that abound today. Many have long acknowledged an obligation to God over all else, including political obligations. This was the teaching of the ancient Hebrews. Yahweh was the center of their life and their central obligation, a God who decided the legitimacy of all other obligations. This is true as well of the teaching of Christianity. There political obligation is respected and sometimes—as in Romans 13—demanded. But one's obligation to God transcends every other obligation. Such is the doctrine of Islam and numerous other religious faiths also.

Here we cannot address the issues of whether there is a God or which religion, if any, may be the true one. These are matters of faith. What we must do is recognize that obligations based on religion can clash with political obligation. They have been the ground of most conscientious objectors to war (in the United States), the basis for revolution (in Iran), and the energy behind defiant settlers seizing land (in Israel's occupied territories).

It is no easier to establish that there is an obligation to nature than that there is to God. Yet it would be equally foolish to ignore the enduring strength of this popular idea.[8] The claim that we are obligated to nature comes in multiple, almost endless, forms. Often today it comes in the language of environmentalism. Increasingly, people argue that we are obligated to nature because we belong to an interdependent natural environment whose interwoven parts are all essential, equal, and fragile. From this perspective, no obligation could be greater. That would include any political obligation that might take us to war or justify exploiting natural resources or damage the ozone layer.

Given the reality of serious challenges to survival on Earth, we can expect there will be more and more recourse to nature as the standard of obligation in the future. It will increasingly be proposed as the supreme obligation—superior to any political or national obligation—and, in practice, celebrated as the proper guide for political action. Yet arguments for an obligation to nature need much work. Some depend on religion, that God expects humans to look after and protect God's entire creation—the stewardship theory. Others are utilitarian, making the case that without an ethic of obligation to nature, all life will die. Of late there have been efforts to give nature special normative status independent of religious or utilitarian perspectives. Claims that direct us to "deep ecology" and "biocentric" views see nature as a whole as normative, indeed as the only standard of normativity. They call on diverse predecessors from Thoreau to Aldo Leopold. Why nature should acquire such privileged status is not obvious. Intense environmentalist conviction that it has this status does not eliminate the perpetual need to argue.[9]

Other obligations that are less controversial are personal: obligations to friends, family, or groups to which one may belong. In some cases—as with friends and spouses—the origins of these obligations are consent. We choose these people to be part of our lives. Moreover, we can say that often we choose them over and over again, often deeply and over a long period of time. Thus these can be serious obligations, hardly to be ignored if they conflict with political obligations. Thus if the state requires us to testify against our family or friends, how do we decide morally? How does one choose between such conflicting obligations?

If the state invokes political obligation so that we would act against our other commitments and obligations, who is right? Conflicts will not be routine, but they will happen. Multiple obligations are a reality and no discussion of political obligation can safely skirt them. The point here is not to downgrade political obligation. Not at all. Rather it is to appreciate that it is one obligation among many. It may be far more important than most. It may be the most binding of all. Or it may be of little significance. Yet it is not the only obligation most of us have and cannot be treated in isolation from our other obligations.

Each of us needs to know our obligations. To whom are we obligated and on what basis? What is our nation's norm of political obligation and is it legitimate? How should we decide when we are obligated, politically and otherwise, and why? How should we balance our multiple obligations, political and otherwise? What are the limits to political obligation? What are its solemn responsibilities? To address this world, however, we must now turn from the world of multiple obligations and focus on the question, When, if ever, are we politically obligated? When, if ever, do we owe political obedience to the state?

THE SPECIFICS OF POLITICAL OBLIGATION

Political obligation is about the duties we owe to our political community. What each of us may owe the political community is an issue that all citizens must and at times do face, whenever the state puts demands on us. The best approach to this subject is to listen to people speak about political obligation. When we do so, we discover that people think about political obligation in a few fundamental ways and always have. These are the boundaries of our discussion of political obligation.

Frequent among the basic approaches is a utilitarian standard, sometimes described as a benefits or benefits received view.[10] Advocates of a benefits perspective hold that we are obligated if we or the community as a whole benefits from the political system or political community. The idea is straightforward: if the system delivers, we are obligated to it. If it does not deliver, then we are not obligated to it.

The idea is attractive, but there are complications with this argument that must be taken into account. For example, whose perspective will be decisive? Should each individual decide what will count as the standard of benefit for him or her, what we could call individual utilitarianism? Or is the standard to be some kind of common good or public interest, so-called social utilitarianism? If the "common good" is to be what should count, how do we determine what this means in this situation? Perhaps the majority should decide, but opinions differ on the wisdom of this standard.

While some maintain that there must be agreed upon procedures, others accent the necessity of stated definitions of benefit. They have in mind government policies that ensure physical security, religious liberty, basic health care, and the like. Proponents argue that the existence of such established policies is necessary for individuals or, in truth, for whole communities.

It prevents them from rapidly shifting their definition of what counts as a benefit for their selfish convenience.

Many observers insist that some benefits should never count in assessing when one is obligated. Such things as "happiness," "love," "health" cannot be provided by any political system for anyone and it is absurd to judge a political society on whether it does so. But the structure of the basic utilitarian or benefits system remains clear. Once the benefits are defined and the basis for assessing whether they are provided or not is defined, then we are obligated if they are received. And if we don't get them, we are not obligated.

In some ways this approach makes good sense. That is, after all, why it is so often proposed. It does fit with people's view that for something given, something is owed. Granted, there may be problems working through who decides, by what standards, and what those standards actually mean in practice (what is adequate medical care?). But there are problems with establishing any normative ideals in practice. There is nothing new or fatal about that. A problem that is more troubling directs us elsewhere. The social benefit argument seems to deny individual choice. If the community decides on standards of obligation, then we can find ourselves obligated if we have benefitted under those standards even if we vehemently disagree with our government or political community. We may hate the government or just hate some policy or other that we are required to support. The danger is really the old one of majority or community rule. It can put us in a terrible moral and practical bind. These dangers can be addressed by providing procedures to limit the worst possibilities—provisions forbidding slavery or denial of political rights and the like. They can also be addressed by vigorous provision of serious and substantive rights in the society, including a determined commitment to economic cooperation and fairness, political rights, and policies fostering equal human respect.[11] Doubts may also be confronted by honoring the role of dissent and encouraging citizens to speak up loud and clear when they disagree with the decisions of the political community about the common good. Those who fear conformity and repression of dissenters should encourage a society where the probing citizen earns high esteem.[12]

But there is still lots of room for citizens going to war because they are obligated to a country whose policies or political system they loathe. In short, benefit obligation can allow people to be obligated without their choice, something all of us would want to think long and hard about. Yet the substantial advantages of a benefit theory deserve attention too. A benefit theory focuses on the political system and how it is doing, its practical benefits and drawbacks. It is not abstract or philosophical but down to earth. We can all understand it and we know it reflects the way we often think. Moreover, in most forms it does direct us away from exclusive concentration on the individual. It puts us into a mode of thinking that acknowledges that we are social beings and that we are here together. It teaches that the public interest matters. Perhaps serious matters such as political obligation should be resolved in no other light.

On the other hand, many favor consent as the proper standard of political obligation. In Western political philosophy, consent has dominated thought about political obligation for three hundred years, building a tradition that since Socrates in ancient Greece has been a major view. The idea of the consent theory is that we can be obligated only when we have chosen to be obligated. It accords well with Western valuation of individual choice as integral to moral life. It respects each individual as a choosing, moral person and insists that he or she cannot be treated as a means to someone else's ends, however good.

There are some important assumptions in consent theory. Consent advocates assume that we have at least some free will in life. We contend that this is an issue upon which little may be usefully said. Proof either way about free will is beyond us. Here we just note that all consent theories assume some free will and the idea that people can sometimes act other than the way they do.

Consent theorists also assume that choice is connected in some fundamental way with what is ethical. If they did not, there would be no reason for insisting that choice must be present before one can be obligated/not obligated. Why choice is essential for morality is far too often announced rather than argued. This is only to be expected, given our culture's deep commitment to freedom, but the assumption is not self-evident. What can be said here is that those who see choice (and thus in obligation terms, consent) as a necessary requirement for morality believe that such a standard honors each person. It honors each person as an individual and because each can be a responsible, reflective, choosing being. Granting some free will and the ethical nature of choice, it remains a dilemma how free any choice can be. It is one thing to affirm that free will exists, as a matter of faith. It is quite another to declare that human choices are not conditioned in a multitude of ways. We all know that our choices are affected by our family, social and economic background, national origin, schooling, health, and all the rest. Also important are the myriad of short run, immediate, situational factors that influence specific choices. They range from our mood to the external pressures affecting us on any given day. Are we choosing freely when we are consumed by frustration, anger, greed, or for that matter, joy? The fact is that we never choose freely if that means free from historical, situational, or personal context. This would be impossible. Life in such a setting is inconceivable. What we live with is a continuum of constrained choices. What we must be clear about is the point at which a choice is so constrained that it is no choice at all. This point is not self-evident. People argue over it, which is all the more reason for self-conscious determination of that point in any consent theory of obligation.

We need also to recognize that consent theories focus on the individual and not the community. Consent is concerned with whether or not an individual has had a choice. It is input oriented. That is exactly why it has so many adherents. But that raises doubts among those who want to ask about the political community or about the general welfare and political obligation.

Are consent theorists interested in anything but their individual freedom? The test comes in concrete theories of consent obligation. Some are solipsistic, but others try to be as sensitive to the community as they are to the individual person.

TYPES OF CONSENT

What are the standards that have to exist for a person to have chosen to be obligated? How do we decide whether or not to obey according to consent? One view holds that we can never be politically obligated if we take consent seriously. This position is philosophical anarchism. Anarchists insist that we cannot discuss the proper conditions for political obligation until we have addressed whether there can be *any* such conditions. And anarchists assert that there are never such conditions. For them, talk of choice and political obligation is nothing more than a swindle, nor has it ever been anything but a swindle. They maintain that we simply cannot choose to limit our future choice, and that is always what obligation mandates. Political obligation to them is nothing but a device by which rulers and their philosopher lackeys grasp the bodies and even the lives of their fellow citizens for taxes or for wars.

Anarchist theories have come in many forms. Many of the stereotypes of anarchism are not particularly valid. Some anarchist thinkers—such as Henry David Thoreau—are highly individualistic; others—such as Peter Kropotkin—are devoted to communal ways of life. Few have been in favor of "chaos," contrary to a common image. They are united in their suspicion of rulers and most often believe that consent can never lead to obligation because that would be a denial of future consent. Obligation thus denies the human person and his or her basic dignity.[13]

Opponents of anarchism reply that obligation is acceptable if individuals choose to surrender some or all of their will, that is, if they choose to be politically obligated. However, anarchists are not impressed. They insist that one cannot morally choose to limit choice. One cannot choose to deny one's very self.[14] Critics also suggest that without obligation, no government or political society can endure. Anarchists reject this claim too. If they are realistic, anarchists know that history is not kind to their assertion, but they believe that under proper conditions, with people not already corrupted, we could have a flourishing political society without organized government. It just would not be able to require obedience under the claim that somehow it followed from political obligation.

Suspicion of such an optimistic assumption is as common now as it ever was. In fact, proponents of political obligation invariably conclude that political communities cannot endure in practice without a system of political obligation. Thus much of the case for political obligation is utilitarian. Political obligation is necessary to hold societies together even if it can hardly do so alone.

A second consent approach toward obligation also celebrates the individual but argues cautiously that political obligation is possible. Its advocates propose that we can become politically obligated if we decide that we are so obligated. Some versions provide that the standards an individual may use should be determined beforehand; others do not. But all share the common premise that the individual is sovereign. His or her decisions about obligation are definitive.

This individual consent system of obligation is not the same thing as anarchism in theory. After all, it holds that we can choose political obligation, something anarchists deny. But critics do not see much practical difference because, to them, both approaches are far too individualistic and guarantee chaos. Critics worry that the individualism of this form of consent, of individuals deciding on their own—whenever they want and for whatever reasons they want—when they are or are not politically obligated would make it difficult for a political community ever *to count on* the support of its citizenry. This kind of consent makes it too easy to deny political obligation on the basis of individual whim. They wonder whether any society can function with such an arrangement. They know that none ever has.

The defenders of individual consent are for serious individual choice as the basis for obligation and they propose to let the chips fall where they may. They are confident, though, that there are a good many citizens—perhaps too many—who worry about community and stability. These people will sustain society. The advocates' point is that they are serious about choices and suspect that other standards of political obligation love order and obedience at the expense of human freedom and consent.[15]

A third type of consent theory concentrates on direct choice through oaths of allegiance and loyalty. Officeholders take such an oath, soldiers do so, new citizens must. This approach cares less about an individual's open-ended freedom to choose than it does that the choice be straightforward, self-conscious, and public. Enthusiasts of this view insist that only direct consent makes clear that the choice has been made or that it has not been made. It is not in this context a choice which is private, vague and vaporous, and dependent on mood. It is up-front and open. Less often stressed is the fact that it is also sometimes quite permanent. By no means do all direct consent theories provide each citizen repeated opportunities for choices about political obligation. Oaths sometimes are permanent, even though the most reflective of minds do change.[16]

Critics fasten on what they fear are the massive consequences that could follow from any oath that is taken or might be taken. They ask why an oath should bind us when we change our mind, especially when oaths can be mechanical, something people go through in a ritualistic, perfunctory fashion. Sometimes this question is well-grounded, but not always. Attend a swearing in ceremony for new U.S. citizens and you get a sense of how deeply meaningful such a "ritualistic" oath can be. Moreover, direct consent theories have the advantage that they make sure everyone is willing to take a public stand and knows what he or she is doing. They also try to be quite community-regarding. Choice (to take the oath or not) is present, but once it is made, obligation to the community takes over.

Finally we must consider the indirect or *tacit* consent theories. They have been the most popular species of consent theory for hundreds of years. Today almost every government in the world dares to claim that its citizens are bound together by an indirect consent theory of political obligation. Tacit consent is the idea that choice can be expressed indirectly and when it is done so in socially accepted ways, then one is politically obligated.[17] Most often the measures of indirect consent are political participation or the opportunity to participate. At other times they involve economic participation, the provision of central economic protections and opportunities in life. The model always assumes that citizens must understand that if they participate (however defined), they thereby indirectly choose the political system under which they exist. What kind of participation will count is something which indirect consent theorists usually believe society as a whole must decide. They insist that it cannot be decided by each citizen on his or her own unless we do not care about the community as a whole. Thus they conclude that their version of consent provides significant choice for each of us while at the same time being community-regarding.

Indirect consent—an idea first clearly formulated by John Locke, the seventeenth-century English political philosopher—often looks like a benefit or utilitarian theory. One receives a benefit—the opportunity to vote or a good job—and one is then obligated. However, indirect consent theory views this benefit–obligation relation differently. It interprets receiving certain benefits and/or opportunities only as an indicator of consent. Accepting the benefits is what counts. That is a sign of the consent. The benefits themselves do not matter. In short, the indirect consent theory emphasizes choice, whereas the utilitarian theory cares about benefits.[18]

Almost all governments agree that the mere fact of residing in a nation indicates indirect consent and properly leads to political obligation. This is known as the residence test of political obligation. But most theorists of indirect consent reject the residence test and insist that there must be guaranteed actual or potential political and/or economic participation as well. To them, the residence test is way too oriented toward ensuring that people will be politically obligated no matter what. It says little more than stay and be obligated or get out. It sets no standards for a society before one must choose it—no standards about its political system, economic justice, or whatever. This does not mean it is a worthless theory. Far from it. It claims to be the most realistic, granting choice but recognizing the need for order too. What alternative tests to residence are there? The most popular, minimal one demands that at least a roughly equal opportunity to participate politically must be present in society. Its advocates contend that if such an opportunity is present, then we may be considered politically obligated. Their logic is that remaining in a society with such opportunity amounts to a powerful choice, one that allows us the chance to help in society's self-governance.

Others support political participation as another measure of indirect consent. They maintain that if we participate in the political system in a serious manner, we are choosing it and are obligated to it. This is an attractive test since it is so related to the political system to which we would be obligated as a result of participation. But the problem is that participating in a political system does by no means always imply choosing it. We may participate as a mere concession to reality—with absolutely no support for the system intended—or we may participate only to change it radically. Moreover, this standard not only leaves anyone who does not participate not obligated, but it in fact encourages people who seek to escape political obligation not to participate. In this sense the political participation test is decidedly not community-regarding.

WHEN ARE WE NOT OBLIGATED?

All consent theories must confront the question, When are people not obligated?[19] For those emphasizing unrestrained free choice there is no problem. We are not obligated whenever we decide we are not obligated. For other consent theories it depends on what measures consent. Sometimes consent, once given, is extremely hard to terminate; in other instances it can end far more easily. Thus, for residence test theories, residence implies consent and is permanent unless one leaves the country. For participation theories, the citizen is obligated only so long as participation is available within the political system and only so long as the citizen actually participates. What every citizen needs to know clearly from the beginning is when one is— and is not—obligated. Under a consent arrangement, no state may assume that it is automatically and permanently owed political obligation. It must be chosen in some publicly understood way by its citizens. And it must be able to be unchosen, to be rejected, or else there is really no choice after all.

CONCLUSION

The question for the future is whether political obligation makes much sense in the long run. The arguments over alternative versions of political obligation are sometimes significant in today's world, as is the dialogue and sometimes tension between political obligation and other obligation in people's lives. Yet in the future the global relationships among us may—indeed must—become central. The challenge will be to rethink political obligation and our other obligations within a larger, planetary, framework—within what will undoubtedly become a larger global obligation to ourselves, our fellows, and our planet. How this process will develop will be fascinating, and it may be essential for our mutual survival. It will not signal the end of obligation thinking. That seems impossible given the human species. But it may lead to the greatest rethinking of obligation, including political obligation, since Socrates walked in Athens 2500 years ago.

GLOSSARY OF KEY TERMS

anarchists A group of strong libertarians who are generally opponents of political obligation. They often support community and other nongovernmental forms of obligation.

benefit theory of obligation A political theory holding that obligations are owed based on benefits received from society or government.

consent theory of obligation A political theory holding that we are obligated if we take oaths or consent to our political system, either directly or indirectly.

free will The ability to make choices unconstrained by fate or predestination. Usually assumed in political obligation theories.

multiple obligations A situation where we feel obligations to more than one person or institution. Often multiple obligations conflict with each other, causing many problems.

obligation The duties and responsibilities we owe to each other in moral terms.

political obligation The duties and responsibilities we owe to the nation or each other through political communities.

relationships Give and take between two or more individuals that are the basis for any moral obligations.

tacit consent Indirect consent that is assumed if not explicitly repudiated.

SUGGESTIONS FOR FURTHER READING

DeLue, Steven. *Political Obligation in a Liberal State*. Albany: State University of New York, 1989.

Fishkin, James S. *The Limits of Obligation*. New Haven: Yale University Press, 1982.

Kropotkin, Peter. *Selected Writings on Anarchism and Revolution*. Cambridge: M.I.T. Press, 1970.

Locke, John. *The Second Treatise of Government*. Indianapolis: Bobbs-Merrill, 1952.

Nash, Roderick. *The Rights of Nature: A History of Environmental Ethics*. Madison: University of Wisconsin Press, 1989.

Pennock, J. Roland, and Chapman, John W., eds. *Political and Legal Obligation*. New York: Atherton, 1970.

Pitkin, Hannah. "Obligation and Consent." *American Political Science Review* 59 (1965):990–999; and vol. 60 (1965):39–52.

Rorty, Richard. *Contingency, Irony, and Solidarity*. Cambridge: Cambridge University Press, 1989.

Simmons, John. *Moral Principles and Political Obligations*. Princeton, N.J.: Princeton University Press, 1979.

Thoreau, Henry David. *Walden and Other Writings*. New York: Modern Library, 1950.

Walzer, Michael. "The Obligation to Disobey." *Ethics* 77 (1967):163–175.

NOTES

1. Plato, *The Republic*, Book 1.
2. Alan Wolfe, *Whose Keeper? Social Science and Moral Obligation* (Berkeley: University of California Press, 1989).
3. Bellah is good on the subject of Americans and freedom. Robert Bellah, Richard Madsen, William Sullivan, Ann Swidler, and Steven M. Tipton, *Habits of the Heart: Individualism and Commitment in American Life* (Berkeley: University of California Press, 1985).
4. A splendid example of pragmatic political thought in our age, one that rises way above the norm, is Charles W. Anderson, *Pragmatic Liberalism* (Chicago: University of Chicago Press, 1990).
5. For a number of definitional discussions, see J. Roland Pennock and John W. Chapman, eds., *Political and Legal Obligation* (New York: Atherton, 1970).
6. Richard Rorty, *Contingency, Irony, and Solidarity* (Cambridge: Cambridge University Press, 1989), chapter 9.
7. One interesting discussion is Wolfe, *Whose Keeper? Social Science and Moral Obligation*, op. cit.
8. See Roderick Nash, *The Rights of Nature: A History of Environmental Ethics* (Madison: University of Wisconsin Press, 1989).
9. Ibid.
10. Steven M. DeLue, *Political Obligation in a Liberal State* (Albany: State University of New York, 1989), chapter 1.
11. Ibid., chapter 8.
12. Ibid.
13. See, for example, Henry David Thoreau, *Walden and Other Writings* (New York: Modern Library, 1950); Peter Kropotkin, *Selected Writings on Anarchism and Revolution* (Cambridge: M.I.T. Press, 1970).
14. See, for instance, Robert Paul Wolff, *In Defense of Anarchism* (New York: Harper & Row, 1970).
15. A version of this kind of individualistic consent theory is Hannah Pitkin, "Obligation and Consent," *American Political Science Review* 59 (1965):990–999, and 60 (1966):39–52.
16. Philosophical defenders of direct consent appear to be scanty, but it has the defense of practice: it has been and is often used and accepted.
17. For an interesting discussion of tacit consent, see John Simmons, "Tacit Consent and Political Obligation," *Philosophy and Public Affairs* 5 (Spring 1976):275–291.
18. John Locke is the great early theorist of indirect or tacit consent. John Locke, *The Second Treatise of Government* (Indianapolis: Bobbs-Merrill, 1952).
19. An interesting example may be found in Michael Walzer, "The Obligation to Disobey," *Ethics* 77 (1967):163–175.

Chapter
9

Political Theory and Challenges: Patriotism, Disobedience, and Revolution

*I*ssues of patriotism and revolution are the most vexsome political issues that people ever confront in their political lives. Often they are literally a matter of life and death. Governments and other sources of political authority constantly demand loyalty from us and tell us how we ought to behave in the public realm. Patriotism is not asked of us; it is simply expected. Though these citizenship demands can become a considerable burden, most of us accept them routinely (though we may occasionally grumble) because we think our political system is good. Hence our conditioning leads us to believe that we, as good citizens, have a duty to support it.

However, despite our patriotic habits, most of us will reluctantly rebel (or want to) after what the English political theorist John Locke called "a long train of abuses."[1] When we are thoroughly fed up with our government, especially if we feel it is corrupt or selfish, we will grudgingly become political challengers who reject the authority of our political system.

Patriotism, challenge, and political change have always been constants in a shifting world.[2] And they will remain so in the future. Whether this change is swift or slow, peaceful or violent—and officially sanctioned or not—it goes on and we all face it sooner or later. It is not something that happens only to others who are unlucky enough to live at history's cutting edge. What is more, political change is always traumatic because it is wrapped up with the vexsome issues of loyalty and revolt. These are visible and emotionally charged issues. No wonder they are taken very seriously by political theorists, rulers, and sometimes citizens.

In part to evade the pain of making perilous choices about potentially disastrous political situations like whether to participate in war or revolution, citizens and rulers often surround such issues and events with dogmatic ideological cliches. For example, "All those who oppose the law are anarchistic revolutionaries" or "It is the moral duty of the true man of the people to take arms against the illegitimate dictatorship that has seized our nation" are common historical utterances. Another frequent response is simple denial— "It cannot and must not happen *here*. Our civilized people will obey because our society is uniquely by, for, and of the people."

Such evasions do not work. Political theory and political conflicts surge equally around political activists and apathists. Wars and revolts are analogous to tidal waves: They do not inquire about political efficacy or practices before storming ashore and altering all in their path. Because political theory can assist us in using reflection and judgment, it can help us to manage traumatic politics and to avoid both ideology and denial. Patriotism and political challenge are very much part of our world. Consequently, we need to think about them before they happen to us.

In 1989, the Chinese students who defied tanks around the "democracy wall" in Beijing to demand changes in the political system of the People's Republic of China stood figuratively alongside jubilant Berliners watching the Berlin Wall fall after massive, unprecedented demonstrations by citizens in Leipzig and other places. Issues of political theory linked them despite time and distance.

All of them stood with Soviet citizens who pushed for reform in the early 1990s; with the courageous, stubborn rebels in the Baltic republics of the USSR; and with Nelson Mandela as he helped to dismantle South African apartheid. They were also linked to both the American anti–Vietnam War demonstrators of a generation ago and the U.S. soldiers who volunteered to fight in that war. They were as one with civil rights demonstrators in the American South in the 1960s, Confederate troops of the Civil War, those who fought at Guadalcanal in 1943, those who joined the Continental Army in the war of independence against the British in the 1770s, and the Tories who remained loyal to the British.

They also had much in common with Oliver North—who violated laws on presidential orders—and those from emerging democracies of Central and Eastern Europe who ran for office and organized politically for the first time in their lives in the early 1990s. Surely they are allied, too, with the Canadians who struggle to preserve the Canadian union against secessionist sentiments from French-cultured Quebec, with the native (precolonial) Canadians who feel ignored, and with the people from other provinces who feel economically disadvantaged by populous Ontario and Quebec. The common bonds of all of these revolutionaries, civil disobedients, and citizens living (and dying) voluntary political obligations are the issues of revolt, partial obligation, and patriotism—part of the concerns of political theory. Political theory considers values in politics. Therefore, it is not just in the library; it is a feature of the lives of millions of ordinary people in extraordinary times, whether they recognize it or not.

It is not enough merely to label these things as important and ubiquitous, though. We cannot think sensibly about patriotism or rebellion without examining the political values that lead to political obligation. Reason is our best asset as we face momentous political change because it can help us obtain better understanding of rebellion or loyalty. Political theory and systematic reasoning can help us craft a political theory of loyalty and challenge for all who need it.

LEGITIMATE POLITICAL COMMUNITIES AND POLITICAL THEORY

A political theory of loyalty and challenge rests on a foundation of values. As we saw in the chapters on authority and community, citizens interact and build political communities on the basis of what they believe and value. Loyalty and challenge are not exceptions. They can be rallying points for consensus or barriers which divide us, as Eastern Europe has seen in the aftermath of the breakup of USSR-dominated communism. Often, what matters more than anything else in society is political legitimacy and authority.

Legitimacy is sense of properness, legality, and morality. Legitimate political systems are recognized by law, popular culture, or political argument as worthy of recognition. Illegitimate ones are not.

Authority is a parallel concept. An individual or institution that has authority has our permission to be and act. Robert Paul Wolff calls it "the right to command and the right to be obeyed."[3] He distinguishes it from power because the *right* to command is far more sweeping than the mere ability to compel obedience. Citizens who recognize it obligate themselves to obey because they empower a polity or leader with an inviolable moral right to issue orders that must be obeyed by definition.

Authority can and often does exist without resort to force. For example, if all of the students in your political theory class decided to study the issues and facts diligently and write the laws for the nation for a year or so, what would happen? Even if the resulting laws made as much or more sense than those emanating from Congress, society would not take them seriously or follow them and they could not be enforced. Why? Because society accepts the legitimacy of the U.S. government and assumes its authority to make laws, quality of laws notwithstanding.

Like most political rights, authority has limits even among its adherents. If those with authority abuse it, citizens will eventually become disenchanted and even angry. Leaders then find their authority and legitimacy evaporating. As a result, loyalty also may evaporate. It may then be replaced by force without moral sanction.

Ultimately, legitimacy rests on intricate judgments about political institutions, people, and practices that are not beyond the intellectual grasp of citizens. Such judgments by thinking people rest on a foundation of fundamental values like justice, liberty, and so forth. Moreover, such values can have serious political consequences. Ideas about legitimacy or authority can lead us toward patriotism or to challenge political authority. They become both a meaningful responsibility and an opportunity for all citizens and a factor for leaders and governments who want legitimacy to maintain their jobs or regimes.

The significance of political values is not determined solely by how many people hold them. Numbers do not make morality. Even if some form of citizen consent is important to a regime, other factors also count. Even if a majority sees a regime as legitimate, it is not if it regularly violates values of legitimacy rooted in appropriate standards of political theory. Similarly, if the majority think their government's policies are illegitimate because it is doing something unpopular, they might not be right. It may be doing what needs to be done. Ultimately, legitimacy and authority are political judgments about values by individuals. The principles of utilitarianism (the greatest good for the greatest number) and natural law (values which are self-evident truths from God or nature) are prominent examples of legitimacy values in political theory. Each has been applied to government actions many times in history and will remain with us in the future.

Which values are the "right" building blocks for this kind of political thinking? While there are no definitive answers, some obvious candidates are those that have been analyzed in these pages. For example, when the issue is whether a given political system merits patriotism or challenge, a logical starting point is our personal theory of political obligation. As we have seen earlier, our theory of political obligation serves as a blueprint for a good regime, as a standard by which to gauge the finished product. Polities that measure up deserve political obligations. Those that do not may be opposed.

Often, the matter is not simple. While it is hard to imagine a regime that meets our threshold values but still does not deserve our obligation, it can happen. One which fosters several of our important values might not merit our obligation if it violates other critical values for us or for those to whom we are politically obligated. Perhaps it respects our rights but not those of others. Under such circumstances, we might feel a limited pull toward political obligation, but we still could not declare the regime fully legitimate.

We need to maintain high standards of political legitimacy and authority if we are going to foster the best possible governments and policies. If the values of liberty, equality, justice, the validity of human life are important to a better public life, they are important enough to be integrated with our obligations. In effect, legitimacy requires us to reject the authority of a regime that fails to pursue adequately legitimate values, no matter what good things it might otherwise do. Clearly, political theory helps us to think about the values of legitimacy carefully so that our ideas about political loyalty are both rational and meet the challenges of our real political world.

Sometimes even this is not enough. Our principles appear to require contradictory actions simultaneously, compelling us equally to be patriots and challengers. The daily headlines might cause us to want to support the government by paying taxes that will be used to defend our nation from foreign enemies. At the same time, we might oppose paying taxes that will be used to support a justice system that condones police brutality and does not provide equal treatment for all. Unfortunately, a perplexing situation like this can never be resolved completely satisfactorily. Fortunately, political theory can help us deal with such agonizing dilemmas. It can encourage us to search for fresh perspectives on some of the analytical approaches and values we have already examined.

For example, using the approaches and insights of positive versus negative freedom gives us a way to examine a conflict between liberty and equality in our values and obligations. It shows that our opposition to a state that suppresses legitimate revolutionary movements or drafts pacifists is justified by laissez-faire values that give each citizen the right to be left alone and pursue individual values. Simultaneously, it verifies our patriotic obligations to the same state because it intervenes on the side of justice for the many when it restrains economic exploiters, violent revolutionaries, or polluters who do not deserve to be left alone because they exploit others.

Thus by using political theory to sort conflicting obligations, we see the appeal of each. Moreover, we see that individual values that oppose the polity but do not exploit others are fundamentally different from identical values that do exploit. Accordingly, we have at least the preliminary guidelines of a theory of loyalty that says, for example, that pacifism is a more moral exception to state authority than an industrial polluter's individual rights because the pacifist is not directly harming others to as great a degree. While this does not resolve our obligation conflicts, it gives us a handle on what to do when we confront options of challenge and patriotism.

Another example might bring this into sharper focus. Suppose that our political obligations are based on values that uphold for all the equal right to believe in and display any patriotic symbols they wish. Furthermore, we oppose desecrating such symbols so as not to offend others' rights, much as it is a crime to profane churches or synagogues or temples in many nations. Suppose that we also believe that desecrating nature is morally wrong.

Given these as our starting values, suppose that our polity (which protects racial, religious, sexual, and economic equality by law and policy) allows loggers to clear-cut and destroy the last virgin forests in the nation. Furthermore, loggers and the government will not respond to our vigorous legal protests against deforestation policies. So, to escalate our protest, we build a small, rough house of commercial lumber from the virgin forest (to represent the houses built with the precious virgin timber), paint it with the nation's flag (to attract media coverage and show our patriotic love of the nation's forest), and burn it in front of a logging camp. The laws which prohibit flag desecration are invoked and we are arrested.

Which of our conflicting loyalties (to nature and to the right to practice patriotic-symbol veneration as enforced by anti-symbol-desecration laws) is right? Are they both right? We can use political theory to help us discover and define the conflict between the equal right to practice patriotism unmolested and unprofaned and the values that give absolute legitimacy to nature and demand government protection for the natural environment.

While this use of political theory does not solve our problem, it gives us paths to reexamine such issues and find an approach that helps us to relate and even to rank conflicting allegiances. Unfortunately, this example is more common than we might think. It raises subtle issues and illuminates rationales for several positions. It helps us think about why we follow a particular position and gives us a point of view and some criteria to ask why or when any position (or related action) might be best.

Frankly, the best advice that political theory can supply in such situations is simply to recognize the potential tension among multiple or conflicting values and to deal with them tolerantly and patiently, using reason as much as possible. Political theory counsels us that when we have conflicting values or obligations, we should hesitate before we support irrevocable actions like war or killing. Sometimes that is enough to allow us to detour satisfactorily around our dilemmas. At other times, though, the best that we can do is to remind ourselves that patience and tolerance can help prevent clashing norms or obligations from destroying any more than necessary.

VALUES AND POLITICAL ACTIONS: THE IMPLICATIONS OF AUTHORITY

While values underlie our political-allegiance obligations and political theory can help us sort out conflicts, our values do not float in a vacuum. They help determine our behaviors as patriots, rebels, or ordinary citizens. They give us an observation platform from which we can view the political landscape and assess our attitudes. Thus the remainder of this chapter deals with the kinds of political behavior of support and challenge available and helps us to assess which are appropriate when.

Obligations and Patriotism

Political obligation entails a voluntary responsibility to support a given political community. It implies that we have a moral duty to be patriotic to communities that follow our values—and that our values are right.[4] But what is patriotism? What are its limits and boundaries? The popular notion of a patriot is one who loves his or her country and defends its institutions and policies by whatever means available, no matter what the cost or foe. It is usually associated with those who serve their country militarily or who defend national policies and symbols (especially the flag) with a zealousness that pushes aside concerns about the morality of patriotic acts. Other types of patriotism are often viewed skeptically by supporters of this popular view.

Tracing the word back to its classical Greek origins, *patriotism* originally meant love of the fatherland or one's nation and its peoples. But in modern

American terms, it has evolved to mean loyalty and support for the political system or the nation that transcends leaders, policies, or tactics. In this sense, the patriot follows orders and does whatever needs to be done to protect and defend the nation. Such was presumably the motivation of Colonel Oliver North (famed for his part in the Reagan administration's Iran-Contra scandal) when he told Congress that he knew his acts violated the law but that they were justified, in his opinion, by a patriotism that demanded serving the national interest as he and his superiors saw it. Such is also the motivation of many who are willing to go to war and do whatever is ordered, even if they have doubts as to tactics or goals.

This popular notion differs from the way many political theorists have often understood patriotism. They usually use the term to cover far less ground than did Colonel North. Patriotic love of country is one value, but reason suggests that there are other, equally fine, values. Political theory calls us to consider, balance, and choose among values—not to totally surrender our intellect to leaders or symbols of popular patriotism.

As we see it, patriotism embraces love of country and loyalty to national institutions, policies, and leaders. But it simultaneously embraces respect for others' liberty of expression, equal treatment of other citizens, and accommodation of dissidents who oppose policies or personalities in their patriotism. This limits narrow-minded patriotism by accommodating acts and values of those who love the country differently. Those who carry a gun for their country or obey it, right or wrong, may be no more patriotic than those who conscientiously oppose war or pursue their values via dissent about the morality of national actions.

Questions about what patriotism is and how it is justified are two sides of the same coin. Real patriots voluntarily support the nation and its people because they are motivated by love of country and the values that encompasses for them.

Consequently, genuine patriotic obligations have a powerful logic which does not dissolve otherwise valid allegiances simply because they appear to motivate the patriot to pursue a better regime. As uncomfortable as that might be to thinking patriots accustomed to reflexive regime support, political loyalties can compel patriots to rebel against illegitimate regimes as much as they can compel support for legitimate ones.

At the very least, allegiances strong enough to oblige patriotism are strong enough morally to compel the patriot to withdraw his or her patriotism from a political entity which has turned evil. Our values remain in force when our polities turn sour and violate the norms that originally earned our allegiance. Only the target of our loyalties changes.

But do we "merely" have a responsibility to withdraw our loyal behavior or do we have a more sweeping responsibility to overthrow an illegitimate regime and to replace it with a better one? Here, too, while easy answers are not forthcoming, political theory can supply at least an instrumental answer. If the costs of failing to oppose a regime are clear and weighty because the regime is actively damaging innocent people, then we feel there is a responsibility actively to oppose it. Failure to do so makes us morally culpable to some degree, as we argue at the end of this chapter. If we do not speak out in the face of evil that we could effectively oppose, then we allow that evil to happen. Thus we do not live up to our values.

However, if the regime is just not worthy of our loyalty because it fails to pursue our values diligently, we certainly do not owe it allegiance. But the case for a patriotism requiring opposition is so much less compelling in these circumstances that it does not convince us that we must rebel. The standard of clear and weighty harm has not been met in such a situation. The obligation for a patriotism of rebellion exists only in carefully defined and relatively rare circumstances. Nevertheless, it is part of the relationship between patriotism and allegiance.

It is important to note in this context that this patriotism is not the same as a reflexive patriotism that supports regimes unconditionally. Blind patriotism can lead to zealotry and chauvinism that destroys, whereas patriotism linked to sound values can lead to political obligations that build.

Full and Partial Challenges

Examining the issues surrounding political challenge in more detail, we see that despite some common bonds, all challengers are not alike. They fall along a continuum that ranges from those who maintain their political obligations as they challenge the polity to revolutionaries who want to smash the state.

We call constitutional challenge provisionally obligated behavior because it is patriotism that supports regimes provided that they support the right values. The constitutional challenger supports the polity deeply enough to stop it from violating its laws or from being overthrown, despite its violation of some worthy values. He or she is obligated to the polity because and provided that it follows the right values. The constitutional challenger's obligation is inspired by his or her fundamental values and remains in force only as long as it is deserved. That is, the obligation is provisional upon the state's moral behavior.

To remain law-abiding citizens does not call for us to suspend our reason or political skepticism by supporting each and every stupid scheme or policy

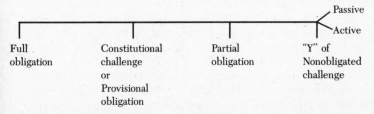

Provisional Obligations. At one side of the continuum is full obligation. Next to it is constitutional challenge or provisional obligation. Next is partial obligation. At the far end is the "Y" of nonobliged challenge.

that comes along just because we are provisionally obligated. To the contrary, the values imbedded in our political obligation drive us to oppose policies and leaders that violate our norms. We have a moral duty to use any constitutional means of dissent and opposition in order to steer our polity on a moral course. To fail to do so is to fail to uphold our genuine political obligations.

In democratic political systems, provisional obligations frequently lead patriots to try to influence elections through vigorous campaigning for the candidates and parties that oppose those who are in power. It also leads to lobbying those in power to change their policies, as well as attempting to influence public opinion through robust exercises of freedoms of speech, press, and assembly—including marches, demonstrations, protests, rallies, organization of political movements, and so on. In other words, the constitutionally obligated challenger in a democracy may do everything short of violating laws in order to get the job done. Such a challenger is never compelled to practice automatic, unthinking support of regimes and policies. This kind of opposition is a clear, consistent form of patriotism.

All of this also applies to those who live in nondemocratic regimes. However, there are usually (though not always) fewer legal paths available for opposition in these polities. As a result, challengers who want to be both effective and law-abiding in such a state must be more clever in order to do what needs to be done. They often must hide their dissent and challenge through stealth and subterfuge but are never licensed to disobey the laws of the polity. They remain provisionally obligated. Since all polities demonstrate a disturbing tendency to repress unwelcome dissent and to violate the civil liberties of challengers, the provisionally obligated challenger never has it easy. But regardless of the kind of political system involved, supporters of provisional obligation must demonstrate their patriotism through nudging the political system to live up to values that deserve obligation.

Constitutional challenge can come from above or below. When those in power change things in opposition to the policies and personnel of other powerful elites, this is challenge from above. Though opposition from below arguably is more common, change from above can be easier to accomplish, all other things being equal. After all, elites can be just as moral and dedicated to effective political change as those who do not walk the corridors of power. The elites are also in a position to accomplish change through the rulers instead of against them. Thus lawmakers, executives, and bureaucrats can become "whistle-blowers" by publicizing bad practices, introducing policy changes, educating citizens about better government practices, convincing their fellow elites to change, and so forth. Despite the dangers to those who pursue such opposition, it can be and has been done, albeit not often. As political scientist Zbigniew Brzezinski recently observed about Gorbachev's impositions of changes from above in the then Soviet Union, "True democratization has to involve . . . initiatives from the top down [and] also spontaneous democratic aspirations from below."[5]

All the styles of constitutional challenge covered in the preceding discussion are linked because they challenge but stop short of breaking laws. They are not unreflective acts by zealous patriots. Nor are they disobedient acts by those who feel their political system no longer deserves full obedience. Instead, they occupy a middle ground.

Partial Obligations   As we move along the path of patriotism to challenge, we come to a major chasm as soon as we put provisional obligation behind us. This chasm represents the predicament of patriots who are forced to deal with a nominally good polity that pursues an act that cannot be condoned. Perhaps our nation is waging an unjustified war. Or maybe it is guilty of overt and brutally unjust racism or sexism in some of its public policies. What are we to do? Our dilemma is clear. Provisional obligations cannot be stretched to justify support for unjust acts even if the good being done by our state precludes complete withdrawal of obligation. But surely, full revolt is not licensed here either. To overthrow such a state is to declare war on something that we admit is more good than evil.

Fortunately when we face such quandaries, we have an option of partial obligation, a middle ground between provisional obligation and genuine revolution. Our political obligations remain operative because their value infrastructures have not been violated. While political theory does not bind us to obey the immoral, it does not license opposition without substantial justification. For example, a state that provides resources for the suffering is commendable even though it is unworthy in other policies. Thus, we are morally compelled to obey its laws to the extent that they do not flagrantly violate our fundamental political values and so long as its leaders respect the rights of citizens.

Our values of provisional patriotism imply a civic duty both to obey what is good and to try to correct what is improper through acts of civil disobedience. We become partially obligated citizens who want to steer a course between the rock of limitless loyalty and obligation and the hard place of unjustified revolution.

Civil disobedience is a controversial—often risky—choice to violate publicly an act, order, or policy. As a personal act of disobeying the law, it has very serious consequences. While political scientist Carole Pateman's skeptical generalization refers to it as "an essentially symbolic activity that, in itself, makes no impact on the law or policy at issue,"[6] that is not necessarily the case. Civil disobedience can be a radical, sweeping act that so disrupts the everyday patterns of the state that it cannot be ignored by even illegitimate leaders. If civil disobedients are sufficiently persistent and clever in their legal defiance, they can be stopped only by repeal of the offending law or policy or by state coercion atrocious enough to kill or maim them under the glare of the international press coverage so common today during public ferment. Most states are not willing to incur such bad publicity, though the 1989 Chinese repression of pro-liberty dissidents in Tianenmen Square or the former Soviet Union's suppression of Baltic nationalism in 1991 shows that even in the television era some states will risk highly negative publicity because they feel that capitulating to the partially rebellious would do more damage.

Genuine acts of civil disobedience have certain common characteristics that bear examination. First of all, as Michael Walzer pointed out, they are morally serious acts.[7] A civil disobedient does not violate laws lightly or for personal advantage or benefit. On the contrary, he or she faces severe sanctions and makes a considerable sacrifice in order to project acts as an example designed to end evil policies.

Civil disobedience is also inherently political. The civil disobedient differs from an ordinary criminal (the embezzler or the robber) because the person does not profit from his or her acts nor try to escape capture. He or she wants to be arrested, charged, and publicly tried for violation of the offending law or policy in order to have a forum from which to criticize the policy and embarrass the accusers with the injustice of their laws and enforcement. The goal is to embarrass the state by forcing it to conduct an unpopular and highly visible show trial and thereby discredit its own policies.

In effect, civil disobedience is a form of political communication. It is an urgent, costly cry of anguish by those who want to be politically obligated but choose not to put their other values on hold. Civil disobedients refuse to allow their love of country to lead them to declare, "My country, right or wrong." By the same token, they will not jettison what is good about the polity by rejecting the whole thing in order to excise what is bad.

In essence, a civil disobedient has a duty to retain as much of his political obligations as circumstances permit. Legitimate opposition to specific policies never gives us the right to violate speeding laws while driving to our act of civil disobedience. We cannot justify violation of laws (traffic laws in this case) that are eminently justified because we are angry at other, evil, laws. Like killing in the name of life, that would commit us to an unacceptable logical and moral contradiction.

There is a long-standing debate in political theory about the role of violence in civil disobedience. Some, like Bedau,[8] argue that morally justified disobedience must be nonviolent. They argue that any violence[9] is so intrinsically savage and hostile to public order that it leaps across the line between obligation and revolt that the partially obligated citizen wants to straddle.

In terms of this debate, violence is clearly coercive and can irrevocably damage people. It should never be relished or celebrated. But advocates who suggest that violence against property is not as serious or irrevocable as violence against people have a point. Steel and glass are worth less and can be more easily replaced than flesh and blood. Furthermore, it is unfortunately true in an often mean-spirited world that violence captures headlines—and political agendas—more effectively than nonviolence. What is more, it often does not incur any more violent response than does nonviolence. While we can never justify violence for its own sake (and counsel its avoidance when possible), we cannot reject totally the logic of those who argue that it is an effective way of opposing state acts that are themselves violent and irrevocable. While it is an open moral question whether civil disobedients should commit violence or not, an act that fits the definition of civil disobedience is not automatically disqualified as civil disobedience by the amount of physical coercion it involves.

Nonobligated Challengers   There are times when even civil disobedience will not be effective against an evil polity. It is an effective political tactic and catalyst for change only in states that are responsive (however reluctantly) to strong public demands. It is folly in states that ignore it. Citizens who live in such unresponsive states have no reason for even partial obligation to the state as they pursue their civic agendas. Some political systems are so thoroughly committed to bad policies that they cannot be deterred. Others have so little moral worth that the personal sacrifice and loyalty of partial obligation only result in perpetuating the bad.

Serious pursuit of political obligation in such circumstances forces us to leave partial obligation behind and enter the non-state-obligated realm of rebels. Though our values link us to continued political obligation, reason uncouples us from a malevolent state. What is more, it may also allow us to direct our values elsewhere through positive support of alternative regimes. In other words, this end of the continuum branches out into a Y: One direction "simply" withdraws our obligation to an evil state and the other withdraws it and also directs it toward attempts to overthrow the evil state and replace it with something better.

The simple withdrawal of obligation is called passive rebellion because it stops short of actively opposing the polity. Though it tries to overthrow the government by refusing support or by limited, nonphysical means, it is not necessarily weak or timid politics. Frequently, it manifests itself in flight into exile to oppose the polity from safe haven and, hopefully, to direct invective or other weapons toward those who remain. Sometimes rebels have no other choice because they are either so vulnerable that their remaining would result in almost certain death or imprisonment and, therefore, render their opposition impotent. An exiled rebel's support of the regime might be missed and contribute to its downfall. Or perhaps his or her voluntary exile and continued agitation and propaganda might inspire others to flee. At any rate, exile—when it is deliberate and made visible—is a conscious political act of rebellion that dissolves any obligation toward the regime. Surely it can be an effective thorn in the side of regimes.

Another form of passive rebellion is "dropping out" or noncooperation by those who reject physical exile. As the poster implies that asks, "Suppose they gave a war and nobody came?" no state can remain viable for long if citizens will not pay taxes, obey laws, or otherwise contribute to public order. Obviously, a bad state can cope if only a few decide to drop out as citizens and live by private resources alone. But if many do so—even less than a majority—a critical mass is reached that endangers the state. If sustained, such noncooperation can bring a powerful state to its knees permanently. Treasuries soon empty and the public order system (police, courts, and jails) is overloaded and collapses in short order. The critical foundations of state authority simply disappear.

A more organized and effective form of passive noncooperation is the general strike. Rather than an individual act, it is a collective enterprise designed to enlist every person in the nation to withdraw all services and citizenship simultaneously to bring the state down. All workers, shop-keepers, bureaucrats, operators of key infrastructures like transportation and communications—even the police and army—simply sit down and refuse to do anything for the evil state. Though general strikes are very difficult to organize, they do happen. Through them people can deal the state a blow without becoming active, violent aggressors. While passive revolutionaries do not engage in active overthrow of governments, they surely do withdraw obligations with productive purpose.

To some nonobligated citizens, these indirect tactics are not enough. Revolutionaries feel that the best way to act against a state which does not deserve loyalty is to try to overthrow it by any means that can do the job. They hold that passive measures merely give the manipulative state an advantage, thereby perpetuating evil. Nevertheless, revolutionaries who revolt because of rational political values do not embrace violence and aggressiveness for their own sake. Instead, they suggest that the ends justify appropriate means. A strong enemy requires strong measures.

Such zealous tactics are familiar to viewers of nightly news broadcasts. Assassinations, terrorism, pitched battles by revolutionaries and would-be military juntas are quite common today. Actions involving the intifada in the Israeli-occupied West Bank of the Jordan River, the Irish Republican Army in Northern Ireland, and the Russian revolution are too familiar.

Embracing both the coup d'état (an overthrow and replacement of a regime, keeping the political system) and full-scale revolution (a change in relationship between government and citizens, accompanied by regime changes), such revolt recognizes few limits. Its unswerving goal is to smash the apparatus of the existing state and erect a better one on its ruins. Tactics are only measured by their effectiveness in accomplishing the goal. Passivity or kindness is rejected because it only stands in the way of attaining the just cause.

Sharing this burning passion to overthrow and replace the state with a better one are revolutionaries with a different attitude toward tactics and their consequences. Algerian-French political theorist/activist Albert Camus calls them rebels to distinguish them from full-tilt revolutionaries.[10] He says that fanatic revolutionaries who use any means toward a good end are almost certain to become as evil as their enemies as they shoot and blast their way to the promised land. If our enemies are evil because of what they do, asks Camus, why are we justified in doing the same thing to oppose them?

Why indeed? Camus suggests that even the most noble ends can never justify evil means. Killing in the name of life is a moral and logical contradic-tion. If the ends justify the means, what will justify the ends? To this nonrhetorical question, Camus answers, "The means." He suggests that nihilism (the lack of values) results inevitably when we do not recognize a doctrine of limits that teaches us that means cannot be separated from ends in revolution.

Camus counseled revolutionary restraint in both his underground resistance to the Nazis in occupied France and his demands that both sides be less violent in the Algerian war of anticolonialism against the French. He was not a pacifist but felt that radically minimizing violence in active revolution through intelligent, patient, and effective tactics is best because it avoids the twin tragedies of being either a victim or an unjustified murderer. Fully as patriotic as any loyalist, civil disobedient, or nonobligated challenger, he has burned the relationship of ends and means in patriotism and challenge into our consciousness so effectively that we dare not ignore it.

Throughout history, political theorists who have disagreed on everything else have seen the merit of the value of life as a basic foundation for political thought. For example, Hobbes in his *Leviathan*[11] says that the sovereign can do virtually anything to keep the peace except take a subject's life. Camus, too, makes the importance of human life a centerpiece of his *Rebel*. They are telling us never to undervalue human life. In terms of issues of obligation and revolt, this means that we should always try not to kill or hurt anybody in our acts of opposition if it can be avoided. Inconvenience is no excuse.

In resolution, a very basic judgment about what ought to be done by active challengers to evil governments is whether our right to withdraw political obligation from a bad polity also licenses or compels us actively to work to overthrow it. The choice is always personal and never easy. What is more, the consequences are often frightening and permanent: Rebels can die and become maimed and do the same to others. Political theory counsels convincingly that you should seek the best paths and tactics in any situation.

ISSUES AND PERSPECTIVES

Now that we have seen some choices available to potential patriots or challengers interacting with imperfect political systems, we can begin to put these important and confusing matters in some perspective. The first issue involves giving the polity the benefit of the doubt. We should approach political challenges carefully because even harmful political systems can also do a lot of good. Declaring war on them (or even partially withdrawing obligation) is likely to trigger coercive defenses by states and will cancel their advantages with their disadvantages if our war succeeds. Therefore, we do not advocate partial, passive, or active challenges easily or lightly. We simply point out that challenge is a double-edged, sharp sword. One edge can bring down a bad state and the other can be very harmful to those we defend by our challenges to established political authority. Challenge only when truly necessary—and then recognize costs. A similar issue involves what economists call opportunity costs,[12] which are incurred when we fail to challenge illegitimate authority. Failure to oppose wrong policies is not costless or neutral. We, in effect, validate and legitimate evil because we do not use resources to oppose it, thereby giving it some assistance, however inadvertently. A case can be made that if we see political wrong and simply turn away, we are guilty of acquiescence in evil. Always we need to balance reflections on the harm our opposition might bring with the harm our failure to oppose may cause.

Yet another perspective on this involves the relationship of morality and effectiveness in challenge. The conventional wisdom is that passive (even active) challenges that are limited by consistency with the value of life and a doctrine of limits are necessarily weak. Therefore, they have greater opportunity costs than do more militant measures. But sometimes with careful planning and attention to tactics (and a healthy dose of courage), moral challenges to evil polities can be effective and powerful and can bring the evil state to a screeching halt. General strikes, organized boycotts, denying offending police and military units access to their victims, and similar tactics can do the job that needs to be done.

One more issue that has become important in an age of what media expert Marshall McLuhan calls the global village[13] is that of self-interest and challenge. People all over the world now have access to television and other information media for the first time in history. The same technology that brought the 1991 U.S. bombing of Baghdad to the world as it happened also brings viewers knowledge of how others live. Thus some revolutionary zeal today may be motivated by self-interest (some would say envy) that comes from seeing that others live better and wanting what they have and challenging a polity that fails to provide a good life. They say that it is just to try to improve your material lot and your neighbors' too.

Such justifications do need to be stronger or purer than other justifications because they involve self-interest. All forms of political challenge seek to advance their advocates' values and thus promote their self-interest. As long as the challenger's self-interest coincides with that of fellow citizens, any benefit the challenger might get from the outcome of his or her challenges does not invalidate the moral worth of the act of opposition. Economic desires are just as legitimate as any other. It is neither more or less more moral to oppose slavery than to oppose starvation. People need food and rights. What is at issue is whether the means and measures of opposition are supported by what they oppose. If evil is serious, whether economic or not, its opposition is warranted.

What conclusions may we draw from these observations? Where do one's political obligations lie? Clearly, as the discussion in our chapter on obligation indicates, these are complex issues that need to be considered carefully. In the political context, a citizen can have legitimate obligations no matter where he or she falls on the progression from patriotic constitutional challenger to total revolutionary. In other words, a revolutionary or a rebel can be and often is as fully obligated as a civil disobedient or a patriot. The former are obligated to fellow citizens, a would-be replacement for the state, or a similar entity instead of the state, whereas the patriot remains definitionally obligated to his or her fellow citizens or their organizations through the state. We point this out because behavior that is not bound by careful political obligations is very dangerous. It is prone to the nihilism that Camus warns about, when clear values do not support and unambiguously mandate goals that are consistent with them.

A CITIZEN'S HANDBOOK ON ISSUES AND IMPLICATIONS OF THE PROGRESSION OF CHALLENGE

We have argued that the moral citizen should choose only provisional patriotism or, if necessary, turn to some form of challenge in his or her relationship with every political community. We end with a series of maxims and observations about what a citizen who is both moral and thoughtful should do about this progression of choices. What are the major issues surrounding a good citizen's moral responsibilities and actions in the face of offensive state behavior?

One important question is whether we should be held morally responsible for passivity in the face of evil. Should we blame the citizens of a country who say nothing (because of fear for their own personal safety, presumably) as they watch their leaders commit genocide or wage an immoral war of conquest? We think the answer can be yes. Citizens who do not speak out against evil might be wrong and could be held accountable for their failure to act. We understand that challenge to the actions in question might be costly to the potential challenger and we can sympathize with his or her reluctance to try to stop what seems inevitable. But we suggest that people remember that failure to challenge has consequences—it legitimates the offending behavior.

Clearly the passive citizen's failure is not nearly as serious as the evil committed by perpetrators of genocide or aggression. Nevertheless, there are certain conditions that lead to moral responsibility and, hence, culpability for silence. If the evil is clear and present enough for the average citizen to see it, and if our opposition has a reasonable chance of helping to slow or stop it, we insist that there is a moral obligation to challenge it because that is the most direct way to live up to our values. If we fail to seize this unwelcome but real moral opportunity, our behavior is wanting. If more of us speak out against genocide, international terrorism, brutal occupation of captured territories, and racist oppression—especially in their early stages—perhaps these abominable policies would not succeed now as they have in the past.

Another aspect of this position on the moral culpability of quiescent citizens involves the relative moral worth of solidarity as opposed to individual opposition. Political theorists from Hobbes and Locke to Rousseau[14] and Bentham[15] maintain that challenge is most legitimate when it is done in concert with others. Singular challengers are sympathetic victims, perhaps, and may be entitled to challenge. But they are not in the same moral league with those who act with kindred spirits to represent the public interest because political opposition is both more visible (hence more dangerous) and more effective than solitary opposition to political evil.

We are only partially persuaded by this argument. Surely challenges by many victims of arbitrary public or even private authority carry more weight than challenges that are the acts of one or a few. After all, they represent a large bloc of citizens. Nevertheless, that fact only makes them more politically meaningful, not more morally meaningful. The rightness of a challenge turns on its validity, not its number of supporters.

The Methodology of Minimalism

We conclude with a methodological perspective as a form of useful advice, a kind of handbook for citizens who must deal with powerful and not always just political communities in daily life. The conclusion of our handbook is basic: citizens should begin with small measures in challenging the polity in hopes that they work. As we have seen, challenges are always coercive and sometimes dangerous. They should never be undertaken lightly or without healthy respect for their negative and positive consequences. Thus the prudent citizen should neither overreact or underreact. He or she should avoid the undesirable opportunity costs of underreaction and the equally undesirable costs of nihilistic overreaction.

But how can we know when a reaction is about right? The only answer we know is to try the minimum that the target action warrants (in terms of depth of wrongness of policy and the mean-spiritedness of policymakers) and hope that it is effective. If it is not, then gradual, incremental escalation of tactics which move across the progression from patriotic challenges to active assault on the polity is in order. If each new step is just a small notch more serious than its predecessor, and sufficient time is given to make sure that it is not working, then that is reasonably good empirical evidence that you need to notch up your assault against the state again. If the next step accomplishes its goal, then obviously a more coercive step would have been, by definition, unwarranted overkill. The goal is to be on the right side in the right way. We should try desperately not to resemble one's enemies as we oppose them.

This raises the interesting question, How long do obligations to be patriotic or to challenge last? If we are obligated, are we bound indefinitely? We think so, as long as the original conditions that merited the obligations in the first place persist. However, if there are major changes either in values or in the behavior of the political community, obligations may be changed or dissolved. Obligations (and any moral relationships) depend on mutuality, reciprocity, and choice. Consequently, changes in these foundations of obligation merit modifications of our obligations. Consistency here, as elsewhere in political theory, is only a proximate virtue, not an absolute.

THE PRESENT CENTURY—AND THE NEXT

The only task left for us to explore is to assess how these important, enduring principles of patriotism, disobedience, and rebellion link with some of the critical issues facing us in the contemporary world—and how they will link with similar issues in the next century. One particularly worrisome issue is how our emerging ability to brainwash and manipulate people with modern techniques of advertising and mass communication affects the political theory of patriotism and challenge. If people can be brainwashed or hoodwinked into hysterical patriotism or challenge, then our whole notion of thoughtful obligation and rational, measured responses to illegitimate state behavior loses meaning. Values would be rendered moot in such a tragic situation. While we have no magic solution, we hope that the act of voicing our worry will cause you to be alert for efforts of governments, interested private groups, or coalitions of would-be challengers to lie or use agitation and propaganda to short-circuit thinking. The emerging technology that makes this an even greater danger than in the past makes the need for a sensible political theory of authority and revolt an even higher priority than in the past. We must guard against any and all efforts to prevent people from thinking and forming defensible values and tactics.

Political theorist Sheldon Wolin voices that we will be so fearful of some of the social evils that plague our society that we will overreact and limit.[16] Wolin is distressed that our fear of such scourges as illegal immigration, crime, AIDS, and the drug epidemic might lead us to erect a "new surveillance and control state" with the sophisticated technology of snooping and security now available or on the drawing boards. If we let our desire for security outrun our desire for a legitimate, fair, and open society, then we will have handed those already in control of the state a justification to extend and develop their already massive powers. If we give them permission, even encouragement, what guarantees do we have that leaders' new abilities to control populations and ferret out and destroy state opponents will not be turned against legitimate challenges or even constitutional dissidents?

The only safeguard against such excesses is not to allow states or private groups to violate critical civil liberties when they pursue social ills. The cliché that eternal vigilance is the price of liberty applies here—we must be ever vigilant against those who would erode the precious rights that we have to challenge through the system. If we do not succeed because our passion for security at any cost gives the state awesome powers of social snooping and control, then we will have maneuvered ourselves into a situation where we have a massive need for revolt and a severely reduced capacity to do anything about it. We should also keep in mind, however, that a prominent necessity of every polity is order and that we must balance liberty and order in a good polity.

We also need to consider a parallel question, Are challenges from above as legitimate as challenges from below? Some argue that only those out of power have the objectivity and the perspective to keep government honest.

They feel that revolution led by elites within the system is intrinsically flawed because leaders have self-interest in mind and cannot empathize with victims of state authority. Hence they cannot effectively represent the common citizen, which results in flawed challenges that—at best—coopt citizen needs.

Frankly, while the preceding assumptions accurately describe many attempts to foster political change from the top, such an outcome is not inevitable. While leaders have a difficult time empathizing with followers, the whole edifice of democracy depends on their ability to do so with sufficient incentive as a catalyst. Granted, their position of power can lead to damaging self-interest and greed, but the powerless are hardly immune to such temptations. What is more, we have seen that the powerful can get the job done. If their perspectives are rooted in effective political argument, they can be very both effective and just. While we do not know whether the challenges to orthodox political and economic values and structures put into motion by Mikhail Gorbachev will ultimately succeed, he surely moved the Soviet system quickly and almost certainly pushed it beyond the point of no return. The subsequent efforts of the coalition surrounding the first democratically elected president of Russia, Boris Yeltsin, appear to have contributed to the initial development and institutionalization for a key part of the former Soviet Union. Many problems and dangers lie ahead there and in other former Soviet Republics. Revolution from below has its powerful attractions, but we must realize that what counts is whether a challenge is moral, its origins notwithstanding.

CONCLUSION

In the final analysis, whatever drummer we march to, however measured or far away,[17] we cannot evade the need to make judgments about political systems and political values. To paraphrase a revolutionary slogan of an earlier time, you may not be interested in the revolution, but it will be interested in you. Apathy does not buy us immunity from political events. Whether we are patriots or challengers—on behalf of the environment, all of humanity or our fellow citizens, the rich or the poor, our neighbors, or ourselves—we need to make judgments about politics—about political theory. Our task is to address the competing claims. Political theory can be a reliable beacon, no matter how diffused its light may become in the maelstrom of events.

GLOSSARY OF KEY TERMS

active rebellion Overt attempts to overthrow a government.
authority A concept involving the right to govern and to be obeyed because of respect for or legitimacy of position.

civil disobedience (type of partial obligation) Deliberately and publicly disobeying a law and accepting the consequences in order to pressure the polity to change the offending statute.

constitutional challenge Working legally within a political system to change policies and processes.

coup d'état (French term) The act of changing the rulers by extra-constitutional means, frequently violent, while leaving the general form of government intact.

full obligation Being politically legal to the state provided that it meets individual criteria for good political values.

legitimacy Sense of properness, legality, and morality in a political context.

negative freedom A concept envisioning a night-watchman state with little government interference in citizens' lives. It assumes that liberty is secured by preventing government from denying people their natural rights to liberty.

opportunity costs A measure of the real costs of spending our resources. It precludes using them elsewhere.

partial obligation A situation of loyalty to the state generally, with the exception of being so opposed to one or a few policies that obligation in that area must be withdrawn. (See civil disobedience.)

patriotism Love of country and support for the political system. It may be displayed in many different ways.

passive rebellion Indirect ways of trying to overthrow a government, such as refusal to participate in obligations of state or disobeying orders.

political obligation Loyalty and feelings of moral duty that one holds to a government, political group, or fellow citizens.

positive freedom A concept of liberty envisioning a state that actively works to provide for the public interest. It assumes that liberties are assured when the state actively prevents private exploitation of individuals and promotes their positive development.

revolution, revolt Terms used to describe the attempt to overthrow a government and replace it with a different kind of polity. More extensive than a coup d'état.

SUGGESTIONS FOR FURTHER READING

Berlin, Isaiah. *Four Essays on Liberty*. London: Oxford University Press, 1969.

Camus, Albert. *The Rebel*. New York: Alfred A. Knopf, 1961.

Dahl, Robert. *After the Revolution: Authority in a Good Society*. New Haven: Yale University Press, 1970.

Dunn, John. *Western Political Theory in the Face of the Future*. Cambridge: Cambridge University Press, 1979.

Hobbes, Thomas. *Leviathan*. Introduction by H. Morley. London: G. Routledge & Sons, 1885.

Locke, John. *Second Treatise on Civil Government*. Edited by Maurice Cranston. New York: Collier Books, 1965.

McLuhan, Marshall, and Powers, Bruce. *The Global Village*. New York: Oxford University Press, 1989.

Moore, Barrington, Jr. *Social Origins of Dictatorship and Democracy*. Boston: Beacon Press, 1966.

Pirages, Dennis. *Managing Political Conflict*. New York: Praeger, 1976.

Smith, Michael P., and Deutsch, Kenneth L. *Political Obligation and Civil Disobedience: Readings*. New York: Crowell, 1972.

Rousseau, Jean Jacques. *The Social Contract and Discourses*. New York: E. P. Dutton, 1950.

Wolff, Robert Paul. *In Defense of Anarchism*. New York: Harper & Row, 1970.

NOTES

1. John Locke, *Second Treatise on Government*, ed. Peter Laslett (New York: Collier Books, 1965), p. 323.
2. We are examining the limits, degrees, and boundaries of obligation in this context. In the chapter on obligation, we discussed its kinds and bases. Here, we are examining the values of patriotism and challenge. Obligation is sometimes used in this context, but it is also used in very different ways.
3. Robert Paul Wolff, *In Defense of Anarchism* (New York: Harper & Row, 1970).
4. We do not mean to imply that because we believe in particular values they are automatically right. Many standards and arguments of values exist in political theory, and each must be considered carefully before it merits application to patriotism and challenge.
5. Zbigniew Brzezinski, "On the Breakup of the USSR," *World Monitor*, November 1990 (Boston: Christian Science Publishing Co.), p. 33.
6. Carole Pateman, *Participation and Democratic Theory* (Cambridge: Cambridge University Press), p. 59.
7. Michael Walzer, *Obligations* (Cambridge: Harvard University Press, 1970).
8. Hugo Bedau, "On Civil Disobedience," in Donald Hanson and Robert Booth Fowler, *Obligation and Dissent* (Boston: Little Brown and Co., 1971).
9. Violence is usually defined as killing or maiming other persons, though it is sometimes extended to incorporate damage against the property of others.
10. Albert Camus, *The Rebel* (New York: Alfred A. Knopf, 1961).
11. Thomas Hobbes, *Leviathan*, intro. Henry Morley (London: G. Routledge & Sons, 1885).
12. An opportunity cost is what we incur when we spend our resources on one choice and, consequently, do not have them available for pursuit of other choices.
13. Marshall McLuhan and Bruce Powers, *The Global Village* (New York: Oxford University Press, 1989).
14. Jean Jacques Rousseau, *The Social Contract* (New York: Dutton, 1950).
15. Jeremy Bentham, *Introduction to the Principles of Morals and Legislation* (Oxford: Clarendon Press, 1876).
16. Interview with Sheldon Wolin, in Bill Moyers, *A World of Ideas* (New York: Doubleday, 1989), p. 97.
17. A theme espoused by Henry David Thoreau in his essay *Civil Disobedience*, in Hanson and Fowler, op. cit., pp. 176–196.

Chapter
10

Political Theory and the Tangible World of Politics

*T*he issues of political theory and politics are vital elements in our lives. But only a few of us devote our lives to studying or being active in politics and government. The rest of us simply do not perceive the issues of political theory and politics to be as central as other personal or professional concerns. Political theory's issues do not seem to be as clearly tangible to us as the things that we deal with in our daily lives. Not quite as real to us as our friends, our jobs, and our taxes, they can strike us as part of an abstract and bookish world that is not genuinely engaged with the nitty-gritty political and economic environment of *our* lives.

Yet, appearances deceive us in this case. Our familiar (and very real) structures of government and politics, our economy and its patterns of exchange, and even today's trends in political communication have their historical roots in political theory. Today's form of government is connected with yesterday's debate over events and values. Moreover, our contemporary political economies remain connected to political theory because they are regulated and steered by political ideas and institutions.

Regardless of whether we recognize or appreciate it, political values affect our lives as deeply and subtly as life's other values. Just as our moral values affect our personal relationships and business ethics, and just as our views about God inspire our religious outlooks and affiliations, so do our views on the values in political theory affect our relationships as citizens, soldiers, and taxpayers.

What analysts of comparative politics refer to as political culture[1] is the critical area of our lives as citizens. It is the place where our deeply held political values interact with the real world of our political environment.[2] This pattern of institutions and public relationships is not very visible because our "choices" about them—for example, which political and economic institutions we live under and value—are habitually dim and passive. Most of the time, our beliefs and loyalties attach almost automatically to what we are familiar with and have been socialized[3] to believe as we grow up and/or acquire citizenship.

Our socialization is not necessarily bad because it allows us to work together in institutions that give us comfort. This makes it easier for us to act together politically to accomplish many valuable social goals. Without shared beliefs and loyalties, we would have no community. However, while this is how political theory lives for most of us, the process is not always voluntary or conscious. Politics and its values affect us whether we act on or think about them regularly or not. Whether we have examined and evaluated our choices and loyalties in political economy or just let them happen to us does not matter. Somebody thought of them and put them into practice at some time and place in history. Somebody also got others to believe in and reinforce them. Thus our political choices and loyalties have evolved to define and reinforce our contemporary political and economic institutions and are how political theory lives in our tangible political world.

Accordingly, this chapter examines the subtle but important relationship between political ideas and institutions. In dealing with some keystone concepts and issues about this relationship, it also offers us some insights about how to think about and deal with it as we experience real political situations with very real winners and losers. While it helps to organize our thinking to ponder political systems[4] and political economies[5] separately, we believe that they are not separate in reality. We use the integrated term of political economy.

FORMS OF GOVERNMENT AND POLITICAL THEORY

The tremendous assortment of governments that people experience around the world has not just germinated naturally, like so many seeds scattered by the wind. Each has been conceived and debated in its evolution through a long tradition of political theory. To give a few examples, Locke, Rousseau, Bentham, and John Stuart Mill have affected the development of modern parliamentary democracy. Moreover, the ideas of Aristotle, utopian medieval Christian thinkers, Rousseau, and Marx (among others) have affected modern communist systems. The political theories of Plato, Hegel, Neitzsche, De Maistre, and others have also surely affected the development of modern oligarchic systems.

In further illustration, the principal values that drive Western institutional variations of democracy (including the British parliamentary system and the American presidential system) are the worth of the common man, individual liberty, and equality of citizens. The concept that people ought to rule directly or at least select who rules them and consequently hold rulers responsive to public judgment was developed in arguments by political

Participatory   Dictatorship
democracy

The first continuum describes political participation and refers to how many
govern. Participatory democracy (where the many govern equally and directly)
and dictatorship (rule by one, with all others being subjects) mark the poles of
this continuum.

Pure   Completely
laissez-faire   government-guided
capitalism   economy

The second continuum is economic and refers to how resources, property, and
material values are organized. Pure laissez-faire capitalism and a completely
government-guided economy mark its poles.

theorists over the last twenty-five centuries. As they explored questions of
who ought to rule and why, some thinkers fashioned strong arguments that
people have moral value and that government is justified only insofar as it
facilitates just public relationships among them.

In turn, these ideas about rulership inspired political theorists to examine
institutional arrangements of governments. As a result, they prescribed
forms of government they felt would best make democratic values operational.[6] Many of these forms are so familiar that they are taken for granted by
citizens of contemporary democracies. Nevertheless, the democratic institutions embodied by the common practice among the Swiss people of using the
ballot box to override the national legislature on policy, the directly elected
bicameral legislature, executive leadership by cabinet, separate executive
branches, general elections, staggered elections, were all first described and
advocated by political theorists.

These practices put the ideas of political theorists into the public domain.
Constitution writers, revolutionaries, and/or reformers were thus free to coopt and incorporate them (with modifications and compromises forced by the
realities of governing) into existing political institutions. As these institutions
evolved, most of the enduring worthwhile changes to them (such as the
British Reform Act of 1832, which ushered in the modern parliamentary form
of government) also originated in political theory and entered government by
a similar route.

Today the analyses and proposals made by political theorists continue to
advocate changes in democratic theory and practices, such as those of Pate-

man and other advocates of economic democracy and more participatory democracy.[7] Advances in the technology of communications also inspire political theorists to imagine what the ability to have highly interactive communications systems could do for the next century's democratic institutions.[8] Though these have not yet led to major modifications of our democratic institutions and practices, they have infiltrated the political agenda. They stand as challenges in the public domain that may become more intense and affect future political practices and processes as political theory moves into its twenty-sixth century.

Political theory has been important, too, in developing contemporary communist polities. In communism, the institutions of political economy that dominated the Union of Soviet Socialist Republics before Gorbachev—as well as Yugoslavia and other Eastern European neighbors of the former USSR before the fall of the Berlin Wall—and still hold sway in China[9] felt the direct influence of such leaders and political thinkers as Lenin, Mao, Tito, and others.[10] These disciples of Karl Marx, Friedrich Engels, and their followers were attempting to put into practice the Marxian values of classlessness, equality, and economic justice. While the demands of local cultures and coalitions led to institutionalization of values that Marx did not anticipate, his historical influence is tangible. Furthermore, while communism is currently undergoing rapid and substantial changes in the wake of the apparent failure of its original institutions, the values that drive its transformations are much the same as those that inspired communism originally. While personalities and historical experiences differ, the values of social justice and equality are still major actors, albeit now sharing the stage with liberty.

Similarly, much of political thought has justified oligarchy. The values in the abundance of oligarchic nation-states today have been inspired by political theorists from many eras, including the present one. Some theocracies found in many parts of the world were surely influenced by political and theological thinkers like Muhammad and some readings of the Bible.[11] Also, Plato's advocacy of rule by the brilliant and educated (to prevent the stupid from leading the smart), Machiavelli's promotion of the virtues of bold, opportunistic leadership, Hegel's defense of a key role of leadership in society, and Nietzsche's veneration of the role of extraordinary people all justify oligarchy's constitution builders. Despite disagreement about the best principle for determining who is best suited to rule, such political theory supported constructing political institutions in pursuit of principles defending the legitimacy of government by the few.

Even the mixed or hybrid forms of government that dominate contemporary political institutions have been encouraged by centuries of political theory. Their hybrid form suggests that their philosophical antecedents are eclectic. Examples of the hybrid forms are some emerging governments in formerly communist Eastern Europe, which are attempting to institutionalize a democratic political system and a mixed economy. Similarly, the United States has representative democracy in its Congressional elections but follows oligarchy when it appoints its national judges for life and tries to follow capitalism (in spite of the presence of a few nationalized economic activities like Amtrak) in its economy. France has both a president and a prime minister in its institutions, and the former Soviet Union has had an uneasy parallel existence of the legislature and the Communist party as governing bodies.

Each of these systems has institutions of political economy (democracy, oligarchy, capitalism, communism, etc.) first articulated by political theorists. The constitutional engineers of these polities have thus borrowed from a wide variety of sources. While that gives them a wide menu of choices, it forces them to risk juggling concepts and structures that are potentially conflicting despite their individual worth.

FORMS OF POLITICAL ECONOMY AND POLITICAL THEORY

Economics and politics are merely terms of classification. The political and economic institutions and practices called political economies are rooted in both the economic and political sectors of society. The "real world" of public experience exists as an almost seamless whole, wherein economic decisions are often made authoritatively by political institutions and vice versa. As an economist wrote, "Economics arose in response to questions of political interest about the national economy. . . . its vitality and development continue to stem from this central concern."[12] Put bluntly, politics and economics each spill over into both polity and economy. To recognize this fact is to enhance our understanding of complex public interactions even though we are not used to the perspective this manner of analysis yields.

Political economy has benefitted from the ideals and values of political theorists as thoroughly as has the purely governmental. Aristotle, Adam Smith, John Maynard Keynes, Karl Marx, John Stuart Mill, and others have helped us think about political economy regardless of whether we place them in the pantheons of political science or economics. They paid substantial attention to both the material and public dimensions of public interactions because they realized that politics and economics differ only in the arena of the interactions.

What has been called a political theory of public utilities (and many economic subtheories derived from it) has influenced generations of political theorists. In this context, public is the political dimension and utilities are what is useful and functional. They include energy and power-generating networks, telephone and postal systems, and other infrastructures we customarily call public utilities.

But they also encompass other basic public needs, including public passenger and freight transportation, highways, railways, airways and waterways for private vehicles, housing, medical care, food, environmental protection, and the like. Various political economists argue that such infrastructures are really public utilities because they are necessary for a decent public life.[13] Furthermore, they hold that the state is justified only to the extent that it provides for the public interest as opposed to the private greed of its rulers.

Consequently, legitimate political systems should provide adequate and affordable public utilities for all citizens. Good polities should also finance public utilities equitably, taking ability to pay as well as need into account. Beyond this, most political economists assume no obligation for the state to provide luxuries or substantial ease for a few, especially at the expense of the many. They posit only an obligation to foster a political economy that promotes provision of these desirable goods by private interests at market-determined prices.

While these observations form the general parameters of the theory of political economy, there have been many different historical approaches to political economy. The two most familiar examples are capitalism and socialism, but there are others, such as decentralized and mixed political economies. Each of them is driven by its own set of values rooted within political theory.

Capitalism is a system that assumes that private individuals and groups should provide goods and services in a free-market political economy in exchange for payments from consumers. Profits after expenses are felt to be legitimate and are either plowed back into the enterprise and/or converted to private use of owners. A complex series of individual perceptions and transactions known as a free market is felt to regulate the whole process. Its values rooted in political theory include the importance of individual economic liberty and the legitimacy of polities that foster free enterprise for entrepreneurs. They also include endorsement of a limited direct role for the polity in public utility provision and a night-watchman function for the protection of property. Equality and fairness receive less emphasis than liberty and property rights from this system, though they are recognized.

Socialism (frequently existing symbiotically with democratic government in Western history) is a model of political economy wherein economic allocation relies on direct government control (or strict regulation) of the production of public goods and services. Private interests or individuals play a marginal role under socialism. Regulation takes place through law and bureaucracy rather than free markets. The principal influence of political theory on socialism is the value of equality. Socialists generally assume that all citizens are morally valuable and equally entitled to an equal economic life. Rights *to* rather than *of* property (at least basic-necessity levels thereof) are emphasized. Also, they feel that the state should intervene in the market on the side of justice and the public interest rather than merely as a night watchman protecting the property of the wealthy. Liberty of individuals and entrepreneurs is not valued highly as it is under capitalism.

As interesting and influential as ideas as they are, neither pure capitalism nor pure socialism is a reality in today's globally interdependent world. The complex and important political economies we see out there are actually hybrids which embrace substantial elements of both these theories of political economy. Quasinationalized political economies (where capitalism dominates but coexists with a few government-owned but profit-oriented enterprises that compete with capitalist enterprises in the marketplace)[14] are common. So are various government-enhanced market political economies which feature different degrees of government guiding of markets through regulation, antitrust regulation, subsidies, and so forth.

Each of these hybrids combines the major features of the polar political economies of capitalism and socialism. Each embraces both free enterprise and government economic intervention as circumstances and ideologies dictate. But, in so doing, each carries the others' philosophical baggage in the guise of a sometimes uneasy coalition of values. Thus hybrid, mixed political economies are nurtured and driven by both liberty and equality and both negative and positive economic and social roles for the state in a legitimate society. Their relative emphasis differs between each political economy and over time within each political economy. Nevertheless, each is an interesting and sometimes unruly combination.

Related to this but difficult to place on our continuum is the model of a decentralized political economy. It appears to be related to capitalism, but it is quite different as well. It takes its values from the wing of political theorists and classical economists who distrust any concentrations of power (especially government, but business also).[15] Their prescriptions for a political economy envision economic activity taking place in small, decentralized communities that emphasize social justice, participation, and economic democracy. This romantic (some would say utopian) notion of political economy—not as well developed as the others—lives in "underground" and barter economies and a few present or past communes like those of the famous "hippies" of the 1960s era or the nineteenth-century Swiss watchmakers in the Jura mountains. Surely it occupies the attention of some political theorists and is driven by values of personal liberty and radical equality. The decentralized political economy also serves as a straw-man symbol of opposition for many orthodox popular economic ideologues even though it is not a major factor in today's political economies.

STYLES OF POLITICS AND THEIR ORIGINS IN POLITICAL THEORY

Political theory's influence on us is not limited to our values about government and political economy. It also has a sometimes subtle but pervasive effect on our political environments: our styles[16] of contemporary politics. In order to accomplish their political agendas, citizens, politicians, governments, and quasi-governmental institutions like political parties and interest groups regularly interact and deal with each other in a complex society like ours. Interestingly, though these political relationships are inevitable, they are not random or dependent upon the whim or mood of the communicator.

To the contrary, the customs, practices, and even the ceremonies of our political lives constitute predictable styles of politics that shape basic communication patterns among the many actors in a political system. These styles matter. They constitute a common political culture and language that politically differentiates U.S. citizens from Canadians, French, Germans, Japanese, Nigerians, or Pakistanis, despite their obvious species and common-planet similarities. These political styles are analogous to modern roads because they are practical paths between destinations best utilized by effective and appropriate vehicles. Hence, each style of politics is a cultural vehicle, a product of political theory, that carries us down the roads of politics.

Most of the political styles visible from our Western-facing windows on the public world are rooted in some facet of democracy and its political history and values. This should not be surprising. Indeed, the principles (if not the practice) of democracy have become a common political goal throughout the world. The parliamentary democracy of the United Kingdom is one type of democratic style. It has a long literature of political theory that advocates institutions without separation of powers, stresses the need for general elections, has elected representatives deciding constitutional issues, and a figurehead monarch. It is by far the most common style of democracy. Another type of democratic style is the United States-inspired Presidential system. Its scholarship and practices indicate that democracy is best served by competing, separately elected legislative houses, a separate executive with veto powers, an appointed-for-life judiciary with the power to decide constitutional issues, and elections that are staggered in time and scope.

Beyond their democratic roots, Western political styles have grown to maturity in the soil of political theories and practices like justice, equality, liberty, efficiency, and policy development. All of these political flowers grow in the soil of political theory.

Western political systems trying to pursue modern styles of political theory have found it far easier to implement values negatively—by legislating against behaviors (making it illegal to discriminate against individuals because of sex, race, or religion, for example)—than to implement them positively, by mandating what must be done (by implementing rules demanding respect, aggressive integration, etc.). At least in the United States, people are far less comfortable with mandates for actively creating equality than they are with mandates that merely restrict liberty by prohibiting certain behaviors.

Perhaps this is because styles of politics in liberal democratic environments have developed a positive cultural bias toward liberty as natural and a negative one toward forced equality, despite any similarities of the two in political practice. Whatever the reason, when Western political institutions try to legislate morality through bureaucratic prescription and mandate, they usually find that the road is bumpier than it appears to be despite almost universal agreement on the worth of the ultimate driving values.

It is beyond our descriptive and analytical needs to include an exhaustive catalogue of political styles, even just democratic ones, in these pages. Instead, let us examine a few characteristic styles and parts of styles from our political culture that illustrate how effectively political theory lives through our political institutions, processes, and practices.

Campaigns and elections are very common phenomena in our political system. Hence the most common political style in our contemporary political system(s) pervades their processes: who runs, how they run, and why x instead of y wins are not chance occurrences. The electoral style in each of today's Western, industrial democracies is a factor in both the practical requirements of the rules and structures of the political system and our customary expectations. In the English parliamentary system,[17] successful candidates for national legislative office usually rise through the ranks of local party organizations and are expected to campaign mainly by highly inter- active personal appearances and street-corner rallies. By contrast, candidates for the United States Congress frequently have no significant political party organizational ties and often raise vast sums of money which they use to hire professionals to engineer primary and general election victories using mass media and direct-mail advertising instead of personal voter contact. Each is a style of politics rooted in values about the value of politics and politicians. And each affects such critical democratic variables as candidate recruitment, training, platforms, campaign intelligence (including polls) and tactics, fi- nancing, and media-shaping of messages.

Different electoral styles have real consequences that encourage differ- ent types of individuals to run for office and certainly affect the type and quality of campaigns. In turn, the electoral style of the system affects the directions and degrees of responsiveness and the nature of public decisions in the polity as well. For example, the British parliamentary style generally produces politicians with more governmental experience (for better or worse) and the British citizen is consistently more interested in and knowledgeable about complex political issues than his or her U.S. counterpart.[18] The presi- dential style, on the other hand, generally produces politicians who are successful at raising a lot of money and using media to "position" their images. Experience and knowledge of public policy processes and issues are not prerequisites for success.[19]

Another stylistic precinct (and further example of political theory's impact on our public lives) involves efforts to influence government. Here, too, there are distinguishing patterns among polities; one may be termed open and the other covert. Lobbying is the legitimate, common process of complaining to governments about grievances or advocating policy. It takes place in all political systems, and it is so common and well-defined in democracies that we need not detail it here. In authoritarian political systems, however, elites often try to repress its mass manifestations (driving it underground) and usually tolerate channels of influence peddling that suit the particular elite patterns of power and institutional labyrinths. Open lobbying tends to pro- duce policies that represent compromises among several group demands because interested groups can see if and how their competitors are involved and jump into the fray and influence policymakers. Covert lobbying is usually not visible until its effects are felt in policy. As a result, the successful lobbying group usually does not have to compete with other groups for policymakers' ears—and usually carries the day by its singular access.

Lobbying sometimes is an internal governmental process as government agencies and departments compete for funds, policies, and defense against other agencies and other groups within the precincts of the government. For example, the role of the Soviet military in decisions about responses to Baltic desires for independence and/or the surrounding moves toward or away from economic reform illustrated a different style from one which drives the process of military influence peddling within a third-world military dictatorship. In the latter, the military is usually the dominant political force and sometimes threatens to overthrow the government if its demands are not fully met. In the former USSR, the military has had a tradition of following civilian policymakers' wishes regardless of whether its negotiation for change succeeded.

A probably more common pattern of lobbying is an external one. This complex of influence styles occurs when individuals and (especially) groups[20] pick from an arsenal of political weapons of influence, including access, rewards and/or sanctions, reason, public relations, information, and knowledge of the process to get governmental officials to do (or not to do) something. Here, too, values and styles are intertwined. Single-party systems like Mexico have quite different styles of influencing governments than weak-party/strong interest groups like the United States, or authoritarian communist systems like the People's Republic of China.[21]

Moreover, views on the legitimacy of individual and group claims on public policy vary; they appear to be more important values in democratic political systems than in authoritarian ones. Different styles of political systems also differ in emphasis on the political obligations of groups as well as the legitimacy of governmental responses to public opinion. For example, in the United States, it is considered legitimate for business firms or labor unions to press their particular agendas of political economy through government. In England, however, individual firms or unions traditionally have had loose affiliations with political parties, but it is not considered as legitimate for them to lobby the government directly. Furthermore, different cultural norms of justice affect views of the substantive worth of lobbyists' claims in different polities. In the United States, lobbying effectiveness is increased if legislators view the requesting party as a victim of unjust discrimination, as when American women's groups like the National Organization for Women lobby for equal pay for equal work. Success also is enhanced if legislators share the lobbying group's belief that its cause is particularly just, such as the right to affordable medical care in Canada or the condemnation of nuclear weapons as instruments of war in Japan.

Another important complex of political styles involves descriptions and critiques of public policy in the mass media and by various public and private dissenters. Each society has a different tradition and tolerance of policy assessments from those outside of the government. While a lively and free press and a tradition of citizen willingness to make demands through constitutionally protected rights such as freedom of speech, press, and assembly are prerequisites for modern democracies, that is neither widely appreciated by publics nor always tolerated by states. Such differences are more than symbolic: Open and democratic political systems promote greater liberty than repressive or authoritarian systems. Furthermore, there are differences even among equally liberal polities. Prior restraint and military censorship of the press are tolerated more in England than in the United States, though there has also been strict military censorship in times of war in the United States.

Different styles of civil liberties are associated with varying degrees of freedom of speech, press, assembly, and academy in a given polity. They are also associated with differences in traditions of information and education. Styles can be placed on a continuum from free to repressive. Polities like the United States—which have a style of reasonable tolerance of freedom of press, speech, and assembly—are fairly effective at holding government responsive to the public interest. Authoritarian systems that do not value civil liberties are more prone toward the sort of repression that the Chinese committed at Tianenmen Square.

Why is this so? In classic essays like John Stuart Mill's *On Liberty*,[22] political theorists have made the case that a free marketplace of ideas is an indispensable component of a good political system, particularly a democratic one. The first thing that most dictators do after taking power is to begin media censorship because truth about their activities can be a powerful weapon that can lead to popular disapproval, opposition, and their downfall. Similarly, the ancient tradition of academic freedom maintains that universities must be free from social and political interference as they work or they cannot examine ideas and expand the knowledge base that allows societies to progress. Moreover, loyal dissidents driven by political obligations to try to change odious governmental policies by demonstration and protest—and the corresponding government reactions—operate within a style firmly rooted in political theory. The bottom line is clear: Degrees and traditions of liberty and dissent make a difference in the quality of life among polities.

Important variations of political style among polities are also found in program origination and implementation. The inquiry that goes into identifying problems that need government attention depends on values and perceptions of the public interest. Because problems are not facts, both the acknowledgment of a problem and its perception and definition depend on values. What problems are considered important varies because values differ sharply among political systems.

The values found in political theory also influence who is responsible for initiating programs to deal with social problems—how and by whom they are designed, which social goals get maximized by public policy, and how policies are implemented and sold. The centralized government style of France (which leads Paris to dominate what goes on in the provinces) is a style far different from the policy dominance of Canada's ten provinces and Switzerland's cantons. While policy implementation styles are very complex because they respond to many more variables than do some other aspects of political style covered in the preceding discussion, they are just as important in shaping the overall direction of a polity.

Political theory plays a major role in political change as well. An important set of variables in this political area involves judgments about the values, pace, and means of change. Polities responsive to public opinion and change have styles that reward evolutionary activities and oppose those who wish to overthrow or even radically change the established order. Clearly this is the attitude shown in the United States toward war protesters during the Vietnam and Iraq wars. They were urged to "work within the system" and protest lawfully and quietly, irrespective of the effectiveness of their dissent. Those who advocated overthrow and replacement of the whole system or who undertook campaigns of civil disobedience (or even legal mass protest) have often met criticism as being disloyal and unpatriotic.[23] This contrasts with styles of political change widely practiced and advocated by a significant sector of opinion trend-setters (though definitely less widely tolerated by the government) in France in 1968, in East Germany in 1989, or in the Palestinian intifada in the early 1990s in the Israeli-occupied West Bank. There, mass protests and civil disobedience have been generally more accepted by the people and felt to be less unpatriotic than in the United States. Perhaps that is why they have ultimately been perceived as less threatening to the survival of the polity. In yet another example, in Iran during the 1970s and 1980s, mass protest was even officially sponsored.

But in the United States, those who only wanted to change the country's foreign policy goals and tactics—and not to overthrow the system—were cautioned to go more slowly. They were judged to be violating the prevailing theories of patriotism and political obligation that form the foundation of this pro-regime style.

The particulars of morally valid changes are components of this aspect of political style. Stability and justice play out differently in polities that tolerate more sweeping demands for institutional and policy change than those which do not. More tolerant polities place greater emphasis on justice and less on stability. Some will tolerate or even institutionalize sweeping changes of institutions and processes pushed by massive mobilizations of public opinion. Whether through referenda—as in the case of secessionist sentiments by the French in the Canadian province of Quebec—or by general strikes and other mass actions leading to the downfall of governments in Italy, France, or England[24] at various times, political styles do indeed differ. The tradition of revolutionary overthrow of regimes in European communism, for example, surely contributed to the revolutionary ends and means associated with the apparent end of communism in Eastern Europe during the late 1980s and early 1990s. The values of equality and justice and the lure of liberty as a missing ingredient were also factors of political theory in that historic transformation.

CONCLUSION: A DEFENSE OF POLITICS

Let us end this chapter by returning to its original theme: Political theory ultimately is about politics . . . and politics matters. Far more than a set of great thoughts or historical curiosities, political theory dwells in our public lives and can make a positive (or negative) contribution to our vital public relationships. Regardless of which political style dominates our experiences at a given moment, we are in a political environment and part of that world is political theory.

We believe that is as it should be. The tendency now in our political culture to downgrade the utility of politics is unfortunate. Why? We see politics as an honorable, defensible activity that can allow us to relate to each other in more satisfying ways than by any other alternative. For us to deny the worth of politics is to deny a very effective tool for a better life.

Politics and political theory at their best share the admirable purpose of enhancing and defending human life. The political obligations we form toward each other are neither neutral nor abstract. They can and should be positive moral goods that are building blocks of forming and operating governments. When functioning at or near its full potential, government can be a robust, beneficial public force. Because of its power and representativeness, legitimate government is well suited to attack a wide spectrum of social ills.

Government also allows us to accomplish collectively what cannot be done by us in isolation or in small groups. Together we can pool our resources and learn to accommodate each other's needs. Even in this age of skepticism about government, we have the capacity to collectively attack the regional and global ravages of pollution. Also, providing cost-effective water for parched neighborhoods and fields, fostering economic development, providing public education, defending against enemies, bridging raging rivers, putting out fires, fostering human dignity, and providing medical care are but a few of the potential accomplishments of government.

We should not forget that government is the institutionalization of politics. The polity cannot be separated from the values, relationships, and the patriotism that form its sinews. If we value the social protection and opportunities achieved by the best of governments, we must also value the political theory and the politics that drive and guide them. To appreciate government's worth and to participate in it for that reason serve to validate and perpetuate its positive features.

Government at its best synchronizes our individual self-interests. It can couple the motive power of our synchronized self-interest to the public interest and help us live a better life. Furthermore, the alternative to this kind of political commitment is unappealing. If a large proportion of those of us who have a stake in politics are not involved in it, we clear a path for the organized remainder (special interest groups) to capture political processes and turn them to their own advantage. They fill the vacuum created by the general public's sense of inefficacy and apathy and acquire the power to make public policy serve private goals.

Using their resources to hire a powerful array of pollsters, campaign consultants, and public relations people, these interest groups can and do couple their own narrow—though not necessarily evil—interests to the public interest. Unfortunately, society can suffer in the process. After all, what is good for a powerful special interest is not necessarily good for the nation. While truckers, for example, will make more profit from triple-bottom trucks, the nation's roads may be punished by them and traffic safety may deteriorate.

For these reasons, we view politics and government as a legitimate and useful process. In fact, we personally participate in American politics. We try to bring our individual concerns to the political sphere and try to steer outcomes in desirable directions in many different ways. We urge you to consider doing the same. After all, we do share a small and fragile planet.

GLOSSARY OF KEY TERMS

capitalism A political economy model wherein distribution of goods and services is in private hands and government plays a light regulatory role and provides order.

civil liberties Freedoms of speech, press, and assembly are usually included. A concept that guarantees the right of political participation by minorities and gives them a chance to participate in a free marketplace of ideas. It is usually considered an integral requirement for stable democracy.

democracy A form of self-rule. Government by the people.

dictatorship A form of government characterized by rule of a single individual.

government-guided economy A political economy characterized by a substantial amount of government planning and intervention into the economy.

laissez faire capitalism A free-enterprise political economy characterized by minimal government intervention in the economy.

lobbying The act of petitioning government officials to enact certain policies. It is usually done by interest groups and individuals.

oligarchy A form of government characterized by rule of a few.

parliamentary democracy A British-invented form of representative democracy with no separation of powers and legislative supremacy. The prime minister executive is elected by parliament and is leader of the majority party.

participatory democracy The form of democracy where the people make policy directly, without elected officials. Also called direct democracy.

presidential democracy A U.S.-invented form of indirect democracy that has separation of powers, staggered elections, an independent executive, and—in the United States—a nonelected, life-tenure judiciary.

political culture The dominant attitude of a nation's citizenry toward their politics and government.

political institutions Organized forms of political relationships that define the powers and roles of political leaders. Governments are prime examples.

political style The term the authors use to summarize different political behaviors and techniques found in various political cultures and forms of government.

political theory of public utilities A political theory holding that government has a moral responsibility to allocate (directly or indirectly) basic needs like housing, food, and public transportation for its citizens.

regulation A tool consisting of government commands and legislation that stipulates market or public safety behavior. It usually consists of rules for economic providers in capitalistic societies.

representative democracy Indirect democracy. The people select rulers and hold them responsive to public opinion through lobbying and periodic general elections.

socialism A model of political economy wherein economic allocation relies on government distribution of goods and services either directly or through extensive regulation.

SUGGESTIONS FOR FURTHER READING

Bloom, Allan. *The Closing of the American Mind*. New York: Simon and Shuster, 1987.

Dahl, Robert, ed. *Political Oppositions in Western Democracies*. New Haven: Yale University Press, 1966.

Dolbeare, Kenneth M. *American Political Thought*. 2d ed. Chatham, NJ: Chatham House, 1989.

Dubnick, Melvin J., and Bardes, Barbara A. *Thinking About Public Policy: A Problem-Solving Approach*. New York: John Wiley and Sons, 1983.

Dye, Thomas R. *Who's Running America? The Reagan Years*. 3d ed. Englewood Cliffs, N.J.: Prentice-Hall, 1983.

Hartz, Louis. *The Liberal Tradition in America*. New York: Harcourt, Brace, Jovanovich, 1962.

Herson, Lawrence J. R. *The Politics of Ideas: Political Theory and Public Policy*. Homewood, Ill.: Dorsey Press, 1984.

Norton, Philip. *The British Polity*. 2d ed. New York: Longman, 1991.

Pateman, Carole. *The Problem of Political Obligation*. New York: John Wiley and Sons, 1979.

Phelps, Edmund. *Political Economy*. New York: W. W. Norton, 1985.

Ranney, Austin. *The Doctrine of Responsible Party Government*. Urbana: University of Illinois Press, 1962.

Roth, David, Warwick, Paul, and Paul, David. *Comparative Politics*. New York: Harper & Row, 1989.

Sibley, Mulford Q. *Political Ideas and Ideologies*. New York: Harper & Row, 1970.

NOTES

1. David Roth, Paul Warwick, and David Paul, *Comparative Politics* (New York: Harper & Row, 1989), chapter 3.
2. Political culture is defined by us to mean our dominant attitudes about politics and government that we have received from the society around us. It embodies our political values.
3. Socialization is a sociological term that refers to the patterns of learning about cultural norms that family, peers, media, churches, schools, and the rest foster in us as we grow up and absorb the norms of society.

4. What political scientist David Easton referred to as the authoritative allocation of values in *The Political System: An Inquiry into the State of Political Science,* 2d ed. (New York: Alfred A. Knopf, 1971).
5. Political economy is defined operationally by examining the relationship of its political and economic components. Both involve public relationships and inter-dependence of strangers who have to deal with each other in some way in order to survive as fellow inhabitants of the same small planet. Wars, values, and political and economic institutions are neither political nor economic; they are both. Thus political economy describes the fact that most economic institutions have a political component and vice versa and that it makes sense to think of them as a seamless whole. See the discussion of these in Jeffrey Orenstein, *United States Railroad Policy* (Chicago: Nelson-Hall, 1990).
6. Of course political theorists do not agree on how to make values institutionally operational even when they agree on similar values. Theorists are influenced by their own assumptions and socialization patterns (which contribute to their personal values), their reading of human nature, and their assessment of the opportunities and/or limitations presented by population, education, technology, among other things.
7. See Carole Pateman, *The Problem of Political Obligation* (New York: John Wiley and Sons, 1979), and Michael Walzer, *Obligations* (Cambridge: Harvard University Press, 1970), for example.
8. See the following chapter on democracy for a little sample of this.
9. The People's Republic of China still has a highly centralized political system, despite the moves to decentralize some markets.
10. Nikolai Lenin, Mao Tse-tung, and Joseph B. Tito were influential political leaders and institution-builders of the Union of Soviet Socialist Republics, the People's Republic of China, and Yugoslavia in the twentieth century.
11. St. Thomas Aquinas wrote *Summa Theologica,* and St. Augustine wrote *The City of God,* among other major works. Both were advocates of rule by kings who were agents of God and the church and who had to follow extra-worldly values. Muhammad was a prophet of the Muslim religion and his thoughts are found most prominently in the Koran.
12. Edmund Phelps, *Political Economy* (New York: W. W. Norton, 1985), p. xiii.
13. This definition assumes a Western, classically liberal viewpoint shared by most political economists. For a more thorough discussion of these issues and ideas, see Phelps, *Political Economy,* or Orenstein, op. cit., especially chapter 2.
14. See Orenstein, op. cit., pp. 26–28.
15. In the literature of political theory, they are sometimes known as philosophical anarchists; in popular jargon, they have been called libertarians.
16. We define a style of politics as a paradigm or dominant trend of political ideas. It is similar conceptually to political culture. As we use it, *style* incorporates the sociological context of most comparative politics and adds a stronger component of political ideas to the mix.
17. Phillip Norton, *The British Polity,* 2d ed. (New York: Longman, 1991), chapter 5.
18. Ibid.
19. Surely values examined in other contexts in this volume—about the importance of the individual and the saliency of politics in the lives of U.S. citizens—contribute to the American democratic style and are affected by it as well.
20. Such groups are called special interests or interest groups. They most often have economic agendas, but they have been known to have symbolic or noneconomic desires as well.

21. Roth, Warwick, and Paul, *Comparative Politics*, chapter 5.
22. John Stuart Mill, *Utilitarianism, on Liberty, and Representative Government* (New York: Dutton, 1951).
23. See the description of this tendency toward intolerance in U.S. political culture in Louis Hartz, *The Liberal Tradition in America* (New York: Harcourt, Brace, Jovanovich, 1955).
24. In England, riots protesting the hated poll tax and demanding the removal of Margaret Thatcher in 1990 were evidently effective since Prime Minister Thatcher resigned under their pressure.

Chapter
11

Political Theory and Democracy

*D*emocracy—the very word has stirred passions down through the ages. It means self-government. Such a simple idea has ignited centuries of thinking and controversy. Virtually all political thinkers (and some intellectual giants who were not explicitly political thinkers) have put democracy on their agenda. So have many reformers and revolutionaries. As a consequence, we have a rich legacy of democratic political theory and a lively public interest in democracy. Self-government has held such a powerful sway over the popular imagination and needs that even those hostile to democracy, like Plato, were forced to deal with and try to refute its elements.

Democracy has been an idea that will not go away, in spite of repeated attempts by the powerful to suppress it. It is older than Pericles' defense of public participation in ancient Athens. It is as contemporary as the demands for democratic reforms in the new Russian Parliament, the struggles for democracy in Poland, or the courageous students gunned down while demanding democracy in Beijing. Thus its future in political theory seems as bright as its past.

While we discussed democracy in Chapter 3 in the context of community and authority, more discussion is needed. This is a subject of great importance in this age of spreading democracy.

Since democracy and the machinery used to empower it change with morals and events, our thoughts about them also change with the times. It must be so if we are going to continue to ask valid questions about democratic polities in an age of computers and satellites. Without asking the right questions, we have no real hope of recommending how to adapt democracy to a changing world.

For example, changes with potentially revolutionary implications are the burgeoning modern developments and progress in communications and transportation. This new climate of rapid information processing and dissemination has made political theory's classical analyses of participation and representation in democratic theory empirically, if not normatively, suspect. It is scarcely too strong a claim to state that it has rendered them obsolete.

Now it is finally possible to have direct citizen policy-making in large, complex polities. (Before the microprocessor age, it was only physically possible in small polities with a leisure class supported by an underclass who did the mundane physical things necessary to give full citizens the time to devote to the practice of democracy.) Just as this chapter has been "penned" with the assistance of a computer, future democracy may be "penned" with the assistance of analogous machines. In both cases, the overall goals (communication of ideas and making public choices, respectively) do not change with the advent of new technology. What changes is the ease with which previously difficult tasks ("cutting and pasting" and "consulting, articulating, and aggregating public opinion," respectively) can be accomplished. With greater ease of performance, the tasks are done more often and can be done more effectively since improvement often accompanies practice. Our ability to implement the laudable goals of democracy has made a quantum leap. Therefore, political theory is challenged to think about new technology that gives ordinary people the time and means to learn about far-off events and personalities and to engage in face-to-face debate and voting on the issues. To put it in practical terms, successful democracy should mean something different to us than it did to the classical masters of democratic theory because it no longer need result in unprepared people making important public decisions.

This example demonstrates that a task for the modern political theory of democracy is "simply" to continue to take the seminal thoughts of Rousseau, Locke, Mill, Green,[1] and other theorists of democracy and adapt them to the world we live in. What is true for the relationship of participatory democracy and technology is also the case for many other issues which surround democracy. Times change and so must democratic political theory. The tradition of democratic theorizing must continue by reexamining and interpreting enduring democratic concepts in a spirit which looks to recombine old ideas to apply to new circumstances as a valid approach to political thought.

Clearly such an enterprise will raise far more questions than it settles since the moral questions surrounding democracy and the contemporary physical realities of participation are complex. Thus the need for political theory about democracy in the future will surely be as great as the need for it today or yesterday. Democratic theory has a historically pivotal place in Western political thought because it examines what people want to know about the best form of government and the proper relationships of citizen and ruler. These weighty issues have not been—cannot be—settled definitively. Therefore, our times continue to bear witness to the power of democracy and the vitality of its theorizing.

DEFINITIONS AND COMMONALITIES

It is necessary to start with a clear working definition of democracy in order to think creatively about which ideas are sensible in a democracy. Without knowledge of what democracy is we cannot understand what to do with it today. Democracy is generally defined as rule by the people in a political system, that is, self-government by adult citizens. This radical notion of the people governing is accurate, but it is also the tip of an iceberg—merely a signpost directing us down the path toward the theoretical, philosophical, and institutional richness of self-government in this twenty-sixth century of political theory.

Even though those who value democracy—known as democrats—do not think exactly alike, they share a belief in many principles which are reflected in the literature of political theory. Very prominent among these is the idea that citizens are morally entitled to band together with their neighbors, to speak out on the issues of the day, and to attempt to convince a majority of their fellow citizens of their intellectual and political objectives in what English political theorist John Stuart Mill referred to as the free marketplace of ideas.[2] In other words, elementary civil liberties like freedom of speech, press, and assembly (those rights which allow minorities a fair chance to bid for majority status) are valued by all democrats, and they are especially important to those who trace their roots to the Western liberal tradition of individual rights. Even if the ideas of people are offensive or even wacky, true democrats believe that they should be heard. To fail to guarantee this right is to open the floodgates of repression, as history has shown. In short, the best exception to the free exercise of ideas is no exception because democracy cannot flourish without a lively tradition of these civil rights.

All serious democrats also share the conviction that citizens have a moral right and the collective, if not individual, capacity to pick the rulers, if not the policies, of government. They feel that people count and that it is morally and empirically right to ensure meaningful citizen participation in the government in which all have a common stake. It is a matter of simple arithmetic: To fail to pursue democracy is to allow the few to tell the many what to do. This offends democrats because they believe that all have a moral claim to help steer society since it does control their lives and fortunes. If people are of equal moral worth, they should have equal political empowerment.

In addition, all good democrats feel compelled to abide by the outcome of a democratic process regardless of how personally distasteful the results may be to the player and his or her supporters because the process itself is intrinsically valuable. The name for this commitment is democratic political culture. Political culture is a subset of general culture that concerns the dominant political values, beliefs, and emotions shared by a nation's citizens. It is the major predictor of our attitudes about political values such as liberty and equality, whether we vote, whether we vote for the person or the party, and whether we support democracy, monarchy, oligarchy, or another political system. A democratic culture is a subset of the subset since, in effect, it defines the dominant values and attitudes associated with a particular kind of political system, a democracy.

Holders of democratic political culture feel that the process of self-government is so good in the long run that they rank it higher than their immediate self-interest of winning or losing in a given case. They reason that it is better to risk losing an election that was conducted fairly and openly than it is to "fix" the process, thereby guaranteeing the outcome but attacking the very system norms (values) that democrats cherish and which provide the hope of political justice. Similarly, real democrats always place willingness to abide by administrative decisions, legislative votes, and other expressions of public opinion over and above whatever advantages might or are alleged to be found in coups d'état, assassinations, electoral fraud, dissolving of the constitution, setting aside unpleasant election results by angry executives, refusals to vacate an office upon defeat, or other acts of frustration of the public will.

Adherents to democratic culture feel this way because they know that the game of democracy is worth playing since participants can win something just by playing, even if they lose on some or even many issues. They believe that a democracy that is fair enough to avoid automatic winners and losers morally binds its participants to agree in advance to play the game according to its rules. Any subversions of the game itself are abhorrent for representative and participatory democrats alike.[3]

Even though they are very valuable, democratic cultural norms are quite fragile. It is difficult to get them to take root and they are easily destroyed by violations, especially when a cultural tradition is young. Once they are established, however, they can be very powerful. Such norms cause a defeated president or legislator to surrender his or her office and cooperate with the transition to a successor even though there is personal hurt and a (perhaps not articulated) belief that the voters did not choose the best person for the office. After a presidential election in the United States—as in other countries with a similar democratic culture—there are no tanks ringing the White House and no one wonders whether the armed forces will obey the new chief executive. Instead, transition teams are quickly formed and the new president-elect is brought up to speed on policy and programs by the defeated occupant of the oval office. Similarly, in a smoothly running democracy, citizens believe in their right to be heard and do not hesitate to take advantage of it. As democratic practitioners, they feel the need to (and sometimes actually do) keep informed and get involved in the political system by voting and other legitimate forms of political participation.

DIVERGENCES

Even though the significant democratic theorists generally unite on most of the basic concepts of democracy, they do not think exactly alike. Democrats are seriously divided on some important concepts as well as some fundamental institutional prescriptions for implementing democracy.

The principal split is between participatory and representative democratic theorists. Participatory (or direct) democrats feel that authentic self-government can only happen when citizens participate directly in the institutions and policy-making of a nation. On the other hand, representative (or indirect) democrats feel that citizen selection and periodic reselection of governing elites (as opposed to direct decision making) fully satisfy the requirements of democracy. Participatory advocates often label the process of representation—in which one person represents or speaks for others—a danger point for citizen rights, a figurative (if not literal) act of tyranny whereby elites vote their own interests and ignore the public interest.[4] Their pro-representative brethren respond by suggesting that representation is not only not tyrannical, but that it is a good, practical way to make government responsive to public opinion and citizen needs because the elites will listen to the public when the public has the choice to reelect them or not.[5]

THE PARTICIPATORY DEMOCRATS

In examining the case of participatory democrats, it is evident that they interpret the requirements of self-rule in democratic theory quite literally. They hold that all legitimate adult citizens who are affected by policy—virtually all who are not ruled out because of youth, criminal, or alien status—should have an equal say in debating, making, and implementing policy in a truly democratic state. To do otherwise would be to needlessly introduce elements of inefficiency, unresponsiveness, and perhaps even tyranny into the system. They maintain that only face-to-face contact (or its electronic equivalent) by citizens can produce the give-and-take and compromise that result in good democratic practice and policy over the long haul. Moreover, they believe that the very act of direct participation leads to a heightened sense of efficacy and interest that becomes a self-fulfilling prophecy. That is, citizens rise to the task of becoming good policymakers (equal to or better than their elite counterparts) because they are given the tools and the responsibility/opportunity of so doing. They use their talents to do the citizen's job well because a good job is in their self-interest: it affects their lives positively. New England town meetings; the Landsgemeinde in Switzerland (annual public meetings in some entire Swiss provinces that serve the same functions); the widespread use of binding votes (referenda) by the citizens at large in Swiss national and provincial politics; and the occasional (and not always binding) use of similar votes in some U.S. cities and states for policy issues and constitutional amendments are some examples of this kind of democracy in practice. Those who advocate it today suggest that it is quite practical in any size political system. They also maintain that it is as efficient as any other kind of democracy. More importantly, they think it is morally best because it is the only kind of democracy that avoids the tyranny or ineffectiveness of some speaking in behalf of others.

In other words, contemporary participatory democratic theorists answer the widespread criticisms about its being impractical to implement—and, therefore, just an idealistic dream—by advancing the modern claim that electronics (interactive cable television systems, computers, telephones, videocassette recorders, etc.) make this form of democracy possible today. They think it has reduced the size of even the biggest democracy to a manageable level, where information can flow from government to citizens and vice versa with ease, accuracy, and speed. The time-shifting capability of VCRs even answers the objections of sympathetic critics—like the political theorist Michael Walzer—who have asked whether the demands of policy-making will outstrip the amount of time ordinary citizens might wish to devote to information gathering and participation in a direct democracy. Information televised while citizens are at work or play can be recorded and viewed later, and votes can be registered at the convenience of the voter through the capabilities of modern electronics.

To them, a giant nation like the United States today is practically as small in terms of the physical requirements of democracy as classical Athens ever was—or maybe even smaller. Thus to them the question about how big or small the ideal participatory democracy should be has been answered. It is of any size as long as it is knit together electronically.

However, the fact that we can have a kind of participatory democracy in this age of the microelectronics revolution does not answer the question of whether we ought to have it. Participatory democracy requires a lot of citizen competence, knowledge, and interest. It is unclear whether the self-fulfilling prophecy hypothesis (that citizens will rise to the occasion of being good participants because they can and because their participation matters) is sufficiently valid to ensure enough good participation by citizens to avoid elite rule and, in effect, the tyranny of representation.

Modern democratic theory does not answer this question. Therefore, the topic should occupy a prominent place on our research agenda for the near future. Pending the results about how it might work out over time, there are enough results known now to suggest that participatory democracy is a candidate for national referenda and local and regional governing, even if no nations adopt it as their form of national decision making.

THE REPRESENTATIVE DEMOCRATS

Opposed to participatory democracy's champions are those democrats who advocate indirect democracy. They frequently claim that direct democracy should be rejected because it is inevitably accompanied by low turnout, low voter competency, and the impracticality of operation. They suggest that these scourges can be avoided by the practice of representative democracy.

These are unfair criticisms to level at participatory democracy alone. Unfortunately, while representative democrats are right about these problems (which are hard ones in modern times), the practice of representative democracy does not cure them. It, too, suffers from low turnout, poor citizen preparation, and additional problems of lack of effective representation. It is just as difficult for citizens to determine which group of people pledged to what ideas should rule as it is to decide important policy issues. Such problems are part of all forms of democracy. Luckily, the advantages of all forms of democracy help to offset these democratic problems. Thus it is unfair for one brand of democrat to saddle another brand with problems common to both of them. Also, we still might want to embrace democracy, in spite of these problems.

It is less easy to brush aside another issue representative democrats raise against direct democracy. They suggest that it is morally wrong to have a system of government where the expert yield to the lowest common denominator and, in effect, create a decision-making structure in which a majority of fools lead a minority (by definition) of experts.[6] The representative democrats suggest that their kind of indirect self-rule will allow elites to rule, subject only to the broad outlines of public opinion.

This objection is not fully convincing, however. It is certainly true that every society is populated by some people who are wiser than others, whether by environmental or hereditary advantage. However, the wise group is not the same for every issue. In order to make sure that all those who have wisdom have their say on issues over time, it might be best to enfranchise everybody, just in case everybody is an expert on something that may come up in the course of governing over the long haul. In addition, it is not proven fact that the majority will always be wrong or foolish. Sometimes the majority can be right and smart. It is also a sensible moral claim to suggest that all have an equal stake in the outcome of decisions made by a democratic state and all, therefore, should have an equal right to participate in those decisions. Clearly this is an issue that has always evoked a lot of passions in democratic theory and it is not easily settled.

Representative democratic theorists are a very influential group. In our times, they have won the intramural debate among democratic theorists since they advocate the kind of democratic polity that most democratic nations have adopted today. There is little public debate on the topic. They have convinced most Westerners that a representative democratic system is fully democratic, provided that people are allowed to select their rulers and force those elites to be responsive to public opinion through a periodic reselection process.

Indirect democrats assert that tyranny need not (and will not) result from representation as long as certain common sense arrangements are followed. They hold that a system in which elites (representing but not actually being all of the people) make policy decisions and have complete practical sovereignty is as democratic as any participatory scheme. This is so, they claim, because elites in a representative democracy are held responsive to public opinion through a political process which involves periodic elections and other reliable, effective means of public choice. This forces elites to govern in the public interest rather than their own. Thus the many parliamentary and presidential systems of government found today are deemed democratic by definition if they have the minimal institutional mechanisms necessary to secure responsive rule by elites.

This claim by representative democrats suggests that as long as the institutional democratic safeguards and techniques are maintained, representation will be both responsive and effective. Even though citizens cannot make policy directly in such democracies, they can influence the broad outlines and directions of policy through compulsory mandates placed into the system by voters at the ballot box. It is assumed that if elites ignore these mandates, they will be out of a job, though this assumption by representative democrats ignores or discounts the possibility that representatives may conceal the truth or blur the lines of responsibility. These theorists also do not confront the problem of how to deal with split public opinion—or cases in which no clear mandate is evident—as has occurred in recent elections in such diverse systems as Israel, Italy, France, and in the divided U.S. system, wherein one party frequently controls the legislature and another the administration.

Indirect democracy advocates further claim that citizens are better served by this kind of democracy because they are not overtaxed in either time or knowledge; the people are asked "only" whether they feel that elite group A versus group B or C better fits their image of what they want and who they trust. It is suggested that citizens do better under this system because their occasional participation—though it is a valued citizen right—is not intensely time consuming, and thus they have more time for the other parts of their lives.

Since this kind of system has been adopted in so many modern democracies and its principles are effectively part of most Western political cultures, these claims need to be examined carefully.

To begin with, many citizens in such systems choose not to participate in even such minimal acts as periodic voting. In the United States in recent times, about half of the eligible citizens vote in presidential elections; still fewer citizens vote in state, local, and nonpresidential federal elections; and even fewer lobby the elites, work in campaigns, contribute money, run for office, or participate in other ways that go beyond voting.[7] Many other democracies also have alarmingly low rates of participation, although few are so low as in the U.S. polity.[8]

While this does not mean that representative democracy cannot work, it is a signal that not all citizens feel represented or efficacious enough to participate even at the low level required by this form of democracy. The mandate transmitted to elites surely is weak if it comes from a small portion of all adult citizens, even if they are a majority percentage of those who actually vote in a given election. Citizens must be educated, interested in the democratic process, and have access to information in order to have a chance to control the elites effectively, whether in an indirect or a direct democracy.

Also, examination of the constitutions and operations of a good cross-section of political systems that consider themselves to be representative democracies shows that not all of them have purely democratic institutions. Frequently, representative institutions share governing power with elites appointed by elected elites and—more undemocratic yet—with elites who are not even indirectly responsive to public opinion. In the latter category are the lifetime appointments made to the U.S. Supreme Court and overall federal judicial system and the life and hereditary peers in the British House of Lords. These officials have a great deal of power (especially the U.S. judiciary) and are not forced to respond to citizen mandates. Appointed elites who go out of office once their appointers are defeated at the ballot box are not such a serious problem since they are at least indirectly responsive to public opinion. Every layer of indirectness, though, makes the system that much more cumbersome to steer through the mechanism of public opinion. Since representative democracy must be somewhat responsive to public opinion if it is going to work, the more a supposedly representative democratic political system contains nondemocratic elements, the closer it veers toward the quicksand of potential tyranny.

In other words, the performance and political theory surrounding modern representative democracy implies that Rousseau's dictum that representation is tyranny is not necessarily true. Representation can be effective and democratic, but there are no guarantees: it is often not so. Only careful attention to some minimal criteria of representation and a set of institutional arrangements can guarantee that public mandates rule even indirectly in a system where elites make the rules. In effect, representative democracy can work effectively if representative democrats work very hard at keeping it responsive. While there are many variations of the institutional path to effective representative democracy, all of them share a couple of major components. The first necessary institutional requirement is that citizens must have an extremely reliable mechanism to hold all governing elites responsive to public opinion. In the evolution of modern democratic states, this has come to mean (in practical terms) that there must be an election process which is both fair and effective.

This can only be accomplished by a system that provides effective, meaningful citizen choice among competing elites in order to hold elite feet close to the fire of public opinion. If the entire governing team of elite A is thrown out of office (not reelected) for poor performance or dishonesty, it is assumed that the lesson of what happens to a dishonest or incompetent elite group is not lost on the elite group that replaces it. The act of "throwing the rascals out" creates the incentive for elites to remain on the electorate's good side by delivering what they have advertised, speaking to public opinion to a reasonable extent.

The best practical way to ensure this is to elect whole, interchangeable governments, not just individual offices. That way, elites are given the incentive to work within the group to pick good leaders in the first place and to make sure that they are following the public interest once in office. In other words, there must be collective responsibility wherein a unified and clearly identifiable elite group with a clear set of policies stands ready to assume all of the offices of a government for a finite term and is prepared to stand or fall upon the performance of its people and policies at the next election. If only a few are elected at a time, the lines of responsibility are blurred, the electoral mandate is seriously weakened, and citizens are divided. Frequently this results in loss of the public interest. Since this kind of electoral concept suggests that one rotten apple spoils the barrel and the whole barrel must be replaced, elite barrel tenders must put good apples in it or suffer the consequences.

A like-minded group of barrel tenders and occupants prepared to govern—with a collective standing on its platform of policies and programs—is, of course, a political party. The relationships of parties to each other within a given democracy characterizes a party system. To put it simply, the most practical way that has evolved to implement the first minimal component of representative democracy is a genuine system of general elections that allows all adult citizens to be able to vote on a whole government. In other words, real indirect democracy must have a universal franchise and a functioning party system with at least two competing parties who not only campaign but can also govern if elected. This gives citizens a simple, effective choice among competing elites. (Logic dictates choice between at least two, but more are acceptable, as long as the practical requirement of garnering a majority via coalitions or the like is addressed.)

The key is that citizens must be able to replace an entire government, not just individual parts of it. To do otherwise creates the ability of elites to evade responsibility. More critically, it destroys democracy's incentive for them to respond to the citizens' collective wishes.

Taken literally, a general election is one that has universal sweep. In a truly representative democratic system, all citizens (all adults who are not aliens, criminals, mentally incompetent, etc.) can go to the ballot box on a certain day and remove (or reelect, if they so choose) the whole government. Any electoral process that is staggered in time or scope fails to be adequately democratic, no matter how fairly ballots are counted, how often the polls are open, or what percentage of citizens they attract. If rulers can hide under the cover of divided authority and/or actually do share authority with appointed governors (or even those elected by separate constituencies or at separate times), citizens cannot hold the government responsive to public opinion because they can never throw all of the rascals out at one time—and the rascals know it. In other words, separation of powers may check some kinds of tyranny by setting elites against elites, but it frustrates the critical general electoral component of the most effective controller of tyranny known to humanity: democracy. Divided government dilutes citizen voices in a representative democracy. Unfortunately, this weakens democracy's crucial translation of the effective self-interest of citizens into public policy. The point is not widely understood in America, but it is still true. The mere presence of openly and fairly conducted elections does not make a political system a representative democracy. Only general elections can do so, as long as at least one other element is also present.

The other element necessary for indirect self-rule is a free, sufficient climate of information. If citizens are to be effective sovereign electors, the ultimate decision-makers in the system, they must have the ability and the freedom to get knowledge about public officials and affairs so that they can make informed choices. This kind of knowledge can only be guaranteed by a shared commitment to civil liberties, of course. Consequently, both partici- patory and representative democrats ought to value a healthy information climate.

The costs of obtaining information about such matters as policy perfor- mance, veracity, and competence of policymakers must be low (in terms of time and effort required for the average citizen) in order to have a good information climate. Full and understandable analyses of all major public issues need to be widely available from redundant and competing sources like an unfettered electronic and print press if citizens are to have the necessary information to know what is going on. If there is only a party line or an official government press, those who sponsor it often use it to make themselves look good, smear would-be opponents, and generally withhold embarrassing information. Only a truly free press allows the citizen to be shown if the emperor has no clothes.

Similarly, the sovereign people in a representative democracy must have full freedoms of speech and assembly. These civil rights allow the mobiliza- tion of effective (usually loyal) opposition and create the free marketplace of ideas that allows truth to surface.[9] As a prerequisite to all of this, citizens must be literate and educated if they are to function effectively as electors. Thus a truly democratic representative government requires a universal, free, and competent educational system which allows the free inquiry of ideas about government and society that is found in political science and other disciplines where there is free academy. As Jefferson believed,[10] citizens need to be educated in order to understand complex events and the subtle personality nuances of elites. They have to have a civic education that trains them to ask the right questions about policies, governors, and processes. They also need to know how to evaluate data about elites who have a self-interest in disinfor- mation or obfuscation. They must understand what democracy is, what foreign and domestic policy is and ought to be, and so forth. In short, effective citizens in a good representative system must be virtually as well educated as their participatory brethren if they are going to do their part to keep and defend indirect democracy. Since the citizen's incentive of directly governing is missing in representative systems, this requirement must be pursued vigorously if elites are to be made to take the electorate and its mandates seriously.

To do otherwise would invite the tragedy of an elite gaining power democratically (as Hitler may have done) and then using that power to destroy democracy. A good climate of information will prevent rulers from circumventing democracy by forcing them to risk elections (and possible losses) by focusing the fire of public opinion on them if they attempt to circumvent fair elections through manipulation or suppression of civil liberties, failing to follow the rules, and suppressing and/or eliminating any opposition which points this out. Ultimately, democratic governments are obligated to accommodate the sovereignty of citizens rather than vice versa. Citizens must obey governments only until the next election. Governments must always acknowledge popular authority.

PERSPECTIVES AND CONCLUSIONS

It should be remembered that the two important representative elements in the preceding discussion operate within the context of and need for a democratic culture. While representative democracy shares this need and context with participatory democracy, it is even more critical for democracies to nurture the fragile roots of democracy in systems where citizens have neither the incentive to participate nor the assurance of self-representation. Surely the established democracies need to promote the use of their highly developed norms of playing by the rules that provide a strong bulwark against the abuse of power by elites in a representative polity. Without them, general elections and a free climate of information would not likely be as reliable as they are.

Taken together, these basic foundations for a representative democracy go a large measure of the distance toward preventing the problems of tyrannical representation that accompany the shift away from direct participation. If understood, appreciated, and defended, they provide a high probability that representative democracy can be made to work as a reliable form of self-government. History has shown that the more a system (such as the parliamentary form of government originated in England and used by many democratic nations) follows these criteria, the closer to the norm of rule by the people it will be. Presidential systems like that of the United States (with no truly general elections and weak party cohesion) have somewhat more difficulty than parliamentary systems in keeping governors responsive to public opinion, but that is by design. Their founders chose to balance democratic and nondemocratic elements in their constitutions—such as the appointed-for-life U.S. federal judiciary with its power of judicial review holding power over the people's elected representatives—because of a fear that "pure" democracy would be unstable or unwise. Interestingly, the general historical trend in the United States, at least, has been to move toward rather than away from democracy, probably because of a firmly rooted democratic culture. It appears that representative democracy is also sinking strong roots in Japan and the nations of Western Europe. (Some, like Switzerland, have been very democratic for a long time.) Many other nations, including some communist ones, are experimenting with various forms and degrees of democratization, but it is impossible to tell how that will trend since it is a very new process. Nevertheless, in the waning years of the twentieth century, democracy seems to be on a roll, although it is worthy of note that in places where democratic culture has not taken deep root—as in China and many (but not all) states in Latin America and Africa—there is still a long, rocky road for democracy to travel.

Most contemporary democratic theorists have made their peace with the pervasiveness of indirect forms of democracy in today's world. In fact it can be said that there is more interest and practice of that kind of democracy in the last few years of the twentieth century than there was in its first few years. Participatory democracies, however, have simply not taken root in this century to anywhere near the same extent, despite considerable agitation for them periodically (especially in the 1960s) and the potential empowerment modern technology brings to direct self-rule. Whether this trend will continue throughout the next century remains to be seen. What can be predicted with some certainty, however, is that democracy in some form will surely be with us a century from now. It is a form of government that is simply too appealing to deny for political theorists, constitution builders, and citizens alike.

Even though democracy's future seems assured, there are certainly controversies and problems that permeate contemporary democratic theory, even beyond the main debate about direct versus indirect democracy. Among the most interesting and highly contested areas of contemporary democratic theory are a series of problems and/or opportunities that all forms of democracy face, be they direct or indirect, parliamentary or presidential. One involves the issues of how you count votes. The issue of national proportional representation versus single-member, winner-take-all districts (or referendum counts) is more than a technicality of vote counting. Giving each party or point of view on an issue its proportional vote strength leads to multiparty representative systems or referenda in cases wherein the maybes might outnumber the ayes or nays. Winner-take-all systems—where the group that gets the majority gets the whole prize (the seat or the referendum outcome)— tend to be less fragmented and hence more stable. But they also tend to deny minorities their true strength. A party getting 49 percent of the vote on such an issue or contest gets the same representation as a party that receives 4.9 percent of the vote: exactly none. That leads to what a prominent early observer of the American scene has referred to as tyranny of the majority.[11] Democratic theorists are still wrestling with the pros and cons of that debate.

Another bundle of issues modern democratic theorists are wrestling with revolves around whom to enfranchise. What age, resident status, classification by mental health and legal authorities, and so on should be required to give a person residing in a given community full citizen rights? In other words, democracy needs to define who should be fully empowered as a democratic citizen and who should be an "associate citizen," otherwise known as a subject, because of his or her immaturity or other conditions. Can a nation be genuinely democratic if its children, resident aliens, criminals, and mentally ill citizens are denied the right to vote or run for office? Or is it sufficient that these individuals who are presumed to be unable to make responsible decisions are protected by civil rights and due process of law? Agreement on these answers has not been forthcoming from modern democratic theory, although a broad consensus on the rule of adulthood has emerged.

Contemporary democratic theory also needs to come to grips with the best techniques of providing a balance between the demands of national security and democratic openness. It is axiomatic that military secrecy and the requirements of the garrison state conflict with the need for openness required by democracy. This topic has not been seriously broached by democratic theorists to the degree required.

In addition, democracies constantly must struggle with the problem of securing good leadership in an environment that makes everyone politically equal and frequently offers greater rewards for talented people outside the public sector than within it. Dating all the way back to Thucydides,[12] political theorists have isolated the problem but have not come up with any widely accepted solutions to it. Surely it needs to be recognized that good leadership benefits any kind of democratic system and such leadership is not secured by wishing it to occur or by magic. Democracy needs to do better in this regard. Modern theorists need to focus more attention on the techniques of modern campaigns and elections (whether for offices or issues) and examine their leadership quality consequences more closely.

Ultimately, democracy is "merely" a system of government, a way of reaching unavoidable decisions about who is going to rule and what the public policies should be in a nation-state. It is a cluster of closely related but sometimes contending institutions of self-government that all rest upon the value of the moral self-worth and right of self-governance of all citizens. Democratic theorists and advocates alike embrace democracy because it allows those with a stake in society to have a meaningful say in the policies, personnel, and institutions that affect their public lives. In effect, the critical value embedded in all forms of democracy is that people are worth something and have a right to participate.

Beyond this, most Western liberal democrats are also attracted to democracy because they have felt that it secures certain other values necessary to a good polity. Liberty, equality, justice (embraced by theorists like Locke and Rousseau), and efficiency[13] are frequently cited in this context. In this sense, the "best" democracies are the ones which go the furthest in nurturing these values in the society. This is yet another perspective in deciding which kind of democracy makes the most sense. The problem is that democratic theorists not only do not always agree on which values are best but frequently also disagree about which values are best secured by which forms of democracy. For example, the laudable goal of efficiency may be best served by a highly elitist representative system that might not be very supportive of liberty, equality, or justice. Or perhaps just the opposite is true. There is simply not enough hard evidence to argue convincingly that any of these variations of democracy is inherently more supportive of one or another value or combination of them. It is enough to conclude that democracy is valuable in itself and it can certainly be made consistent with many other desirable values and forms of political economy.

In the final analysis, modern democratic theory demonstrates that democracy as a form of self-government is a practical and moral kind of political organization. While it has many variations and all of them have common and unique problems, the late British Prime Minister Winston Churchill probably had the best perspective about democracy when he said, "No one pretends that democracy is perfect or all-wise. Indeed, it has been said that democracy is the worst form of government except all those other forms that have been tried from time to time."[14]

GLOSSARY OF KEY TERMS

democracy A form of self-government by adult citizens. It can be direct or indirect.

democratic political culture A cultural component of democracy characterized by citizens and leaders feeling obligated to abide by the results of the democratic processes regardless of personal benefit in the short run.

democratic theory The political theories of democracy. It dates back to the beginnings of the discipline.

free climate of information A climate of civil liberties wherein the electorate has freedom of information unmolested by government and sufficient sources exist to provide enough information to make informed electoral choices.

general election An election in which all of the citizens may vote for or against the entire government.

judicial review The power of judges to declare acts of other governing officials unconstitutional and thereby nullify them. It is an invention of the United States.

mandates Legislative or electoral orders or edicts. In the case of elections, they are often ambiguous.

party cohesion Process wherein parties bind their legislative members to vote the party platform or agreed-upon position. Usually present in parliamentary systems. Allows voters to support groups which closely represent their principles.

political party A like-minded group of people who organize to get their members elected and to govern on the basis of a set of principles once they are elected.

primary election A party election wherein voters select who will be the party candidates in the general election. An alternative is a party caucus or convention.

proportional representation A voting system that gives parties strength in the government in direct proportion to their national electoral strength. It tends to encourage minor parties.

referendum A direct vote by the people on an issue of policy.

town meeting (or Swiss Landsgemeinde) An annual public meeting where all citizens assemble to make policy. A form of direct democracy.

tyranny Illegitimate political domination, whether by a dictator or a larger group.

tyranny of the majority A doctrine that holds that the majority can use its power to dominate others. It assumes that might wins whether it is right or not.

winner-take-all, single-member district representation A voting system that gives the party that takes any majority of the votes in a district the seat for the whole district. It tends to discourage minor parties.

SUGGESTIONS FOR FURTHER READING

Barber, Ben. *Strong Democracy: Participatory Democracy in a New Age*. Berkeley: University of California Press, 1984.

Cohen, Marshall, ed. *The Philosophy of John Stuart Mill*. New York: Modern Library, 1961.

Cranston, Maurice, ed. *Locke on Politics, Religion, and Education*. New York: Collier Books, 1965.

Darcy, R.; Welch, Susan; and Clark, Janet. *Women, Elections, and Representation*. New York: Longman, 1987.

Frantzich, Stephen E. *Political Parties in the Technological Age*. New York: Longman, 1989.

Friedrich, Carl J. *Constitutional Government and Democracy*. Waltham, Mass.: Blaisdell Publishing Company, 1968.

Girvetz, Harry K. *Democracy and Elitism*. New York: Charles Scribner's Sons, 1967.

Lowi, Theodore. *The End of Liberalism*. New York: W. W. Norton, 1969.

Niehbur, Reinhold, and Sigmund, Paul E. *The Democratic Experience: Past and Prospects*. New York: Praeger, 1969.

Pitkin, Hannah Fenichel, ed. *Representation*. New York: Atherton Press, 1969.

Plamenatz, John. *Democracy and Illusion: An Examination of Certain Aspects of Modern Democratic Theory*. London: Longman Group, 1973.

Plato. *The Republic*.

Rejai, Mustafa, ed. *Democracy: The Contemporary Theories*. New York: Atherton Press, 1967.

Rousseau, Jean Jacques. *The Social Contract and Discourses*. New York: E. P. Dutton and Co., 1950.

Thucydides. *History of the Peloponnesian War*. London: Penguin Group, 1972.

Tocqueville, Alexis de. *Democracy in America*. Translated by Henry Reeves. Boston: John Allyn, 1882.

Wilson, Woodrow. "The Meaning of Democracy" (campaign speech, Scranton, Penn., September 23, 1912). In *The Crossroads of Freedom: The 1912 Campaign Speeches*. Edited by John W. Davidson. New Haven: Yale University Press, 1956.

NOTES

1. Jean Jacques Rousseau, John Stuart Mill, John Locke, and Thomas Hill Green, among others, have been major framers of the debate on participation, obligations, and democracy. Their works have been published in many editions and there is a lively secondary literature about them.
2. John Stuart Mill, *Utilitarianism, On Liberty, Representative Government* (New York: Dutton, 1951).
3. Jean Jacques Rousseau, *The Social Contract* (New York: Penguin Books, 1968).

4. Ibid. This is one of Rousseau's major themes in this important work on participatory democratic theory.

5. John Locke, *The Second Treatise on Civil Government*, in *Locke on Politics, Religion, and Education*, ed. Maurice Cranston (New York: Collier, 1965), chapter 1, and John Stuart Mill, *Representative Government*, op. cit., are both important works in the political theory of representative democracy.

6. Plato, *The Republic*, ed. Alan Bloom (New York: Basic Books, 1968).

7. D. Stephenson, Jr. et al., *American Government* (New York: Harper & Row, 1988), pp. 212–217, 281–303.

8. D. Glass, P. Squire, and R. Wolfinger, "Voter Turnout: An International Comparison," *Public Opinion*, December 1983–January 1984, pp. 49–55.

9. John Stuart Mill, *On Liberty*, op. cit.

10. Thomas Jefferson's political theory is discussed in Charles M. Wiltse, *The Jeffersonian Tradition in American Democracy* (Chapel Hill: University of North Carolina Press, 1935).

11. Alexis de Tocqueville, *Democracy in America* (New York: Mentor Editions, 1956).

12. Thucydides, *The Peloponnesian War* (New York: Penguin Classics, 1954).

13. An excellent discussion of the value of efficiency and how it is integrated into one set of democratic institutions is contained in Joseph Stiglitz, *Economics of the Public Sector* (New York: W. W. Norton, 1986), especially part one.

14. Winston Churchill, speech in the British House of Commons, November 11, 1947.

Chapter
12

Political Theory and Public Policy

*T*he institutions and processes of government sometimes are cumbersome, expensive presences dominating our social horizons like a range of foreboding mountains. But they are necessary and active social agents that affect all of our public relationships regardless of our personal level of awareness or support for them. For us as citizens, the critical public policies that comprise our political environments virtually control the quality of our public life.

Political systems generate public policies (in the form of laws, regulations, etc.) in an attempt to improve the political environment as policymakers react to and deal with citizen demands and supports. Public policies consist of government programs, procedures, and strategies that wrestle with public problems and attempt to solve them in the public interest as seen by policymakers. They are what politics and government do (or wish to do) to modify their social environments to pursue the best political outcomes. They have been referred to by important political scientists as "authoritative allocation of values"[1] or "who gets what, when, and how."[2]

Since public policies and the processes that accompany them have impact on our lives, they have long been studied by political theorists and political scientists. Twenty-five centuries ago Thucydides wrote one of the first manuscripts in political theory in an effort to evaluate his Athens' foreign policy.[3] As we move into the twenty-sixth century of political theory, one political scientist has called the art and craft of public policy analysis speaking truth to power.[4] Another says he " . . . did not wish to spin out political ideas in a policy or institutional vacuum. We quarrel over political ideas in order to have an effect on the political life around us."[5] Yet another has said that she cannot separate politics from policy and that policy goals (like equity, democracy, and security) are aspirations for the community which unite us.[6]

Public policy has always interested political thinkers because of its central role in determining the values, goods, and services necessary to our coexistence as people who share time and space. Since public policy often determines who wins and loses on issues, it can literally allocate abundance and security for some and condemn others to poverty and peril. It also decides contentious issues like taxing and spending and selects who will have access to social utilities like education, justice, and sound housing. Accordingly, it remains a proper theme for political theory.

POLITICAL THEORY AND POLICY ANALYSIS

Doing political theory and doing public policy are not, however, the same tasks. For one thing, policy practitioners or strategists are usually not political theorists by training or concern. Typically, they are government administrators who consult (and sometimes even listen to) substantive experts and practitioners in the area under policy review as they struggle with policy issues. They are preoccupied with policymakers' goals, such as husbanding scarce resources, satisfying constituent needs, keeping key policymakers happy (or quiescent), and accommodating important interest groups. While they are not unconcerned with the values of equity, efficiency, fairness, liberty, and so forth that worry normative political theorists, their interest in public policy responds to a different (not necessarily opposing) agenda of practical politics.

Political theorists and public policymakers have an uneasy natural affinity whether mutually recognized or not. Each shares a common interest in what government ought to be doing, but each is steering on a different value course. While political theory can bring perspective and assistance to the process, that is not universally welcomed or sought by either the theorist or the policymaker. But when the two types do work together, it can be fortunate for the public interest as well as for public policymakers and analysts. Normative political theory so engaged with society must grapple with the same political agendas and problems that hold the focus of policymakers and scientists.

There are also differences between political theory and public policy as subfields within the academic practice of political science. First, policy analysis in political science has had a preoccupation with the policy process. As Thomas Dye puts it, "the major focus of attention of political science has never really been on policies themselves, but rather on the institutions and structures of government and on the political behavior and processes associated with policy-making."[7] Political theorists, on the other hand, are primarily interested in values rather than bare facts. That is, they are primarily normative rather than empirical. They have tended to focus on the impacts of politics and political institutions on citizens instead of focusing on institutions and behavioral generalizations.

Second, to the extent that values concern both groups of analysts as they examine public policy, political theorists and empirical policy scientists often emphasize different ones. The latter view process norms such as efficiency, smoothness of process, interest satisfaction, and conformity to procedural rights and norms as top priorities. Traditional values in political theory like liberty, equality, justice, political obligation, and democracy are either not recognized as important policy criteria or are thought of as desirable values to be pursued only after the "higher-order" process norms are maximized. If values conflict or there are resource constraints, the process-norm values take priority. While political theorists often accept and even appreciate the process norms of most policy scientists, they rank them as less significant than their own traditional values and pursue them as second-order priorities.

Inauspiciously, the linkages and separations between policy scientists/ practitioners and normative theorists have resulted in some distrust between them. This missed potential of unity of purpose and cooperation among professionals with parallel interests has caused many public policies to suffer. Without a clear path toward critical public interest values, such policies tend to reflect practices and needs of policy insiders more than of citizens. We can only start to correct this by getting involved in the policy arena and supporting those public interest values that normative theory at its best can contribute to the political environment.

As advocates of an engaged political theory, we believe that policymakers should consult normative political thinkers because they can be quite thoughtful experts in political values. Political theorists should not wait to be called on, however. Public policies affect the ends and means of politics and government in important ways. Thus political theorists who believe in an engaged discipline have an obligation to research and formulate practical ideas about how to help policymakers steer policy toward the public interest in an environment of competing priorities and scarce resources.

Political theory can contribute to the analysis and implementation of public policy in several ways. An obvious one with important impact is the formulation and discussion of problems. Political theory excels in dealing with values and ranking which ones to pursue first, to what degree and why. Such concerns are the heart of public policy formulation and thinking. The literature and experience that give political theorists the ability to illuminate and mediate the conflicts between liberty and equality, for example, can help in policy areas on today's agenda.

To illustrate, it can assist policymakers to clarify basic and derivative values and mediate conflicts between them as they design a policy of effective and affordable medical care to all. Political theorists may help untangle knotty conflicts between complex and intertwined interests such as the public interest versus the legitimate private rights of the insurance industry, medical practitioners, employers who pay for fringe benefits, labor unions, and government program administrators. In this case, among the prominent desirable values are certain to be equity, freedom of choice, justice, efficient use of tax dollars, and international competitiveness. "Simply" identifying and examining who has what valid claim to them under which circumstances contributes toward deciphering policy choices. As Stone suggests, policy is often fraught with paradoxes, and the politics of policy cannot be effectively dealt with by the traditional, rationally based tools employed by policymakers who are schooled in economics, public policy science, and public administration.[8] Surely political theory can play an effective role in an optimal policy process.

Political theory can then contribute by assisting with policy program design and implementation. A long-standing debate among policy implementers has been whether a political system should secure policy compliance through incentives (tax breaks, licenses to impact the environment, market protection, etc.) or by mandates of regulation and legislation. Either approach works, but each also displays and fosters different attitudes toward the legitimacy of politics and government. Those who want to minimize the impact of government on private interests favor the indirect way of incentives that preserve the liberty to ignore them. Those who believe politics to be a social good prefer the direct approach of policy mandates, arguing that equality and comprehensiveness are just and legitimate.

Political theory can help illuminate this debate by examining its arguments and counterarguments within the context of the public-interest versus private-interests debate. Thinkers like Aristotle and Rousseau argue that we are political and that we ought to choose to employ government as the logical institutionalization of politics to improve our lives. Political economists like Keynes and Galbraith[9] agree and, along with political theorists like Mill, caution that we should leave room for individual liberties in the process. Others such as Marx, Bernstein, and Smith[10] have different perspectives. By reexamining such issues in the process of public policy implementation and evaluation, the values of a direct approach to policy can be discussed with minimal resort to ideological polemics and maximum use of evidence. Furthermore, contentious issues like funded versus unfunded mandates in a federal system (national or regional governments forcing programs on smaller governments without necessarily providing revenue for implementation) can be more effectively discussed in terms of equity, fairness, and other aspects of justice in political theory.

As Herson has pointed out, ideas and ideologies embedded in political culture have effect on policy-making. Since political theorists have some expertise in these matters, they should use their knowledge to add some reasoned reflection to the din that surrounds public policy-making in political systems, especially democracies. The more successful we can be at avoiding unfocused policies with unanticipated and/or undesirable consequences, the better we will be able to formulate and incorporate sound values into useful public policies in the public interest. We do not need a new elaborate methodology to do so. We merely need to keep an eye on our goals and use what we already know to steer a straight course.

APPLICATIONS OF POLITICAL THEORY TO PUBLIC POLICY

A good way of applying some of the insights of political theory to public policy is to examine and analyze some important policy areas. By mapping and beginning to assess the principal components and values of a few major policy areas that will require the attention of policymakers in the near future, we can begin the process of using political theory in public policy design.

The assessments contained in these few pages, of course, are modest, aiming only to explain some of the key value conflicts and positions involved in these critical policy areas. We deliberately avoid detailed conclusions in order to provoke you to think about your own prescriptions on these central issues on the policy fast track. We are "simply" asking and trying to answer questions that help us discover policy goals and strategies that address significant problems with appropriate resources.

As policy scientists Dubnick and Bardes have observed, the first requirement for good policy crafting is to analyze policies before anything else "in the sense that we seek to know and understand what governments are saying and doing, why they are saying and doing those things, and with what consequences."[11] If done right, this kind of policy analysis will be a rich source of data as raw material that policy designers need to consider as they go about their tasks.

Beyond their basic normative and empirical analytical dimensions, policy issues are also judgmental problems and opportunities. Once we understand the fact and value dimensions of a policy area, political theorists have an opportunity and perhaps an obligation to do something with the information generated. As Dubnick and Bardes have observed, there is a need to apply our values and judge whether given policies merit our support or whether we need to advocate different policies or approaches to the problem.[12] But merely asserting our judgments is insufficient. If we are going to convince others of the wisdom of our positions, we must build logical and convincing cases for our judgments within the clear framework of pervasive political values.

Dubnick and Bardes also rightly remind us that substantive areas of public policy constitute strategic problems "in the sense that they call for the development of new or better government actions and statements."[13] In other words, political theorists working as policy analysts must develop usable prescriptions about what should be done, being mindful of practicality, social value patterns, and availability of resources as factors. Hopeless idealism and demands that the impossible be accomplished cannot assist would-be public policy in wending its way through a complex political process.

Nevertheless, we should also avoid the trap of only prescribing the easy or the narrowly possible simply because our goal is to prescribe practical public policy that can be enacted. Ultimately, tactics and actions are only justified if they are means toward morally defensible goals and strategies. We need to strike a balance between the moral and the accomplishable. Impractical prescriptions are likely to be dismissed by policy implementers and supporters while achievable (or very nearly so) prescriptions that make us reach morally can motivate better public policy. After all, public policy is a fertile and appropriate area in which to apply political theory.

Public Policy on Humans and Health

Consistent with the preceding standards and goals of normative political thought, let us draw a few general maps of emerging public policy areas, with the primary focus on the United States of America.[14] Starting with the essential concerns of human health and general welfare, one key concern is the controversial issue of abortion. It is an issue that continues to be the subject of legislative and judicial attention. Even widespread future use of RU-486, the French "instant abortion pill" or its equivalent will only make the issue easier for individuals to resolve. It will not change the basic moral and political issues of abortion policy. As painful and complex as they are, they simply are too salient to be avoided.[15]

Present government policies in the United States can best be described as permeable and permissive, though confused. Abortion is not mandated in any circumstances, but current federal court decisions allow pregnant women to choose abortion the first two trimesters of pregnancy. Though affirming the legality of abortion choices, court decisions also permit the enactment of many local restrictions and discouragements (though no outright prohibitions) of abortion. Many local and some state legislatures have enacted statutes that essentially intend to discourage abortion choosers, but many have also left the area alone. The subject is politically active, with many well-organized advocacy groups that lobby for outlawing abortion or keeping a pro-choice policy and make episodic interventions (with indeterminate success) into elections. New court decisions are likely in the next years due to turnover on the federal bench.

Assessment of the values found buried in abortion issues isolates a major conflict. On one side are those who oppose abortion because they think it is a form of murder. They maintain that abortion violates the value of life. They contend that the public interest demands that the state prevent abortion just as it prevents other forms of murder. No individual, they assert, has the right to judge some human lives to be less sacrosanct than others. Using the value of equality, they argue that all life should be respected and protected by individuals and governments alike. Proponents of this position agree on an inviolable value of life, though they debate its religious versus secular origins. Furthermore, they assume that all fetuses are alive from the moment of conception. They consequently reject the utility of scientific research on when life begins because even sophisticated medicine is a matter of arbitrary definition rather than truth in their view.

On the other side(s) are those who argue that quality of life (both the mother's and the eventual child's) is more important than an absolute value of life and that society has an important moral stake in abortion decisions. They submit that the life of a person who is born and experiencing life is qualitatively more important than a mass of tissue that is dependent on another being for its viability. They contend that mothers should not be forced to raise unwanted children (or those forced on them by rape or incest) and argue that those who are forced to do so face a bleak life of poverty or misery for themselves and their offspring. The public interest is invoked by these advocates when they argue that society needs to be protected from the burden of overpopulation and unwanted and abandoned or abused children. Scarce public resources would have to be expended to provide even minimal care for those who face lives with uninspiring prospects due to malnutrition, mistreatment, and lack of access to opportunities.

Pro-choice policy advocates further claim that a woman has a right to control her own body and the right to choose courses of action. Occasionally their arguments are joined by medical practitioners who want to preserve their freedom to prescribe medical procedures they deem appropriate. A completely different set of claims is sometimes advanced by fathers or parents who demand to be represented and consulted in a decision about abortion in which they have a stake. These claims are advanced by advocates on both sides of the pro-choice issues.

As with many positions, abortion positions are often drawn too dualistically. For example, one can be a strong advocate of the value of life and still doubt that the fetus is alive from the moment of conception. If it can be proven that a specific abortion actually does take life, then advocates of such a position argue that abortion violates their values. Alternatively, it is possible to be in substantial doubt or simply opposed to abortion personally on value of life grounds and still be in favor of a pro-choice public policy position on grounds of personal liberty.[16] The former binds the value-holder; the latter is a position on what the policy ought to do for all. People who endorse this position are free (and might even be obligated) to try to reason with others not to seek abortions. But they do not feel justified in demanding that the state legislate their personal morality for everyone. They prefer to have the state be silent on the issue except for regulating and policing abortions (in terms of cleanliness, safety, licenses of practitioners, etc.) just as is done with any medical procedures that should be subject to regulation for the public good.

This position essentially describes the current state of public policy. Given the evolving state of scientific knowledge about "instant abortion" pills, when life begins and when fetuses are viable, this policy is a practical political response, though it is morally evasive. As knowledge about how these values impact individuals and the community changes with changes in medical research and technology, good policy will need to incorporate what we know as well as what we believe.

The issue of abortion illustrates a general principle that is worthy of consideration. Areas of policy which do not pose a clear and present public danger and involve important areas of personal choice and impact can often be reasonably left to the individual, provided that the state guarantees a free marketplace of ideas about them for those facing important decisions. Political theory should be very cautious about prescribing policies that are based on unsubstantiated and presently unsubstantiable (even if deeply felt) personal opinions. Laws bind others and are backed up by the punitive power of the state. Yet what sense does such a view make to someone who believes abortion is an unquestioned moral issue? From this view, government must act to restrict what is simply murder.

Also relevant is value consistency. Should consistent application of values be a fundamental ingredient of effectively applying political theory to public policy? To the extent that the case is convincing that abortion should be doubted or opposed on value of life grounds, should all other public policies that are analogously contingent on the same grounds be treated similarly? Thus, should capital punishment and war be opposed (or doubted) just as vehemently and for the same reasons by opponents of abortion? Should life be preserved by the best efforts of medical science until there is no hope for the success of continued intervention? We believe that, as with all values, the sanctity of life should cover all of its political situations and manifestations. Unless a convincing case can be made that these various applications of the value of life are not analogous to each other, the values that bind one bind the others. Other values that conflict with them do not repeal the original values, though they need to be considered alongside the original values and taken into account in policy decisions as appropriate. All other things being equal, consistency is a value we admire because it encourages rational and reliable application of political values to issues of proper concern to political theory and public policy.

Other aspects of human health and welfare involve different sets of values. A policy issue currently being debated is individual patient rights versus the rights of the state or psychiatrists to deprive others of their liberty for treatment and/or confinement. This involves a conflict between the value of liberty and the rights of experts to regulate individual behavior and the right of the state to coerce people to protect either them or the public from harm. This is analogous with laws that require motorcycle riders to wear protective helmets for their own good or laws that require use of automobile seatbelts by drivers and occupants. It may be connected with the controversy about regulating smoking in public places. In each of these cases a substantial link must be established between the public interest and regulation of individual behavior (even self-destructive behavior) before such regulations become convincing. The motorcycle debate, for example, is between advocates of individual freedom, even at the risk of personal danger, versus those who argue that high health costs and the emergency resources mobilized in case of accident may lead to a public interest in regulating individual behavior. Mill, for example, is quite convincing when he says that liberty ought not to be tampered with except when its exercise prevents others from using their liberties.[17] Equally convincing are those who say that anything that forces the public to respond is a political act that should be regulated for the public good. The laws about motorcycle helmets or seatbelts should be evaluated in these terms.

Laws restricting or prohibiting smoking in public places are a bit clearer to evaluate. Public smoking can be viewed as a form of air pollution. Laws against it are justified on the same grounds as laws and regulations that prohibit industrial pollution. Such laws protect the air and water which we must all use but still allow businesses other freedoms of product choice, pricing, and so forth. Therefore, are laws that restrict the passive smoke hazards, litter, or fire danger of public smoking serving a public interest if they protect the right of smoking in private? Mill might think so. Regulation of public smoking (or of the analogous driving while intoxicated) is justified in terms of his argument. Is smoking in a way that does not cause others to breathe the by-products of combustion of smoking materials rightly held to be as much a prerogative as driving unimpaired in a legal vehicle? Should it be an individual choice that is part of our claim to individual liberty in a liberal society even if others judge our actions to be stupid?

Another critical policy controversy involves health care delivery systems in the United States. Analysis of the issues produces arguments about the values of equal access to a public utility: whether individual resources ought to give one a moral right to better care, whether individuals or institutions have a right to profit from public need, the individual right to choose, and the best use of public resources. These debates make national versus private health care policies contentious and knotty.

Assessing these claims, the present United States system relies on private health care delivery systems.[18] The only exceptions are the government hospitals organized on a not-for-profit basis that serve a small portion of those in need. Private health care providers are regulated through various public and private bodies but are free to provide the level of service at the place and price they choose. Individuals needing health care make arrangements with the care givers they choose and can afford, and they pay for it either out of pocket or through a combination of insurance and out-of-pocket costs. There are strong interest groups (representing physicians, hospitals, employers, insurance companies, etc.) that are increasingly vocal about whether the nation needs to adopt some form of national health care and/or insurance. Like abortion, it will surely be a contentious issue in the coming decade.[19]

Advocates of the present system argue that government ought to be playing only a night watchman's role, regulating the safety of private health care delivery and little else. They believe that small government is better than big government. They argue that private enterprise operating through the profit motive causes medical service delivery to be cheaper, better, and more technically innovative than public delivery systems. They are not concerned about the access issues, assuming that either employment or public welfare will give the vast majority of those who need medical care the ability to pay for what they truly need. They further maintain that government should not be committing resources to medical care because scarce tax revenues should be spent elsewhere. Other liberties advanced by proponents of a limited government are the rights of patients to choose their physicians, hospitals, and insurance companies or other source of medical funding or organization (health maintenance organization, clinic, etc.) that they wish to patronize.[20]

Arrayed against the present system are those who argue what is essentially a political theory of public utility. They suggest that the government has a duty to provide health care to all regardless of their ability to pay because effective health care is a critical basic necessity for all. They attach a lot of importance to the access issue, arguing that equality demands that everybody have a right to the best care that technology and resources can provide. They claim this by invoking the value of justice, arguing that it is only served when the ability to get that care is separated from one's economic status in life since the latter depends on too many extraneous factors like the job market, family background, health, mental abilities, and so on. Justice gives dignity to all, they contend, and dignity requires access to good health care.

While some of the arguments advanced on this side question whether individuals or institutions have a moral right to profit (often very handsomely) from the health needs and misfortunes of others, most who want to change the current system accept the premise that such profits are not immoral on their face. But most of them also maintain that the present capitalist system is not delivering the care that many need and that costs are escalating beyond reason, with no end in sight.

This area of public policy is likely to become even more active in the future because there are rising perceptions by most groups (including activists on both sides) that the present system cannot continue without either drastic or modest reform. Political theorists ought to help the process by focusing attention on how the values of cost versus efficiency, justice, liberty, equality, and the proper role of government apply here. What should government do to provide medical care? Should government provide national health care delivery? Should it provide a national health insurance and let private providers deliver services? Should it merely regulate private providers? Is there a right to public health care? How should it be organized?

Private Behavior and Public Policy

Another contentious sphere of public policy involves government intervention into traditionally private social attitudes and practices. Increasingly, the public sector is making policies and issuing mandates on what we can see and hear and how we must treat others in our public capacities as employers, governors, and so forth. This has become a highly politicized trend and has made government policy-making a battleground for groups with very different ideologies and agendas. Many of them have been successful in co-opting governments to define and enforce canons of justice and behavior for the entire society that were formerly group norms. The trend has engendered fierce opposition from other groups. It has also led to lively fund-raising battles among groups and alienated many citizens who resent being told what to do by government even as they are being co-opted by groups that have that aim in mind.

Today, Western liberal governments routinely define by law and mandate what sexually explicit material can be sold, used, or even possessed. Closely related to this (though much more explicitly political), some governments also manage and manipulate coverage of events by the news media, though they deny that they are practicing any form of censorship. Governments also routinely step into the workplace and places of public accommodation and define and regulate individual as well as corporate behaviors and expressions of attitude on the controversial topics of equality and treatment of race, sex, affirmative action, and sexual harassment.

Questions about government treatment of sexually explicit material and information censorship have always been prominent in political theory. From the earliest literature of the discipline,[21] political thinkers have considered justice, liberty, and the public interest in evaluating what is proper public entertainment or what the public ought to know of events and policies. Consequently, many of today's policy controversies about censorship can benefit from some of the insights of political theory.

Turning first to the regulation of alleged obscenity, a historical perspective reminds us that sexual mores and standards of societies have constantly shifted throughout the last twenty-five centuries. What was considered perfectly acceptable in one era or society became shameful in another era, only to return to respectability in yet another generation. These shifting moral standards are important because principles governing what should be legal in art, literature, entertainment, and drama have evolved on substantially parallel paths, albeit with some cultural lag. This is probably so because governors respond at least partially to public opinion as a tactic of self-preservation, particularly in democracies.

In the twentieth-century West, due to the widespread acceptance by policy elites of liberal cultural values (such as those embodied in the writings of John Stuart Mill and others[22]), a common public policy practice has emerged, though not without active dissent. Today's policymakers often mandate that obtrusive public displays of pornography (usually defined as sexually explicit and/or objectionable material that offends customary community standards)[23] are prohibited. Child pornography is totally banned in all forms. Otherwise, most contemporary policies allow adults to enjoy materials some would consider objectionable (not including child subjects) as long as they confine their consumption of the material to private homes (especially), galleries, museums, and other places that can be avoided by those who are offended by the material.

Recently, though, responding to many interest groups,[24] some U.S. legislatures and courts have acted to impede severely the availability of or completely ban such material, especially when public funds might be involved. Controversies have raged about whether government agencies should give grants to artists who offend community sensibilities, and some bookstores and newsstands have been raided and clerks charged with crimes for selling material which allegedly violates community standards of decency.[25] While these issues are far from final resolution (and may never be settled definitively due to the shifting nature of public opinion trends on such topics), the increase of censorship of sexually offensive material has accompanied the recent turn of American politics to the right.

There are important values buried in these controversies. Liberty is the value claimed by individuals when they assert a right to read or view any material they deem appropriate. But governments who seek to restrict such material also invoke the value of liberty when they claim that they are protecting the right of citizens to be free from others' more sexually oriented choices and the behaviors they allege they cause.

At the root of some of the claims advanced by those who wish to censor sexually offensive material is a sense of public interest that views pornography as wrong by definition. Other holders of this variant of the values of justice and/or propriety advocate that prudent public policy requires government to maintain standards of community decency. They believe that pornography degrades society, healthy sex, and good family relations and that government should ban it for the public good. Some proponents of this view maintain that exposure to pornography incites at least some individuals to break the restraints of civilization that check such harmful behavior and prevent widespread crimes of passion.[26]

Political theory can play a useful role in such controversies by raising questions and illuminating, balancing, and clarifying the underlying values of the debate. Do we have a right to pornography? What rights ought to be balanced with it? For example, liberty is such a critical value to human beings of different political viewpoints that it deserves a substantial benefit of the doubt when it conflicts with other values or even alternative understandings of the same value. However, no value is absolute, including liberty. Unrestrained liberty can wreak havoc on others and deny the very freedom for some that its advocates urge for all. Many political theorists have dealt with this problem by using equality as a countervailing balance to liberty. Many believe that a sensible public policy in this area is a mandate of equal liberty to choose to take or leave sexually explicit material with no right to force it on others or take it away from them. This is the standard that John Stuart Mill advocates when he advances the right to do what one pleases as long as it does not exploit or unwillingly involve others.

Incidentally, there is nothing in this approach that is inconsistent with the prevailing view that the public interest requires government protection of children and those without power from exploitation by pornography or anything else. Even Mill felt that the prevention of exploitation was so important that it was the only exception he made for an absolute right of individual liberty. Children do indeed need protection by government from adult sexual exploitation because they lack the maturity to make informed judgments and cannot resist adult authority very easily.

Of course, demands for public policies that are claimed to pursue an objective public interest are not automatically valid. Such claims must be carefully justified rather than simply announced since the limitations of individual liberty that they incorporate have serious impacts on citizens. Those who claim, for example, that pornography oppresses all women and demand laws protecting them as a class by restrictions on liberty of the whole society need to demonstrate that protection is needed by the whole of such a diverse group. There is no question that many women (and some men and children) have been exploited and used as sex objects by some. The public interest is best served not by policy overkill but by remedies of clear and targeted public policy such as banning child pornography or unconsenting use of female models. The point is simply that political theorists should prescribe principles and values carefully so that we protect only genuine victims while legally enjoining proven exploiters. Our policy remedies are powerful weapons that should be targeted carefully to minimize collateral damage while they do their job.

The issues and values involved in press censorship are similar. Outlawing the printed or broadcast word has substantial political and public interest implications. Freedom of the press[27] has long been argued to be absolute by civil libertarians because it forms the foundations for a free society. They claim that a free marketplace of ideas is desirable because it gives minorities a right to try to become majorities. They also suggest (with considerable historical justification) that a free climate of information serves the public interest by keeping governments, parties, and politicians honest. Moreover, they suggest that it is a prerequisite to democracy.[28] Governments that practice press censorship are able to use their monopoly of information to hide their transgressions, lie about their accomplishments, and prevent the opposition from questioning their policies. This makes their responsiveness to public opinion unlikely.

On the other side are those who suggest that there is an unambiguous public interest in the value of public safety and security that can only be served by judicious use of censorship. Information about anything that has to do with weapons or military operations,[29] foreign policy, public investments, future public policy priorities, and other similar topics is often felt to be a fair target for censorship in order to prevent enemy advantage or private profit from such data. Similarly, some supporters of press censorship suggest that the potential of libeling either government policymakers or private individuals is sufficient grounds to prevent the press from saying anything it wants. They also suggest that constant criticism of the government undermines patriotism and public confidence in that critical institution and should be made illegal in the public interest. The public's right to know is perceived more narrowly by such advocates. Liberty as a value is far less than the only value.

The present state of press censorship reflects a substantial regard for the principle of civil liberties. Freedom of the press is guaranteed in principle (and usually honored in practice fairly effectively) in most democracies. In the United States, for example, prior restraint of the press is prohibited, but laws against intentional libel and incitement to riot stand as ex post facto restraints against a completely unfettered press. Moreover, the government finds it acceptable practice to restrict routinely release of information it judges to be sensitive.

Many contemporary Western political theorists are persuaded by history and argument that freedom of the press and other civil liberties are important to the kinds of politics and society they want. Thus many argue that civil liberties are so valuable that they ought to be favored over other important values like national security when they are nearly of equal weight in a given situation.[30]

On the other hand, political theorists usually recognize that national security and freedom from libel are legitimate concerns that deserve some targeted protection. In public emergencies like wartime, they might even be given temporary and carefully limited precedence over press freedom. Normally, they argue that general press censorship is an unselective tool. They prefer less harmful and more targeted tools like voluntary restraint, tax or news-scoop incentives for cooperative media, and civil penalties for proven libels.[31] They favor freedom of information in all situations save those rare ones of clear and present public danger.

Another important issue of contemporary public policy involves individual protection against racism, sexism, affirmative action, and protection against sexual harassment. Much of the current debate on private rights versus public interest centers about them. The last decades have seen increasing and historically unprecedented government regulation of employment and public accommodation practices that were formerly left to private contract and choice.

In Europe and the United States, especially, employers and places of public accommodation (stores, universities, hotels, real estate brokers, etc.) have been subject to an extensive set of statutes and regulations. They are prohibited by law from discriminating or permitting their employees to show prejudice on racial, sexual, religious, national origin, or other grounds. Furthermore, they are required to protect employees, customers, and others from sexual, racial, or other harassment by fellow workers even if it is not company policy to condone it. They are also required to maintain internal policies and public postures toward those ends or be subject to pay court-imposed damages to those who convince a jury that they have been victims of discrimination or harassment. In addition, under the general rubric of affirmative action, employers are mandated in various ways[32] to aggressively pursue remedies for past discriminations by seeking out for employment and/ or promotion qualified members of minority groups.

Some employers and a significant block of individuals dissent from this tidal wave of public policy. While most of them suggest that discrimination is wrong,[33] they advocate an individual or group liberty to use their property or institutions in any socially responsible way. They usually reject government rights to enforce what they consider to be only egalitarian social norms of policy elites rather than demonstrated truth. They usually claim (in the face of fierce opposition) that individuals can protect themselves and that there are enough opportunities in today's diverse industrial and postindustrial societies to give all who work hard an opportunity. Rather than advocating discrimination, they argue that the market will encourage equality if the society values it and that government should only intervene when discrimination is clearly proven harmful in specific instances.

The values involved in this area are not readily apparent to the general public, but they certainly exist and have been dealt with at length by political theory. The major value conflict concerns liberty versus equality. Those who make the case for government policies that protect individuals against discrimination argue that human beings are of equal worth and qualifications (subject to individual differences) and that justice demands equal treatment of equals. People left to their own devices have developed a history of prejudice and discrimination that they feel to be wrong. They maintain that only government has the clout and the nerve to protect the weak from being exploited by the strong and that the public interest requires the use of public intervention to shore up the value of equality.

Conversely, many liberals argue that individual rights and choices are so important that they should not be overridden even by legitimate demands for equality. They claim that you cannot and should not legislate morality and that people have a right to feel and act in any way they want toward others as long as they do not directly harm them in any tangible way. They reject the idea that any public interest justifies regulation or prevention of subtle forms of discrimination at the workplace and protecting against a wide list of harassments and discriminations. They do recognize an equality that needs to be guaranteed by government but argue that current policies have gone too far in that direction. They are content with laws that prohibit pay discrimination for equal work, and they suggest that economic opportunities for social victims can be opened by putting more public resources in education of the disadvantaged rather than prohibitions of behavior.

Also embedded in this debate is the value of diversity as an end that many feel is desirable. But as Albert Camus has pointed out,[34] no matter how desirable ends many be, means need to be consistent with them in order to make good policy. The jury is still out on whether means like affirmative action—adopted to reach the desirable ends of diversity and nondiscrimination—are the most appropriate or the best targeted. Do they encourage shortcuts like artificial quotas by employers? Are they too ambitious in their scope? Do they punish the children for sins of their parents or ancestors? What other values (besides liberty) are threatened by them? Political theorists have a ready resource for exploring such questions in our literature about the concepts of equality stemming from desert or merit in justice theory.[35] We also have many discussions about the extent of individual liberty and equality and how conflicts between them can be resolved through strategies of equality of opportunity and other means.

Another important issue involves public participation in democracy. In Western democratic political systems generally, especially in the United States, there has been a steadily escalating crisis in confidence and a serious erosion in public participation in democracy. In recent elections in the United States, participation is often extremely low in local primary elections and lower than most other democracies in general elections. Pollsters also tell us that people have even less than the usual low levels of confidence in government in the current era. It is an open question whether democracy so undermined can be stable and responsive in the long run.

Undoubtedly, one reason for this has been the weak state of public policy regarding the ethics and practices of government service and campaign finance. In the United States particularly, organized interest groups legally hire very costly lobbyists (often former policymakers) to influence policymakers and form political action committees (PACs) which contribute vast sums (currently limited to $10,000 per PAC per candidate for an election cycle of primary and general election, with multiple PACS sponsored by the same set of interests being common) to extremely expensive and often negative campaigns for important offices. The average individual feels powerless and manipulated and often responds by resenting the process and walking away from it. Public policy is left to be made by those who, by definition, have politically succeeded in the present process. The policy that results often responds to organized group pressures rather than more general public voices and further alienates the potentially active citizen. Current policymakers largely ignore the problem, although the U.S. Congress did tighten its outside-income limits recently and the rhetoric of concern (as opposed to more tangible action) abounds.

Political theory needs to investigate a wide range of values and ethics of regulating institutional behavior to ameliorate the situation. What is to be done? Should we abolish PAC campaign contributions? Should we put limits on campaign spending? Do we need to evaluate alternative campaign-finance proposals like public financing? Should we encourage media coverage of campaigns? Should we increase lobbying access by nonrich groups or foster a business ethic of more regard for the public interest? Each of these questions is controversial and complicated. Let us try to avoid hurried reforms like those enacted after the Watergate scandals of the early 1970s (the 1974 U.S. Campaign Finance Reform Act that created the PAC system, among other things). They only make things worse. Instead, political theorists should contribute careful reflection, analysis, and deliberation and help enact reforms that actually deal with the problems. While urgently needed, reforms need to be designed to protect values like individual liberties of speech and press, the public's right to know, pluralist equalities, and the fairness and openness of a good democratic polity.

Similarly, U.S. political theorists should examine and discuss the values as well as the value of public service. Economist Robert Kutner argues that American culturally rooted contempt for government harms our business competitiveness and weakens our public policy abilities.[36] As long as we hold politicians in contempt, inquire into the most private details of their lives, demand they do what we want, and pay them less and give them fewer tools than their private sector analogues, we will not attract the best people to public service. Political theory teaches us that clear standards of public service ethics (banning of outside income, etc.), support of adequate, compensation for policymakers who have important tasks, and—perhaps most importantly—rediscovering the honor and utility of the public sector are good for society. If the corruptions and weaknesses of the present political process are rooted out by careful attention to the values and value of politics, citizens might begin to relax some of their contempt for politics and the whole public sector might begin to live up to some more of its potential. In Kutner's words, "Someday Americans will wake up to the fact that a feeble government as well as an overbearing one can erode our liberties."[37]

CONCLUSION

We believe that political theory is the only academic discipline that is centrally committed to applying values to politics and is schooled in an understanding of the political processes' workings and potentials. Public policy is a fertile and important area for applying our specialized knowledge to problems of political significance. The reward is the chance of a better policy environment for all of us.

The values of liberty, equality, justice, public interest, and so forth that we can apply to pornography, affirmative action, abortion, and democratic participation are equally applicable to the right to die and the moral and political definitions of life and death. They also pertain to reasoned debates on mandated recycling of waste and the search for and dissemination of new sources of water, food, and energy. They can also be useful in evaluating public policies toward regulation of tomorrow's crimes (whether victimless or not). They are appropriate tools of analysis for development of ethics and regulation of new tools of information, the uses of biological modifications, the regulation of future forms of transportation, ownership and uses of the sea and space in the future, and issues of arms control and disarmament, among many others.

There will be many more issues of public policy that we have not even anticipated in the near and middle-range future. We expect political theory will recognize them in a timely fashion. If that is accomplished, the likelihood is high that present and future political theorists will play a useful role in formulating the public policies of the next century.

GLOSSARY OF KEY TERMS

affirmative action A government policy to aggressively pursue remediation of past sexism, racism, or other discriminations.

censorship Prohibition of ideas or publications by government. It is a violation of most concepts of civil liberties.

domestic policy Public policy that applies within a political system.

efficiency in policy A norm of using resources effectively so that as few as possible are wasted as policies are implemented.

empirical Ideas and analysis of measurable and observable phenomena.

equity in policy A public policy value. Treating people fairly and with justice in the design and implementation of policy.

foreign policy Public policy that is designed to deal with the external environment of a political system. Often affects domestic policy and vice versa.

ideology A political worldview. Usually associated with a strongly held and all-encompassing view of political events and values.

libel The legal term for writing something harmful and untrue about another person.

national health delivery policy The public policy that advocates that government should provide health care as a public utility. It is common in Europe.

nondiscrimination A public policy that prohibits discrimination against individuals on account of race, sex, national origins, religion, and so forth. It does not address past discriminations directly.

normative Ideas and analysis of norms and values.

PAC A political action committee. A legal entity in the United States for raising and spending money in order to influence federal elections.

policy process The set of procedures and traditions that political systems go through as public policy is made.

political participation The acts of voting, running for office, campaign volunteering, demonstrating, policy advocacy, lobbying, and other forms of involvement in a political system.

pornography Sexually explicit material that offends community or individual standards. Also called obscenity.

process/procedural norms Norms that require that specific (often lengthy and detailed) processes be followed in making policy in order to protect the rights and claims of all as policy is made.

public financing of political campaigns British practice (proposed as a reform in the United States) of candidates for political office in a democracy having all or part of their campaign expenses paid by the government.

value consistency Using norms and values in the same manner in different circumstances.

SUGGESTIONS FOR FURTHER READING

Annual Editions in American Government—1992–1993. Sluice Dock, Conn.: Dushkin Publishers, 1992 and each year.

Dubnick, Melvin J., and Bardes, Barbara A. *Thinking About Public Policy: A Problem-Solving Approach.* New York: John Wiley and Sons, 1983.

Heilbrun, James, and McGuire, Patrick A. *Urban Economics and Public Policy,* 3d ed. New York: Oxford University Press, 1985. New York: St. Martin's Press, 1987.

Kutner, Robert. "Why Business Needs a Stronger and Wiser Uncle Sam." *Business Week,* June 3, 1991, p. 16.

Mason, Arthur Thomas, and Baker, Gordon E., ed. *Free Government in the Making.* 4th ed. New York: Oxford University Press, 1985.

Mill, John Stuart. *Essential Works of John Stuart Mill*. Edited by Max Lerner. New York: Bantam Books, 1961.

Phillips, Kevin. *The Politics of Rich and Poor*. New York: Random House, 1990.

Pitkin, Hannah Fenichel. *The Concept of Representation*. Berkeley: University of California Press, 1967.

Stone, Deborah A. *Policy Paradox and Political Reason*. Glenview, Ill.: Scott, Foresman, and Co., 1988.

Wildavsky, Aaron. *Speaking Truth to Power: The Art and Craft of Policy Analysis*. Boston: Little Brown and Co., 1979.

NOTES

1. David Easton, *The Political System: An Inquiry into the State of Political Science* (New York: Knopf, 1953).
2. Harold Lasswell, *The Analysis of Political Behavior* (Hamden, CT: Anchor Books, 1966).
3. Thucydides, *History of the Peloponnesian War* (New York: Oxford University Press, 1959).
4. Aaron Wildavsky, *Speaking Truth to Power: The Art and Craft of Policy Analysis* (Boston: Little Brown and Co., 1979).
5. Lawrence J. R. Herson, *The Politics of Ideas: Political Theory and American Public Policy* (Homewood, Ill.: The Dorsey Press, 1984), p. ix.
6. Deborah A. Stone, *Policy Paradox and Political Reason* (Glenview, Ill.: Scott, Foresman, and Company, 1988), p. 310.
7. Thomas R. Dye, *Understanding Public Policy*, 4th ed. (New York: Prentice-Hall, 1981), p. 3.
8. Stone, op. cit.
9. The late John Maynard Keynes was an internationally influential liberal British economist of the twentieth century and John Kenneth Galbraith is a prominent normative economist. Both have written numerous books on these topics.
10. Karl Marx was a prominent advocate of revolutionary, decentralized socialism, Eduard Bernstein advocated socialism through the ballot box, and Adam Smith was an important eighteenth-century laissez-faire liberal economist.
11. Melvin J. Dubnick and Barbara A. Bardes, *Thinking About Public Policy: A Problem-Solving Approach* (New York: John Wiley and Sons, 1983), p. 17.
12. Ibid.
13. Ibid.
14. There is an international flavor in U.S. policies since many of them have been adapted from policies initiated elsewhere, especially in Europe, although Japan and Canada have been models as well.
15. So knotty an issue is abortion that the authors of this text disagree on what public policy ought to be. Consequently, we have chosen to analyze present policies and raise questions instead of recommending specific policies. We hope that this discussion will provoke you to think about the political implications of abortion as much as it has provoked us.
16. In fact, that is the position of one of this text's authors.
17. John Stuart Mill, *On Liberty*, in *Essential Works of John Stuart Mill*, ed. Max Lerner (New York: Bantam Books, 1961).

18. Typically, the U.S. system is organized around a network of physicians organized as private (often corporate) for-profit professional practices. They bill clients according to professional norms and write prescriptions for pharmaceuticals manufactured by for-profit corporations and sold at retail by for-profit businesses. Each of these charges for its products and services separately. Often, privately contracted insurance supplied by for-profit insurance corporations covers these costs. Sometimes, part or all of these insurance premiums are supplied as fringe benefits of those fortunate to have such an employer. Recently, health care costs (including insurance) have escalated alarmingly in the United States and the trend has been to cut back insurance benefits supplied by employers. A new accounting rule from the quasi-governmental Financial Accounting Standards Board known as Financial Accounting Standard 106 has made the situation much worse since employers are now expected to "book" costs and sequester funds for future health care needs of present employees in addition to present needs and costs.

19. This is especially true since the population is aging along with the post–World War II baby boom generation, and an older population has increased health care needs and costs.

20. This assumes a level of choice which is not always present, particularly in poor neighborhoods or rural areas.

21. See Plato's *Republic*, Aristotle's *The Politics*, the Socratic *Dialogues*, and Aquinas's *Summa Theologica* (all available in numerous editions) for examples of early prescription about morality in the early literature of political theory.

22. The most widely cited work in this context is Mill's *On Liberty*, op. cit.

23. There has been widespread disagreement and many court cases in the United States as to who is going to define community standards. Recently, as an experiment, some communities have even allowed a representative panel of citizens to make determinations about specific material and have accepted the panel choices.

24. Such groups are often affiliated with fundamentalist Christian churches and the right wing of U.S. public opinion, but there are many others, including those on the left wing, feminist organizations who advocate protection of women against sexual or any other kind of exploitation, and children's advocacy groups.

25. There has been an ongoing series of arrests of adult bookstore clerks and court challenges to them (not yet resolved as this is written) in Canton, Ohio, that is typical of the genre.

26. The political relevance of these assumptions can be best understood when viewed from the context of our discussion of human nature and politics in Chapter 2. Some religious conservatives and some feminists maintain this position.

27. Freedom of the press is usually combined with functionally similar freedoms of speech and assembly to constitute the whole area of civil liberties.

28. For a further discussion of this topic, see our discussion of it in the preceding chapter.

29. Officially classified and enforced military secrets are supposedly the same thing as valid military security. Unfortunately, there have been instances of material being classified as secret in order to protect the reputation of policymakers or out of habit rather than need.

30. Many conservative thinkers do not agree with this, however, preferring to give the benefit of the doubt to national security and finding press freedom to have in this case less clear value than is found in it by liberals.

31. In the Persian Gulf War of 1991, the U.S. government used devices such as restricting entry into war zones to government-picked and escorted pools of reporters and "laundered" press briefings by military and civilian policymakers to enforce censorship as a tool of national security. A great deal of voluntary cooperation on the part of the press was evident as well.

32. Some say that affirmative action statutes and regulations necessarily lead to quotas in hiring, college admissions, and so forth. Others suggest that they can be satisfied without resort to quotas. The latter is certainly easier if the total pie is expanding and new jobs or spaces can be offered to all who are qualified for them.

33. They should not be confused with advocates of segregation or apartheid who deny any equality of human beings.

34. Albert Camus, *The Rebel* (New York: Alfred A. Knopf, 1956).

35. Our chapters on justice, freedom, and equality discuss these concepts at greater length and can be consulted on the present topic.

36. Robert Kutner, "Why Business Needs a Stronger and Wiser Uncle Sam," *Business Week*, June 3, 1991, p. 16.

37. Ibid.

Chapter
13

Political Theory and the Future of the Discipline in the Next Century

We hope this brief journey through the realm of normative political theory has shown you that it is a form of what one contemporary political thinker refers to as vision.[1] This ability to see in a particular way has built a body of thought that is both timeless and timely. In other words, our final words in this book emphasize the same themes as our first words.[2] Our central theme can be summarized by stating that political theory's vision is as germane to our lives in the microprocessor age as it was to the citizens who argued with Socrates twenty-five centuries ago about what ought to be done in Athens. In its twenty-sixth century (the twenty-first century on our conventional calendar) political theory continues to be a critical, indispensable search for wisdom and understanding about politics and society.

We hope that by this point in our analysis you have a sense of the richness of political philosophy, of its central core of concepts—liberty, justice, equality, obligation, democracy, among others. And we hope that you realize how these may connect with specific problems and policies in everyday political affairs. We also trust that you will appreciate how much everyone is forced by his or her political circumstances to be an amateur political theorist, while many have the desire to be better at it, to develop more aware, more disciplined, and more thoughtful arguments and counterarguments.

To this juncture, however, we have concentrated largely on the past and the present. Yet our goal is to prepare for the approach of the future. As political philosophy looks toward its twenty-sixth century, its (and our) greatest challenge is how to help preserve and enhance our mutual environment on Earth. To some extent, this may merely necessitate a recasting of the themes of traditional political theory. It may direct us to reevaluate traditional perspectives on the good community, the nature of justice, how to operate common life, and the value of equality and liberty, all themes we have addressed. It may also call for drastic new thinking. Our focus may become more directly planetary; the community may now be all of us and our goal may be defined as the survival of nature itself.

We may wonder if political theory comes to this situation well equipped. The substance of the history of political theory is diverse, interesting, and illuminating. But political philosophy traditionally gave little serious thought about the planetary community. There is, in fact, no acknowledged central thinker to the tradition for whom this has been the central concern, though this situation is rapidly changing as environmental political theory unfolds in our own day.[3]

From one perspective, facing the global future is an agenda mandated by necessity. Survival is imperative and only the most foolish will ignore its demands. As we peer uneasily into the next century, how to survive forces us most immediately to confront community and obligation. Political theory will have to—has to now—conceive of the Earth as a community. Who will count as members? Humans, animals, or every living (or nonliving) thing? How realistic is such a planetary community? How would it transcend or integrate the incredible diversity of cultural, linguistic, and national communities (and obligations) that flourish around us now. How could it achieve peace (not to say harmony) among the countless configurations of primary obligations among people, family, friends, and other relationships that envelop most of us? The challenge is deep.

Political theory must wrestle frankly with what kind of case can be made for (and against) an obligation to any kind of global community. As we noted in our obligation chapter, this kind of obligation attracts a good deal of rhetorical support, often in glowing and assertive language. Yet that does not get us far. What the case might be remains open and needs our attention. Nor does rhetoric assist us in ranking any such global obligation with other obligations. Perhaps that will be the most taxing task of all because it will take us from an abstract approval of global community to the concrete balancing of it with others.

An agenda for the future of political theory will meet dilemmas as it considers other issues also. Democracy is one. Political theory may have to grapple with the awful problem of how much we should care about democracy, representation, or democratic compromise among groups if the need for speedy action for the survival of life presses against democratic ideas or practices.

Another issue will be justice. We cannot know, for example, that a new theory of justice will necessarily be required or will emerge. Since Plato's time we have used pretty much the same basic concepts of justice. But how justice will be and ought to be understood in our global future is something else. Perhaps we would not require a new definition but new interpretations and applications of known definitions. We can be as sure that issues such as the relative value of due process or procedural justice in the light of exigencies of immediate action for the environment may arise. Moreover, people may ask how crucial are other conceptions of justice—merit in economics or equality in politics—before the demands of survival of the global community? We may also expect that these disturbing questions will coexist with others, including whether we can sustain great personal freedom given our environmental crises. Has it become a selfish luxury?[4]

Perhaps, too, there will be doubts about the value of the continuing modern tendency for every ethnic, racial, cultural, or other group to seek national justice or "liberation." How to evaluate and deal with this reality may be a central normative puzzle for theorists as they struggle with the nature of justice and community and their contested meanings and applications.

The same challenge will apply to religious, social, ethnic, racial, or political groups that operate outside of a national context but who identify themselves as *the* group who defines justice and, not surprisingly, *the* group most deserving of justice. Indeed, the very idea of justice with its overtones of push-pull, us-them, or "what is due" to me or you, us or them, will encounter skeptics who doubt its relevance for our political vision of the concerns of our global future. Interestingly, justice is not a very common word among today's futurists and globalists. They are clearly more engaged with community, who should be considered in the global community of the future, and how to ensure the survival of the Earth through community.[5]

Yet surely justice will not fade as a continuing human desire in ordinary life or in political theory. Our evidence is the past and the present. Over and over, humans ask about fairness and justice for themselves and others. We can only assume that they always will do so. Political theory dare not forget that survival is not enough for us as humans. We also need a just future for ourselves and our societies.

At the same time, questions of authority will also remain important in the future, perhaps more so than ever. This reality may not be entirely welcome in a freedom-loving culture such as the United States, where currently a continuing disillusion and cynicism are more the norm than are respect for institutions and heroes, though the latter occasionally resurfaces. Authority is very much out of fashion. And yet there is good reason to believe that authority will become a major concern of political theory in the next century. The ethic of expansive individual rights and personal liberties may receive a searching and disturbing reexamination. The hard question is whether fragmentation, subjectivism, and parochialism are likely bases for the fashioning of a world community, much less for crafting a consensus on world environmental action. There is little doubt that global crisis and need will eventually require authority to tackle them. What is in doubt is what role particular freedoms or specific individual rights will have in political theory's next century.

Authority cannot be manufactured as neatly as some hope and others fear. It comes from a feeling that people award to a person, institution, or law. That is hard to decree and not much more effective to preach. Nor is authority something to be casually affirmed and uncritically celebrated. It can be terribly dangerous for individuals and societies. We speculate that political theory will have to focus its vision on it increasingly in the future. We will have to explore the stressful issues of what kind of authority we ought to have in a world grown surprisingly small before we find ourselves hurled into crisis in a world of power rather than authority and force rather than thought.[6]

It is well to remember that political theory is "simply" critical thinking about the pivotal public dimension of our lives.[7] Like all critical thinking, it is a form of intellectual analysis, probing and discovering relationships and regularities, and a search for sensible values. It is unique (and political) because it focuses on the natural, decisive public relationships we all share because we live on the same planet. Thus we all have a stake in our common history, a political culture, and institutions of political economy. In this microprocessor age, even formerly insurmountable separations of language and different polities are rapidly losing their significance because of constant improvement in transportation and communications.

This kind of critical thinking about the ends and means of politics and government is more than a set of manuscripts, values, and prescriptions. It is a humanistic process and an attitude that function as tools to use in attempting to solve some of our public problems. More importantly, it could help us to achieve our unrealized public possibilities and allow us to examine where we are and explore where we ought to be as political animals. Thus it has always been and remains our political eyes and imagination; our vision of ways to improve our collective fortune.

The methods and historical collection of knowledge that we have amassed in these millennia are simply lenses to help us better see politics. Using them will allow you to join the arguments and inquiries about the ends and means of politics that differentiate a critically examined political existence. The broad outlines of how to think rigorously about values and some of the dimensions of political morality that we have touched upon in this introduction need not be memorized or slavishly followed. Use them as they seem to fit the questions that come to mind as you think about politics. Allow them to help you effectively analyze, question, and begin to resolve the major political issues of our time as you see them.

In fact, the best way to learn how to do political theory is on-the-job training. Through this introduction you have learned enough about some of the basic techniques to begin. Now, just do it—with your friends, relatives, and all with whom you come into political contact. Whether you commit your political theory to writing or merely mull it over in your mind, the more of it you do, the better at it you will get and the more of it you will want to do. Moreover, thinking about political questions often has the heuristic effect of causing you to think about critical questions in other areas of life.

Good political theory is a dynamic entity. It is in constant motion because political reality is a moving target. It is an evolving process of evaluating and prescribing for the shifting political sands that we face as we search for the best ways to interact. After all, we cannot have satisfactory public relationships without some common understanding and commitment to values that facilitate our interactions.

Liberty, equality, justice, political obligation, community, authority, the ends and means of revolt and obedience, the rights and proper role of the citizen vis-à-vis society, and the rest are building blocks of political accommodation and understanding that have roots in our living tradition of political theory. As it grows and changes with each new contribution, political theory allows us to develop our political commitments and increases our public opportunities. Rock bands, symphony orchestras, and a good polity have one thing in common: each can make music in ensemble that its individual members could not create alone.

These roles and characteristics make political theory more than just a historical collection of ideas or a set of principles. Because it focuses on both values and politics, it is a practical political tool. Citizens and statesmen use it all of the time, whether they call it political theory or not.

This contribution will not diminish in the coming decades. People will still need to look at the established categories of politics and government and push beyond them in expanding our horizons of critical thought. Political theory has successfully integrated perspectives on political economy, human rights, international solidarities and peace issues, and the control and humanization of technology as they have arisen in human history. Perhaps that is because it alone among the social sciences and humanities specializes in placing vital values into inescapable public interactions.

That is why our enterprise encompasses both continuity and change. Public situations and issues will be a part of our lives as long we coexist on the same planet. But inexorably, new political needs and situations will arise because humans are not static beings. If we work to keep political theory alive and strong, it will be there to guide us in asking the perennial questions[8] and maybe a few new ones as we experience the future. It will remain a practical tool to develop answers to assist our heirs in managing their public relationships just as our ancestors' ideas have helped us.

Consequently, we view contemporary political theory as neither pure philosophy nor pure political science. Rather it is a hybrid synthesis of both. Its unique insights, techniques, prescriptions, and categories have made it an essential feature of our intellectual lives for more than twenty-five centuries. At its best, the art wields facts and values creatively, continuing and expanding the current postbehavioral approach to political science that is analogous to what political theory has always done.[9] Another way of saying this is that the tradition of political theory cultivates values that are realistic because they do not deny facts and facts that are moral because they take consequences into account.

Political theory is a useful prescriptive enterprise. As a major component of our legacy of civilization, it will almost certainly remain useful in the future. This is so because politics and history are still inevitable human processes and political theory has the capacity and will to help citizens improve their political environments as they evolve.

Thinking critically in this manner creates certain opportunities and obligations for us. We have an opportunity to influence the future course of public events. If we contribute with cogent analyses, we will be able to speak truth to power and have power hear us whether it wants to or not. If we perceive an obligation to try to make things better, this opportunity to be players on the political stage creates an obligation to act morally. Consequently, an independent political theory has no business reflexively supporting the status quo or making those in power comfortable. We will be far better servants of the public interest if we use our techniques of critical political thinking to inspire leaders to make changes for the better. Let leaders look elsewhere for rationales for policies that merely serve their own interests.

THE SHAPE OF POLITICAL THEORY IN THE NEAR FUTURE

Political theorists do not have a special talent for looking into a crystal ball and foretelling the future.[10] But we do operate in a discipline that has always kept track of trends and critically viewed the needs that germinate from public relationships. This allows us to take stock of present political styles and needs and extrapolate them into the coming decades.[11] In other words, our disciplinary perspective allows us to make some educated guesses about the shape of political theory in the near future. Without resorting to magic, wishful thinking, or unrealistic views of the public sector, we can carefully evaluate the political present and add sensible estimates of how major political phenomena are likely to develop. The result is a prediction of the shape of tomorrow's political theory.

Opportunities and the Future

The future may pose unpleasant choices and engage us in trying conflicts in service of our planet. Therefore it will affect political theory in ways that not all will applaud. But there is a happier side. The word for political theory's future that may apply best is opportunity. We suspect that its path will hardly be smooth, but we should appreciate that this will give us, as every crisis does, the chance to break free from the conventional, to rethink and to reformulate. Though it may take us to either familiar or new territory, it will yield vigorous and important political theory in either case. Thus the future before us may continue to produce political vision through political theory.

The past is our source for this prediction since most of the great theories of politics resulted from people trying to deal with times of crisis and change. Plato saw his fourth-century Athens in crisis, and so did Marx view nineteenth-century Europe. So did the American founders view their colonial nation in the age of the Revolution and Constitution. In each instance we must recognize the existing crisis to understand their political philosophy, prescriptions, and vision.

We thus argue that the future will certainly provide several significant opportunities for serious normative political thought. One will be about helping to consider and fashion a concept of global community. Given its significance, such a turning to reflection on community in a new context could become a landmark enterprise in our long history.

This is still an underdeveloped topic, despite its apparent importance for our future. Political theory rarely gets around to considering the challenges of globalism, preferring too often to argue solely about the past or to make analytical distinctions about very tired topics in contemporary fashion. The reality of an increasingly interdependent humanity requires us to consider the meaning of a global community and how it might and should fit with other communities of nation-states and the racial, religious, economic, and cultural communities that both divide us and define our personalities. It would not work to abolish all but membership in a global community of humans because people come to the process with socialization and we cannot write on them like blank slates. The objective should be to balance and integrate existing communities and smooth their conflicts. This is a formidable challenge: It will require every measure of our vision and political sophistication.

One approach would be to start from the evident signs of community decay that surround us today, especially declining family structures. As in our following discussion, we must also note how much of modern international order is dangerously tribal in an era of proliferating new nations, the splintering and warring of others like Yugoslavia, and demands by assorted groups for autonomy within existing nation-states. Community is sometimes merely weak. At other times, it is strong but disastrously parochial. We must confront these issues and treat them as opportunities for our learning.

Obviously, there is also opportunity for political theory to go beyond the *idea* of community to explore its substance and what forms it might take. Their ambiguity only adds interest to the task. We must both rely on past experience and walk in new ways. Above all, as we deal with prescriptions for federal or confederated international systems of the future, for example, we will have to perceive and speak to people in the concrete realities of their lives while we nudge ourselves out of the present pattern of decision making.

Opportunities to reflect on what democracy might mean in global terms (and within regions of a global system) and to advocate a more democratic Earth are striking, daunting, and exciting all at once. Does a global perspective cast doubt on democracy of any sort? Is participatory democracy possible in such a context? Or are there new democratic ideas and procedures awaiting our discovery and application as we turn our vision to political theory's twenty-sixth century? We cannot know answers to these questions for certain now, but we do well to keep in mind that political theory excels at visions of the future. Many of today's commonplaces were "unrealistic" visions of political theorists even a century ago.

Similar opportunities exist in the realm of justice. What will justice mean in the next century? How will the traditional legalistic and distributional categories we have considered in these pages change? What is global justice? How would it connect with justice in nature or as nature—defined perhaps in terms of everything in the ecosphere. The questions are many and vexing, but the opportunities for political theory and for your role in its future are many.

One likely challenge will be confronting meaning and morality. At present, there are few places where the meaning of the universe is held to be obvious and where the purpose of human life (much less its definitions) are givens. There are fewer and fewer locales where the skepticisms of modernity and postmodernity have not left their marks. To be sure, close-bounded societies may still be found. Self-confident religions, including Islam and Christianity, are tremendously active and some individuals everywhere rest confident in their beliefs about their existence and purpose. Even among self-consciously "modern" souls, many favor pluralism and diversity only until they discover that their treasured values then will be considered just one set among a host of others.

Still another opportunity is presented to us in the challenge to struggle with the role of politics and government. The major issue is that of government capacity. What can it do? What should it do? We know that governments are effective at distributing money, but they stumble when it comes to changing behavior and, certainly, the underlying values of actions. This is true even as many governments try to undertake more and more, sometimes at their own initiative, sometimes at the behest of others.

The classic, painful example is the modern public school in the United States. In addition to its traditional function of providing basic literacy and numeracy, it now often shoulders a host of other missions: teaching life skills, knowledge of health and sexual life, technical skills, moral norms, emotional strength, and self-esteem, among others. Sadly, there is no convincing evidence of success at any of these projects. Public schools represent a model of government doing almost everything, but few except some educational bureaucrats conclude that it is government working well. This also is a major opportunity for political theory to prescribe lifting some of these misplaced governmental burdens and placing them in institutions more suited to the task if we see it that way.

The disturbing irony is that as we use our vision to peer into the near future, demands on government will probably spiral up to a vast extent. These demands will include saving the environment, providing better health care, better food distribution, coordination of global cooperation, and so forth. Requests for government to promote values encouraging community survival and integration are sure to mount.[12] We have doubts about the capacity of present governments to respond. But, unlike much of the public, we feel that government has unrealized potential that we can help develop with political theory. Politics can offer us some hope and we need to reinvigorate it and perhaps both separate it from and also partially integrate it with civil society, the family, the church, the private association, and our friends.

Life-and-Death Issues

As we enter into what climatologist Stephen Schneider has called the "greenhouse century"[13] of global warming, ecological warnings from credible sources mount. Environmental scientists are making dire predictions about animal, plant, and human health risks from dangerous increases in deforestation, global fresh water shortages, climate changes, depletion of the protective ozone layer and other environmental disasters in the near future. Political systems that have created the conditions that have led to this mounting tidal wave of environmental assault are now beginning to pay attention. Some are even trying to deal with improving the situation.[14] Policymakers are faced with mounting evidence of the accuracy of scientific predictions and the public's new attention to the issue brought about by the activism of political parties and groups like the various Green parties, the World Wildlife Federation, and Greenpeace.

This inherently political area will assuredly be a focus of political theory as polities and citizens ask questions about the ends and means of government and natural environment. The effects of our civilization's practices and standards on the Earth's flora and fauna are an important dimension of public relationships. Now that human beings have accumulated enough technical ability to befoul the planet on a wholesale level, we must turn our political vision to developing a political ecology—a political theory on how we ought to relate to the environment and each other. This should be a fast-track priority of political theory because it is literally a life-and-death issue of politics. If we cannot develop a political culture that will allow us to remain healthy or even alive, there is no sense worrying about how just, free, or equal we ought to be to each other. People who literally are struggling to survive cannot afford thoughts on what constitutes an optimal state of affairs. Even more starkly, dead people have no need to consider any political values.

The value of human life has always been prominent in political theory. We should remember this as we analyze and prescribe liberties to use natural resources. We need to use it as a lens that adapts our political vision to the justice of allocating precious resources and restricting harmful environmental emissions. Life as a value must also play a prominent role as we prescribe environmental latitude for governments and international organizations. It should help us evaluate who should make environmental decisions in response to the demands and supports of whom. But the environmental clock is ticking and we need to hurry before we are too late. Fortunately, we do not need to reinvent the wheel. Liberty, equality, life, justice, authority, and legitimacy will serve us just as effectively in an ecological political theory as they have in the other areas of political theory's focus in the last twenty-five centuries.

Another life-and-death issue that is certain to occupy political theory in the coming decades involves war and peace. Just as with environmental pollution, its urgency is merited by the ability of modern nuclear, chemical, biological, and other kinds of weapons to end life on the planet as we know it.

As astronomer Carl Sagan and others have argued, a large-scale nuclear war is likely to produce enough smoke from burning cities and battlefields to block the sun's rays. This would make growing of crops impossible and create a fatal nuclear winter for a remaining population devoid of its energy and health care infrastructures. Biological and chemical weapons would have similarly lethal effects on a global scale, as would even a very large "conventional" war fought with weapons many times more destructive than those of the last world war.

Even if present arms control initiatives are effective and a war that destroys global life is not fought, smaller wars constantly take place and kill many thousands annually. Also, the world's nations and groups collectively spend trillions of dollars on weapons in "peacetime." This spending is not morally neutral. The research, development, purchase, and maintenance of modern weapons systems constitutes a massive opportunity cost for the polity[15] that renders resources unavailable for health care, food, housing, or other basic human needs. Moreover, military policies mobilize many of the best brains and research facilities for weapons development, thereby holding back research and development of consumer goods and civilian technology needs because there is not enough "brainpower" to go around.[16]

The organization of the present international system is another aspect of the life-and-death issues of war and peace that is not morally neutral. Many reputable international relations experts theorize that the current global system is at least a partial cause of major wars.[17] The contemporary political world is divided into many nation-states and lacks a central authority to settle disputes or enforce international laws or norms. Existing international organizations like the United Nations lack sufficient political or military resources to deter major powers with revolutionary policies from destroying each other and engulfing the world in ruin as they struggle.

This literally do-or-die set of issues provides political theory with an agenda and some major opportunities. Today, increasingly complex technology like high definition television requires international cooperation to fund and implement it and information is becoming more and more global.[18] One of the results of these trends is to forge similar patterns within formerly very disparate nations because each polity faces coinciding stakes and prospects in the evolving world. The so-called global convergence hypothesis holds that this is inevitable and that all major nations are converging on a universal political and economic style that is merely an irresistible adaptation to events.

This hypothesis is probably an exaggeration that does not take the complexities of national political cultures and histories into account. Nevertheless, predictions of global convergence should not be entirely dismissed. Events such as the fall of Marxism-Leninism in Europe and the emergence of some political unity in the European Community show that at least some nation-states are de-emphasizing formerly important barriers of political economy between them.[19] The possibility if not the inevitability of convergence and a concomitant removal of some tensions among nations exists in the next decades. So does the possibility that the poorer nations of the earth will

208 POLITICAL THEORY AND THE FUTURE OF THE DISCIPLINE

dissent from the emerging Northern consensus and form their own Southern consensus and accelerate cries for a new economic order.[20]

A more peaceful world requires developing a future international politics that better meets the needs of all global citizens. Fortunately, political theory excels at explaining and advocating alternative values and the institutional arrangements that support them. It is almost inevitable that the cultural shrinking of the world will place demands on political theory to emphasize political values that accommodate a wide spectrum of cultures and lead to international accommodation. As the discipline responds, the cultural boundaries and limitations as well as war and peace implications of present political theories will be better understood. That ought to lead to some purging of them as appropriate. Tomorrow's political theory is likely to be more diverse and have less of a Western and pro-nationalistic bias. We hope this will lead to future emphasis on how to avoid international conflict and accelerate international cooperation.

Another thing that political theory will probably do (and certainly ought to) is become more pro-active on arms control and disarmament issues. Though thinkers like Thucydides, Rousseau, and Kant[21] have embraced peace issues in our historical discourse, we have not done enough with them to meet world conditions in the next century of political theory. Political theory will be forced by events to recognize the dangers and the opportunity costs of increasing arms spirals and wars. This will lead us to take ethical stances about national and international politics that oppose war unambiguously because it denies the possibility of most of the political values we cherish.

The historical arguments about just wars need to be reexamined in light of the consequences and dangers of modern warfare. Moreover, political thinkers need to establish a dialogue on the topic with those theologians and political leaders who maintain that some wars can be just. Similar dialogue and collaboration with arms control and disarmament experts is also needed on issues like the causes and prevention of war, the morality of various arms control proposals, alternative settlement of disputes, the development of crisis management centers, and the rest. This dialogue ought to result in more effective examination of the empirical and the normative bases of needed innovations. Hopefully, that will hasten better resolution of war-and-peace issues.

As scholars and citizens, political theorists need to learn more about the processes of international political conflict in order to prescribe values and systems that either strengthen existing peaceful institutions or advocate their transcendence where necessary. Political theory as a discipline needs to deal with universal values that are large enough to deflect the dangers that modern military technology and the threat of war and terror have wrought. Only if such issues are ameliorated (if they cannot be solved) can political theory turn its full attention to other issues of human political potential that are not eroded by the opportunity costs and threats of war-and-peace issues in the nuclear age.

The Domestic Political Agenda

Though issues of environmental or military life and death demand center stage, we cannot afford to cast aside the more typical issues of political theory as the discipline adapts to the times. The familiar concerns of domestic political ends and means will probably share the stage as costars in political theory's future because they deal with perennial aspects of our politics irrespective of where or when we live. They will not go away even if we choose to let tomorrow's political theory ignore them. They will simply fester without creative thought and solutions being brought forth to adapt to changing conditions and personalities. Because the near future will not change the fact that we will persist as citizens of a nation-state of some type, we will continue to need political theory's questions and insights into the best political community on a subglobal level.

Technology has changed domestic politics just as extensively as it has affected the realm of international politics. The same microprocessor technology that allows us to make "smart" bombs also allows much more effective dissemination of information about matters of government to the citizenry. It also makes substantially more participatory and responsive government possible in large political systems for the first time in history.[22] What is more, the technology of information gathering and management represented by active political interest groups who mobilize potential supporters or computer bulletin boards, for example, can become powerful political tools. They can let people know about threats to their political values, secure their rights, and even bring discussion of political theory in some form to people whose interests or opportunities might preclude it currently.

At a minimum, political theory has a continuing and even escalating role to play in making sure that the information represented by these technologies does not get distorted or co-opted by those who will manipulate them for their own advantage. Governments or private interests are certain to recognize the revolutionary political potential in these technologies and try to manage them in ways that will benefit themselves and ignore the public interest. Even democratic governments are frightened by the possibility of a public with access to information and an avenue to voice their political opinions and mobilize for change. Political theory ought to educate citizens and future (if not present) leaders about the potential for distortion and manipulation that co-option of these powerful avenues of information represents. Citizens need to be reminded that knowledge is power and that power is both an end and a means that needs to be examined and used responsibly if it is to serve the public interest. Political theory should take the lead on this issue and develop and advocate values that promote the fair and moral uses of such information and secure access for all.

Beyond that, a political theory that remains vital in the future is certain to continue its long and successful tradition of raising radical questions about who should rule according to what criteria of legitimacy. It will also focus on techniques of holding the government and private sector responsive to citizens in a changing climate of information and government powers. Fortunately, tomorrow's political theory will still have a rich literature on the historical manifestations of these perennial concerns. We need to keep the discipline relevant by adding our own voices to the discourse while not ignoring what our learned predecessors have said.

Just as was the case with past normative political thinkers, the vision of our critical thinking applied through technological opportunities and cultural development gives us something to say. Failure to say it will merely allow those in power to govern as they see fit. It will render us unable to ask the right questions that have always helped keep the powerful honest. Our role in developing the next generation of political theory is to remember this and not lose the capacity to ask the right questions. Our ability to come up with the right answers is certain to be undiminished if we take advantage of future political tools as they develop. If we remain as knowledgeable about them as governments and private interests do, we will be fulfilling our obligations to use our political vision effectively.

A related aspect of political theory's traditional focus on ends and means of domestic politics will be useful for both domestic and international politics in political theory's coming decades. Political thought has long been absorbed with values and empirical strategies to reinforce the abilities of people to have or develop a meaningful stake in government. Not restricted to democracy, this aspect of political theory has produced values and inspired institutions of legitimacy and authority. It has also constructed effective ways to represent people and territories within the institutions of government. Majority rule, proportional representation, representation through population and/or territory of residence, representation by "estate," profession, wealth, and so forth have all been developed by political theorists at various points. Moreover, each has played a role in governing somewhere.

As new institutions of government (particularly quasi-democratic ones) emerge in the aftermath of colonialism, wars, revolutions, and the rise and fall of movements like communism, political theory will certainly respond. There will be a continuing and probably escalating need to deal with how citizens are represented and endowed with a stake in the emerging polities of the next centuries. Whether people are going to be counted in politics and government because of what they earn, where they live, what their ethnic heritage is, or any other criteria will be issues that face tomorrow's political theory just as much as they faced Aristotle, Locke, Rousseau, and other political architects.

Whether it focuses on democracy or more authoritarian forms of government, political theory will be studying new forms of government and citizenship and incorporating them into the literature of the discipline. What is more, since change is not always progress, we need to develop values and procedures that will integrate future citizens and their governments and not be afraid to say that some new systems are wrong because they deny proven norms. Change brings choices. Auspiciously using our critical political vision will help us make good ones.

Furthermore, as international organizations and institutions like the European Community or the United Nations develop, they have shifting needs for principles and practices of representation in government. One reason the United Nations is not truly legitimate to many observers is that nations with hundreds of millions of people have the same vote in the General Assembly as tiny nations. In a different way, this is true in the critical Security Council as well. The workable principles and procedures of representation that have been developed within political theory lend themselves to adaptation and application to the problems of international organizations and other supranational institutions of today and tomorrow. It is likely that the discipline will turn toward them as world order becomes more prominent. The values of justice, equality, and the like have as much relevance beyond the borders of nation-states as they do within them.

Another aspect of domestic politics that the political theory of the future will be forced to address involves the issues surrounding violence within the nation-state. Political theorist Mulford Sibley writes that political "thinkers have been perturbed and fascinated by violence. It has played a central part in political speculation of all types."[23] Today the technology of violence and the pressures of crowded life in a stressful environment have apparently produced more murder and violent crime than at any other time in recorded history. Clearly this will draw the attention of political theory.

Among other things, the discipline will be forced to deal more with violence by focusing on the morality (especially the conflicts between liberty and equality) of regulating domestic weapons. More lethal technology and greater populations will cause the discipline to reexamine the issues of crime, punishment, and justice. Allied issues that probably will be placed on the next century's agenda include development of a perspective on whether legitimate fear of crime ought to lead to responses that erode civil liberties or change the extent of government authority over individual lives. Events have a habit of causing us to focus on certain areas as we use our political vision.

In other words, political theory should establish a dialogue and collaboration with criminologists, sociologists, and others that is the analogue of the one that we foresee on issues of international war and peace. Together, political theorists and other experts can increase our understanding of the processes, policies, and institutions that best allow us to live together in an increasingly interdependent but lethal society. Research into the normative and empirical dimensions of new forms of dispute resolution, needed legislation, the proper balance between liberty and equality in the polity, and so forth must continue to keep pace with new social and political trends.

The Agenda of Political Theory and Political Economy

Capitalism and communism are political economies and political theories that were developed by political theorists and economists to cope with the Industrial Revolution. Even though that revolution is still a part of our lives, the nature of industrialization and its impact on citizens has changed dramatically in the last century or so. Today, many parts of the world are entering a postindustrial political economy[24] and more are sure to do so in the future. And even future industrial and agrarian political economies are sure to differ from their historical antecedents in many important ways. Political theory will certainly try to keep pace with these changes by developing visions of how to foster better public interactions in tomorrow's political economies.

We are likely to deal with these issues and their implications in a couple of ways. First of all, we will continue to reexamine and interpret ideas and concepts like capitalism, socialism, and mixed political economies as circumstances change. The realities of decentralization, appropriate levels of government regulation, equity demands by changing work forces, just compensation and working conditions, natural and human resource management, and many others need to be integrated into today's political economies. Traditional categories almost inevitably will be reshaped with these in mind. And perhaps new categories need to be developed as the older political economies change in degrees enough to be changes in kind. Privatization, quasi nationalization, public and private competition, and other political economies now being experimented with will need to be monitored and developed appropriately as political theory keeps pace with events and needs.

An allied issue of political economy faced by political theory involves the knotty issues presented by the apparent crumbling of communism. Is it permanently declining or is this just a short phase in history? What (if anything) has been lost by its passing? What changes in political organization should emerge from its rubble? The nature and role of central institutions of public allocation in an economy will have to be reexamined once again as old answers become less certain.

The potential of efficiency and rationality as advantages of central planning will surely be reevaluated in light of the current century's experiences. So, too, should the linked issue of centralization of political institutions. In terms of both, communications and commerce are becoming more globalized. Therefore, does it still make sense to organize our polities and economies around decentralized units in order to control tyranny? Can we hold power in check more effectively by first centralizing it and them giving the central unit effective controls of responsiveness?

Perhaps a good analogy is to the brakes on an automobile. By controlling the four brakes (one at each wheel) by one pedal, we increase our ability to make the car respond to our wishes. Should we do that with political economies, merging government and economic authorities into one central unit and subjecting it to the brakes of electing an entire government of policymakers? Or should we go the other way and mandate decentralized economic democracy so that workers control their own workplaces and markets and neighborhoods govern themselves and only participate in a loose regional federation as needed? Are there middle grounds that make more sense? These are merely a few of the questions that will occupy political thinkers who have experienced a turbulent couple of centuries since the major writings on the subject have entered the discourse.

Another role that political theory ought to play in coming decades of political economy concerns the humanization of technology. Who will control technological change and how they do it will control our lives in the near future as much as who has the power of information. This formidable challenge is as great as any that has ever faced the discipline.

Among political theorists, Rousseau[25] and Marx[26] wrote extensively on the subject, particularly on how dehumanizing machines and work conditions contributed to worker alienation from the products of their own labor and drained the nobility from political and economic relationships. Though Marx's ideas apply mostly to nineteenth-century industrial technology, and Rousseau's are generally hostile to the emergence of modernism, these ruminations remain as models for what needs to be done by political theory to deal with the emerging technology of today and tomorrow. We need not be Marxists or Rousseauists to recognize the validity of the questions they have raised.

Political theorists will need to raise questions about who ought to have access to work-saving technology and what should be done about workers who are displaced by it. That process should stimulate answers in the form of value clarification and advocacy and prescriptions. Other priority questions for the discipline include the personal or political effects and dangers new technology presents and who ought to sponsor its research and development. We also will be called upon to examine the issues and values of general government regulation of technological issues. The list is almost endless, but the topic presents the polity and the discipline with a critical set of concerns that must be considered if we hope to make technology our servant instead of our master.

Among the myriad issues connected with political economy confronting political theory in the coming decades, the issues of business and government are likely to remain urgent priorities.[27] Here we will need to consider many questions. What is an optimal division of labor and control between business and government in regulating commerce? Who will hold business firms accountable to whom? Who will regulate the regulators and hold them accountable? How should business cycles and political cycles interact? What kind of agricultural and industrial development policies should government pursue in order to maximize economic development and equality among citizens? Should tax policies be used solely to raise revenue or should they also channel behavior through incentives and disincentives? These are but a few of the questions. But they are important and will remain with us as long as people have commerce and politics.

To conclude, we can be sure that political theory will be driven by inclination and events to continue to examine these and associated questions and develop an effective literature on them. The world's political systems and economies are becoming increasingly integrated and the international political economy is well on its way to full-blown emergence. We have an obligation to monitor these events and apply our knowledge to them in order to try to make our future choices in political economy more satisfying than those faced by our peers and ancestors.

Political Theory and Rediscovering the Classical Polis

In the final analysis, political theory functioning at its full potential is a form of political discernment that assesses and advocates the potential of politics. Now and in the future, our discipline will acknowledge the fact that we are political animals. Sheldon Wolin has recently said:

> There is a disconnection between the practices of political institutions and the tempos they require for handling affairs of the public, and the tempos we associate with scientific, technological, and entrepreneurial innovation. . . . Political processes, like marriage and education, really depend on a rhythm that's less frenetic, less innovative, and that demands some kind of respect for how you carry on something. . . . Deliberation, which is fundamental to politics, takes time. . . . you have to consider different points of view.[28]

He goes on to say that this disparity is unfortunate because it means that two major phases of our lives are out of synchronization and that change becomes so frenetic that it becomes meaningless and even conservative. He is right. Something has been lost as we rush headlong into a world of decision making that does not put a great value on deliberation. The historic development of the classical Greek polis and political theory were the result of deliberation and careful vision first and quick decisions second. They produced institutions and outlooks that have served us well over time. We need to rediscover these, our political roots. They have nourished us well over the years and will continue to do so if we cultivate them. As students of political theory, we are proud of our political heritage and look forward to a political future filled with values of similar public interactions.

As we summarize the role that political theory should play in our future, we know we need to bring back the spirit of deliberation and community that was found in the polis and its deliberative processes and institutions. The best way to do that is to rediscover the perspective and thinking about public relationships that can be effectively supplied by political theory.

Most of all, political theory needs to confront and come to terms with the issues of power. As Wolin has said, "defense, high tech, and a strong corporate system can't generate the kind of values that make us really comfortable and that really suggests that the power we have is good and that we deserve it."[29] We should recognize that politics is power over others and it can be used for good or bad ends. The choice is ours.

We need to use political power wisely, as an art and craft. We need to use it to bring back the art of accommodating differences in an interdependent world where conflict is more lethal than ever before. Along the way, as political theorists we should look for ways to celebrate life and speak that truth to those who are using their political power to force conformity.

We can accomplish this by placing values at the center of our political consciousness. While it is a truism, it is still worth remembering that political power that is strong and efficient is not necessarily right. Because the conditions of political theory and politics force us to resolve conflicts between the two, we must give the benefit of the doubt to humane values in order to be good political theorists into the next century. As Camus and other witnesses to the atrocities of politics of the current century have reminded us, the ends and means of power are central issues and define our very humanity.

Our task as political theorists should be to use our minds to understand and advocate a process of moral standard-making that always challenges power. If we succeed at that, we will go a long way toward preventing the shocks and dangers of revolution and the daily obscenities of power abuse. Our dedication to what used to be called civic virtue and what is now called critical normative political thinking can be a major contribution toward a better life for us all.

CONCLUSION

We end this journey into political theory by stepping aside from reflections on the challenges and opportunities for political theory now and in its next century. We must turn now to ask whether there will be much political theory in the future. For there are certainly reasons for discouragement about political theory today. One reason is the formalism and abstractness of so much consideration of the good society and the good political order. Too many political theorists talk and write in pretentious and remote language that avoids the concerns of our time and tomorrow. Political theory can come down to earth. We need it to do so.

Moreover, some of modern political theory is too enamored of the technical and the statistical. Even those who undertake theory that has some normative or policy implications sometimes do not reach a conclusion except through a fog of jargon and crippling qualifications. Still others substitute fashionable, scientific-sounding words for substantial conclusions. Put another way, we sometimes wonder if the more political theory has become a professional enterprise, the more it threatens to strangle itself to death. It may be that the more it has become an academic discipline, the more it edges away from risk and creativity and becomes subject to the capricious winds of fashion.[30]

However, fears that this may cause political theory to miss the chances that are before it are not very credible. Political theory includes but also extends beyond the academic political philosophy profession. Moreover, within academia there are many creative people taking risks and doing normative, analytic, and historical theory. Beyond the ivy walls, political theory fortunately flourishes, being practiced by all sorts of people and from many directions.

Political theory must keep its edges ragged so that it is open to new ideas and new views of the old. Fortunately, it has a solid record of doing so. It should not fall prostrate before every fad, but it requires us to inquire into fresh perspectives whenever they appear, regardless of origins. By definition, creativity will burst bounds and political theory has and will do so repeatedly. We need to think like political theorists and be ready to recognize creativity when it enters our realm.

No one should pretend that we are not in an era of skepticism and relativism where confidence in reason and amity among people is in short supply. Despair makes good sense to many of us in this environment, and we are daunted to undertake the kind of bold political theory that Hobbes or Plato or Marx did. But while these are, indeed, impediments to the future of political theory, we continue to insist that they may just as well (and far more fruitfully) be seen as opportunities. If we strain our vision toward our political futures, it will not fail us. Others have done it and we can, too, if we have the will and acquire the training and the practice.

After all, despite the pessimism and the doubts, political theory continues to attract tremendous interest and good minds. What is more, as necessity creates its own imperatives, today's problems cast a cold and heavy shadow over us as we peer into political theory's next century. This should create a lot of motivation to do good political theory in the years ahead. Sometimes the way will be hard or uncertain, but what is unusual about that in a discipline that has survived over 2500 years? We predict that in its next century as in the past, doing political theory will remain both important and exciting. We hope that all of us do what we can to craft intelligent political theory, whatever our profession or social class may be. If we are fortunate, we may gain some wisdom about the good political community and the good life along the way.

GLOSSARY OF KEY TERMS

arms control and disarmament Practices and processes that reduce the likelihood or lethality of war through control or destruction of weapons.
authority A feeling of legitimacy that people award to a person, institution, or law
convergence hypothesis Prediction that says the world's major political economies will grow more like each other as each deals with similar circumstances and resources.
critical thinking Analyzing, judging, and understanding ideas.
discourse An ongoing dialogue on a topic like political theory. It may span several centuries.
futurism The practice and policy of predicting and analyzing the future.
global community The idea of a polis and society that embraces all of humankind because of environmental proximity.
globalism The practice of viewing problems and prospects of people in context that transcends national borders.

heurism The principle of serendipitous discovery of new ideas and knowledge while looking for something else.

humanism The doctrine that puts human values, creativity, and responsibility at the center of temporal acts.

new economic order The call for a more equitable sharing of resources between the richer nations of the Northern hemisphere and the poorer nations of the Southern hemisphere.

polis The classical Greek term for the political community.

political theory, political philosophy, political thought Interchangeable terms for the rigorous study of the ends and means of politics and government.

political vision Term used by political theorist Sheldon Wolin and others to describe insights and applications of political theory to the polis and society. A form of critical thinking.

prescription The advocacy of public policy goals and processes that is based on the values in a political theory.

rights Immutable moral claims.

SUGGESTIONS FOR FURTHER READING

Celente, Gerald, and Milton, Tom. *Trend Tracking: The System to Profit From Today's Trends.* New York: John Wiley and Sons, 1990.

Daly, Herman E., and John B. Cobb, Jr. *For the Common Good: Redirecting the Economy Toward Community, the Environment, and a Sustainable Future.* Boston: Beacon, 1989.

Dizard, Wilson P., Jr. *The Coming Information Age.* 3d ed. New York: Longman, 1989.

Fowler, Robert Booth. *The Dance with Community.* Lawrence: University Press of Kansas, 1991.

Heilbroner, Robert. *An Inquiry into the Human Prospect.* New York: W. W. Norton, 1974.

Nash, Roderick. *The Rights of Nature: A History of Environmental Ethics.* Madison: University of Wisconsin Press, 1989.

Nelson, John, ed. *What Should Political Theory Be Now?* Albany: State University of New York Press, 1983.

Parenti, Michael. *The Sword and the Dollar.* New York: St. Martin's Press, 1989.

Rifkin, Jeremy. *The Emerging Order.*

Sibley, Mulford Q. *Political Ideas and Ideologies.* New York: Harper & Row, 1970.

Simon, Julian, and Kahn, Herman. *The Resourceful Earth: A Response to Global 2000.* New York: Basil Blackwell, 1984.

Waltz, Kenneth. *Man, The State, and War.* New York: Columbia University Press, 1959.

Wolfe, Alan. *Whose Keeper? Social Sciences and Moral Obligation.* Berkeley: University of California Press, 1989.

Wolin, Sheldon. *Politics and Vision: Continuity and Innovation in Western Political Thought.* Boston: Little Brown and Co., 1960.

NOTES

1. Sheldon Wolin, *Politics and Vision: Continuity and Innovation in Western Political Thought* (Boston: Little Brown and Co., 1960).
2. See the discussion of the themes we have used as an approach to political theory in the first pages of Chapter 1. A review of them at this point will help you to digest the material in this final chapter.
3. Some examples: Donald Edward Davis, *Ecophilosophy: A Field Guide to the Literature* (San Pedro, Calif.: R. and E. Miles, 1989); Herman E. Daly and John B. Cobb, Jr., *For the Common Good* (Boston: Beacon, 1989); Ian G. Barbour, *Western Man and Environmental Ethics* (Reading, Mass.: Addison-Wesley, 1973); J. Baird Callicott, *In Defense of The Land Ethic* (Albany: State University of New York Press, 1989); William Ophuls, *Ecology and the Politics of Scarcity: Prologue to a Political Theory of the Steady State* (San Francisco: W. H. Freeman, 1977); Bruce Stokes, *Helping Ourselves: Local Solutions to Global Problems* (New York: Norton, 1981); Roderick Nash, *The Rights of Nature: A History of Environmental Ethics* (Madison; University of Wisconsin, 1989).
4. For a provocative discussion, see Robert Heilbroner, *The Human Prospect* (New York: W.W. Norton, 1974).
5. See for an overview Robert Booth Fowler, *The Dance with Community* (Lawrence: University Press of Kansas, 1991).
6. On this topic, too, Robert Heilbroner, *The Human Prospect*, is sobering.
7. Many scholars believe that critical thinking is the major product of the Western higher education system. We agree and suggest that a broad cross-section of the literature of political theory deserves a prominent place in any canon of great ideas and/or sensible curriculum.
8. Even though the questions are perennial, the answers to them are not because circumstances are always different. For this reason, no questions are ever settled definitively.
9. Political theory has traditionally looked at both facts and values. The emphasis on facts was called the behavioral revolution in political science. The return to normative questions while maintaining a behavioral set of questions has been called the postbehavioral revolution by the current generation of political scientists.
10. Some of the techniques we recommend are summarized in Gerald Celente with Tom Milton, *Trend Tracking: The System to Profit From Today's Trends* (New York: John Wiley and Sons, 1990). The book is valuable for its catalogue of tools for examining trends, but it has a flawed view of politics that casts doubt on its political advice.
11. Our powers of prognostication dim as time increases. Thus, we are defining the near future as only a few decades because this is all our analysis of trends will support.
12. For an interesting discussion, see Alan Wolfe, *Whose Keeper? Social Science and Moral Obligation* (Berkeley: University of California Press, 1989).
13. Stephen H. Schneider, "Our Waste Free House," *World Monitor* (Boston: Christian Science Publishing Society, 1991), p. 37.
14. Bruce Babbit, "Will America Join the Waste Watchers?" *World Monitor*, op cit, p. 34.
15. An opportunity cost is a term used by economists to describe resources that cannot be used elsewhere even if needed because they are already committed to something. In this case, the something is military spending.

16. Another excellent discussion of this whole range of issues is Michael Parenti, *The Sword and the Dollar* (New York: St. Martin's Press, 1989).

17. An excellent discussion that has become a classic in international relations is Kenneth N. Waltz, *Man, the State, and War* (New York: Columbia University Press, 1959).

18. See Wilson P. Dizard, Jr., *The Coming Information Age*, 3d ed. (New York: Longman, 1989).

19. A note of caution is in order: The apparent failure of one system like communism in Europe does not necessarily lead to the adoption of the Western political economy and convergence.

20. Nations north of the equator are generally richer than nations south of it. The Cancun Summit of the 1980s and the third world debt crisis reflected this condition and led to cries from the South for a more equitable distribution of global resources.

21. Works like Thucydides' *History of the Peloponnesian War*, Rousseau's *A Lasting Peace Through the Federation of Europe*, and Kant's *Perpetual Peace* (various editions) have broached the topic of international relations and war and peace. But it is not a common topic in the discipline.

22. See our discussion of this in the context of participatory democracy in Chapter 11.

23. Mulford Sibley, *Political Ideas and Ideologies* (New York: Harper & Row, 1970), p. 592.

24. See Robert B. Carson, *Economic Issues Today: Alternative Approaches*, 5th ed. (New York: St. Martin's Press, 1991), especially the first and last chapters for a discussion of different kinds of political economies.

25. Jean-Jacques Rousseau wrote on the topic constantly, but his most impressive thoughts on it were penned in the *"Discourse on the Sciences and Arts"* and *"Discourse on the Origins of Inequality."* These are both contained in Jean-Jacques Rousseau, *The First and Second Discourses*, Roger D. Masters, ed. (New York: St. Martin's Press, 1967).

26. A good selection of Marx's views on taming technology can be found in Karl Marx, *Writings of the Young Marx on Philosophy and Society*, Loyd D. Easton and Kurt H. Guddat, eds. (Garden City, N.J.: Anchor Books, 1967).

27. Among the current crop of books on the subject worth noting are Graham K. Wilson, *Business and Politics: A Comparative Introduction*, 2d ed. (Chatham, N.J.: Chatham House Publishers, 1990), Paul Peretz, ed. *The Politics of American Economic Policy Making* (Armonk, N.Y.: M. E. Sharpe, 1987), and Thomas F. Eagleton, *Issues in Business and Government* (Englewood Cliffs, N.J.: Prentice-Hall, 1991).

28. Interview with Sheldon Wolin in Bill Moyers, *A World of Ideas*, Betty Sue Flowers, ed. (New York: Doubleday, 1989) pp. 98–99.

29. Ibid, p. 105.

30. For a good range of opinions, see John Nelson, ed. *Where Should Political Theory Be Now?* (Albany: State University of New York Press, 1983).

Index